Small Town, Big Music

Small Town, Big Music

The Outsized Influence of Kent, Ohio, on the History of Rock and Roll

Jason Prufer

Foreword by Joe Walsh

The Kent State University Press   *Kent, Ohio*

Library of Congress Catalog Number 2018029947
ISBN 978-1-60635-347-9
Manufactured in China

Articles from the *Daily Kent Stater* are reproduced with permission. Some errors were silently corrected for the ease of reading.

Changes to and omissions from interviews were made silently to provide an uninterrrupted narrative, with the permission of the party.

Every effort has been made to contact copyright holders for the materials appearing in this book.

Library of Congress Cataloging-in-Publication Data

Names: Prufer, Jason, 1975- author.

Title: Small town, big music : the outsized influence of Kent, Ohio, on the history of rock and roll / Jason Prufer ; foreword by Joe Walsh.

Description: Kent, Ohio : Kent State University Press, [2019] | Includes index.

Identifiers: LCCN 2018029947 | ISBN 9781606353479 (hardcover : alk. paper)

Subjects: LCSH: Rock music--Ohio--Kent--History and criticism. | Rock concerts--Ohio--Kent--History--20th century. | Kent State University--History--20th century.

Classification: LCC ML3534.3 .P78 2019 | DDC 781.6609771/37--dc23

LC record available at https://lccn.loc.gov/2018029947

23 22 21 20 19   5 4 3 2 1

Contents

Foreword

Joe Walsh

In the late summer of 1965, I was 17 and left my parents' home in Montclair, New Jersey, to take a train out to Kent, Ohio. I joined a bunch of other kids in my generation going to college. We were war babies, and we all sort of looked at the world the same way. None of us really knew what college was, or why we did it. That's just what you did. I just looked at my options and said, "I'm going to Kent, Ohio." I don't really know why. It just felt like it was meant to be.

I lived in Manchester Hall and went to classes when the Measles, my first band, started. There were bands playing downtown already; one band, called the Counterpoints, were from Akron and played at the Fifth Quarter. I stayed in Kent the next summer, and the Measles played and rehearsed, so when school got back in session, the band was really hot, just really tight. Staying in town for the summer, I got to know people in the community. The policemen, the store owners, the club owners. They accepted me. That's when I really felt like I became a Kent resident.

By 1969, I knew the Mothersbaugh guys and Gerry Casale was around; some of them were in art school, and they were on the perimeter. I didn't hang out with them a lot, but that was another part of the young artistic community. The James Gang came out of that. DEVO came out of that. Without Kent, I don't think that would have happened.

Chrissie Hynde was young and wasn't really a musician yet. She wasn't even old enough to get into the club. She would come in and say she was my cousin. And I'd say, "Yeah, that's my cousin." And she would sit and not even drink or anything, and watch the James Gang. It was like Hemingway's Paris in the 1920s. It was an artistic community, there were a lot of musicians, and it was a hugely creative period when you look at everything that came out of it. Just like Hemingway described in *A Moveable Feast*. Then May 4 happened. The May 4 shootings had a lot to do with all of us in that scene becoming who we were and doing what we did, both in life and as artists.

We're all grateful that we had Kent. Kent was very tolerant of us. I still see some of my old Kent friends sometimes, and there is a bond. We have that experience, and that time and place, in common. We knew each other in Kent before some of us were famous. And I love having friends like that, because those are real friends. We kind of grew up together, everyone living in Kent at the time.

What brought all those people—those artists, photographers, poets, filmmakers, and musicians—together? College. Kent State is what made Kent such a magical place at the time and what continued and continues to make it special. And I would never be able to be where I am now without that experience. It was just a magical time.

Acknowledgments

"Joe Walsh's Measles on the Kent State Commons": Richard Underwood, Larry Lewis, Bobby Sepulveda, Chas Madonio, Cory Walter, and Gerry Simon.

"Ray Charles and Louis Armstrong, 1967 Homecoming Extravaganza": Images for this chapter are courtesy of the *Chestnut Burr,* Kent State Student Media (reprinted with permission), the *Daily Kent Stater,* and the Department of Special Collections and Archives, Kent State University Libraries, as well as Paul Tople and Scott White. Thanks to David Bieber and Rich Phoenix.

"Pink Floyd's Dark Side of Kent": Big thanks to Bruce Fulper, Michael Solomon, J. Ross Baughman, and the Department of Special Collections and Archives, Kent State University Libraries, for providing me with much of the great original content for this chapter.

"Paul Simon's 1973 Homecoming in Kent State's Memorial Gym": Big thanks for all the help on this chapter, including J. Ross Baughman, Mark Greenberg, Donna Hess, Shane Hrenko, Michael Solomon, Keith Raymond, and the Department of Special Collections and Archives, Kent State University Libraries.

"DEVO's Seminal 1975 Night on Kent State's Front Campus": Roger Thurman, Gary "General" Jackett, Richard Myers, Pat Myers, Adam Steele, and Michael Pilmer.

"North Water Street High and Lows: Emmylou Harris and the December 1975 Fire": Big thanks to everyone who helped me out with this chapter, including the *Daily Kent Stater,* the *Chestnut Burr,* KSU Media, the Kent Historical Society, Stephen Downey, Mary DuShane, Gerry Simon, Bob Smith, Richard Underwood, and Dennis Rein.

"Bo Diddley Backed by the Numbers Band (15-60-75)": Images for this chapter are courtesy of the *Chestnut Burr,* Kent State Student Media (reprinted with permission), the *Daily Kent Stater,* Mark Hughes Archive, Robert Kidney, Scott White, John Neitzel, and the Department of Special Collections and Archives, Kent State University Libraries. And a special thanks to Bent Tree Coffee Roasters, Byrun Reed, Jack Kidney, Michael Stacey, and Terry Hynde.

"The Red Hot Chili Peppers' 1984 Punk Funk Explosion at JB's Down in Kent": Big thanks to Ernie Smith, Mark and Mary Hughes, David

Jerome Bragg, John Teagle, Michael Purkhiser, Steven McKee, and everyone else who helped me with this chapter. It is much appreciated.

"Legendary Vermont Jam Band Phish Descended upon the MAC Center": Images for this chapter are courtesy of the *Daily Kent Stater* and the Department of Special Collections and Archives, Kent State University Libraries, as well as Dan Soulsby. Additional assistance from Shane Hrenko.

"Black Keys Member Patrick Carney and His Early Days in Kent's Music Scene": Gabe Schray, Philip Swift, Brice Forman, Ryan Brannon, Jon Ridinger, Julie Robbins, Patrick Carney, Robert Petrella, Shane Hrenko, and Jamie Stillman.

My thanks to Olaf Prufer, Trina Prufer, Adam Prufer, Kevin Prufer, Diana Prufer, Keith Prufer, Daniel Medalie, Susan Perry, Ben Medalie, Clara Medalie, Ken Burhanna, Cassandra Saltsman, Kelly Shook, Kara Robinson, Elizabeth Gould, Melissa Spohn, Joe Salem, Amanda Faehnel, Julie Spohn, Cara Gilgenbach, Diane Sperko, Hilary Kennedy, Cindy Kristof, Mark Pike, Karen Ronga, Azeez Bankole, Angela Kelly, Alicia Kay Gelfond-Holtz, Avi Gelfond, Tova Gelfond, Jordan Kay, Mark Hughes, Mary Hughes, Jim Fox, Brian Slease, Scott White, Phil Zimpfer, Dina Zimpfer, Darci Kracht, Todd Diacon, Laura Davis, Mary Mosher, Dylan Tyler, David Elswick, Dianne Centa, Tiffany Harris, Jeremy Garver-Hughes, Scott Calhoun, Stephanie Gaskins, Michael Weber, Mathias Peralta, Betsy Carney, Kyle Jacobs, Patrick Oplinger, Dorothy Peachock, Phillip Peachock, Stephen Buck, Joe Dennis, David A. King, Matthew Weiss, Jason Rulnick, Jim Greco, Bill Rubenstein, Rita Rubin-Long, Michael Pacifico, Kendra Pacifico, Carole Barbato, Alex Gildzen, Christopher Butler, Brandon Andexler, Jeremy Morrow, Chris Graves, Fred Tribuzzo, Robert Lewis, Bill Watson, Clint Alguire, Harvey Gold, Roy Skellenger, Chas Madonio, Roger Di Paolo, Sandra Halem, Henry Halem, Tom Hatch, Patrick Sweany, Bootsy, Michael Staufenger, Brett Davis, Matt Napier, Jona Burton, Kasha Legeza, Mark David, Tim McCoy, Stoney Larsen, Gerry Keefer, Michael Ennemoser, Mike Beder, Evan Bailey, Matt Manus, Mark Watt, Courtney Nething, Bobbie Watson Whitaker, Steve Panovich, Alex Lehner, Ellen Zielinski, David Giffels, Kevin Walter, Peter Heroux, Lauren Heroux, Kristen Mariola Watt, Kyle Thrasher, Robert Kidney, Jack Kidney, Terry Hynde, Kyle Thrasher, Irving Kay, Shirley Kay, Geoff Dee, Tom Dechristofaro, and everyone else who helped me or inspired me to make this book.

I gratefully acknowledge the many individuals who gave me permission to include their material in this book.

I also want to thank Christine Brooks, Will Underwood, Susan Wadsworth-Booth, and Mary Young at the Kent State University Press.

Introduction

Kent, Ohio—is this place extraordinary? Have great things happened here? Have horrible things happened here? Is this just another one of the thousands of towns that dot the midwestern United States? As a Kent native, I have pondered these questions my entire life.

On May 4, 1980, when I was five years old, my father took me behind his Kent State University office to the ten-year commemoration of the KSU shootings. There I saw huge crowds with news helicopters flying overhead. That night, while watching the evening news with my parents, I saw images from the footage those helicopters had taken. It was then I realized that maybe this place was somehow different from other places.

Since then, I have become more and more aware of the shootings that happened at Kent State through the endless amount of books, documentaries, studies, and stories that I have never stopped encountering since that day back in 1970. Through my life when I hear people talk about the history of this town, it's usually dominated by that topic of conversation. Every once in a while, though, I would hear these other vague stories about Kent that weren't related to the shootings: tales of Bruce Springsteen show-

ing up in town once and how DEVO was from Kent, among others.

As a teenager, I had a job at a local record store, and from time to time I would hear these stories from some of the customers: "Oh yeah, we used to see Joe Walsh play around the corner every Sunday night," or, "I saw Pink Floyd play *The Dark Side of the Moon* in its entirety up on campus, like twenty years ago." These anecdotes always grabbed my interest, but the details were scant.

In December 1997, when I took a trip to New York City, I walked into a Greenwich Village poster gallery called the Psychedelic Solution. This unique shop dealt in the rarest of rare posters that mostly focused on the late '60s and '70s. When I started inquiring about the kinds of items it sold, the guy behind the counter told me about how every single show poster, handbill, or ad I saw in an old newspaper for some big show had some kind of worth, whether for monetary, design, or historic value. He told me his favorite band of all time was the James Gang, and he was more than aware that its origins were in Kent, Ohio. He even knew some details about the band's time in Kent that I did not.

When I came back from that trip, I decided to

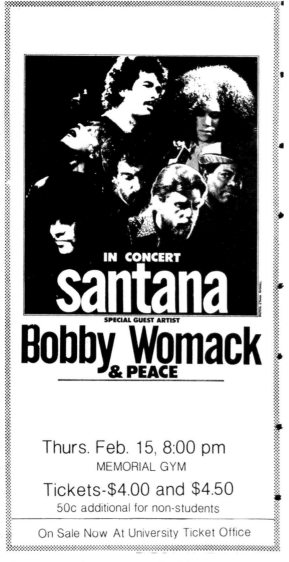

IN CONCERT
santana
SPECIAL GUEST ARTIST
Bobby Womack
& PEACE

Thurs. Feb. 15, 8:00 pm
MEMORIAL GYM

Tickets-$4.00 and $4.50
50c additional for non-students

On Sale Now At University Ticket Office

Advertisement for Santana and Bobby Womack at Memorial Gym (Courtesy of the *Daily Kent Stater*)

follow that guy's lead. I wanted to see if any old *Daily Kent Stater* issues had ads for Pink Floyd's *The Dark Side of the Moon* campus performance. When I went looking at the dirty old microfilm from the spring of 1973, I didn't find any information on that show, but I did find ads for a Santana performance in the old Memorial Gym. What struck me, though, is that this show happened when the artist was vital. Santana wasn't a legacy act—it was an established band. After this initial search I put my curiosities aside for a while, but twelve years later, I started digging again.

In 2010, I received the opportunity to do a gallery show in the Kent State University Library, and I thought, wouldn't it be great to go back and find those original ads for those performances and blow them up into custom posters? As 2010 was also Kent State's centennial, there would be a lot of looking back at the history of the university; this gallery show would fit with all of the other "looking backs" planned for that year.

The show was a huge success. I was able to put up forty panels of original ads and photographs of the likes of Fleetwood Mac, Frank Zappa, James Taylor, Elton John, and the Clash. Every panel was authentic to a Kent State performance. At the opening, a number of people approached me with detailed stories of having attended some of these shows, and some even said the material I was showing was so rich that I should write a book.

I wasn't so sure about writing a book, but I was very aware that as we were getting further away from these times, the chances of these stories and events being forgotten were growing greater. I also seemed to be the only one pursuing these stories, and if I didn't take this further, perhaps nobody else ever would.

So, out of sheer determination to gather this information before it got lost, I just kept research-

Kent State Provost Todd Diacon (*left*), Joe Walsh (*middle*), and Jason Prufer (*right*) look at the manuscript for this book in the Kent State University Library, February 2017. (Photo by Ken Burhanna)

ing. The more I dug, the more I was blown away by the incredible history. As I started going way back, I discovered information about Duke Ellington on campus in the 1950s and Gene Krupa playing an all-campus dance in 1941, complete with a set of photos from the night.

When I began looking into the era when Joe Walsh and DEVO were doing their things in town, I saw many names of locals I recognized with these stories. I followed every possible lead to get to the people who had been a part of these experiences. Amazingly, everyone I approached was more than willing to tell me what they knew—and the stories they told me were gold.

During this whole period of discovery, social media had become a thing, and as I was scanning photos and ads I would post them to Facebook. The more I posted, the more people responded with recollections and stories and unseen photos from private collections. A photograph in a tired old KSU yearbook showing

Bo Diddley playing in a downtown bar would receive new life when I put it on my Facebook wall. All of a sudden, a dozen people knew exactly how the night went down and had stories to tell. Soon, I was writing long blog posts from the best of this material.

This book, then, is a consolidation of my research and supporting archival material. It is not the complete story of rock and roll in Kent but, rather, a scrapbook, with highlights of four decades of music.

Finally, I can't introduce this book without thanking Joe Walsh. He saved this book. It likely wouldn't be in print if not for an encounter I had with him at the Kent State University Library in mid-February 2017. With that said, the story starts with Joe—just over fifty years before I spoke with him. In the fall of 1966, Joe Walsh and his band, the Measles, played outdoors on the old Kent State University Commons.

Joe Walsh's Measles on the Kent State Commons

October 1966

One of the biggest challenges of capturing the stories of rock and roll in Kent was nailing down some kind of real piece about legendary rock and roller Joe Walsh.

But then I worked with local artist, archivist, and entertainer Richard "Ritch" Underwood on a digitization project dealing with many of his long-unseen slides and photographs. I'd never before encountered such an awesome collection of authentic images, showing the likes of Paul Simon, Carrie Fisher, Steve Martin, Bryan Ferry, Stephen Stills, Chuck Berry, Diana Ross, and perhaps a thousand other major stars Ritch had photographed. Leafing through an old photo album from his early days in Kent, I stumbled across a set of five photos with an October 1966 date stamp showing a really young Joe Walsh performing outdoors for a daytime performance at Kent State.

I asked Ritch, "What are these?" and he responded, "Oh, those are photos I took up at KSU of Joe Walsh's first serious band, the Measles, just before I joined." He was more than happy to describe that day, his photography, the band, and his friendship with Joe Walsh:

These photos are just like a diary entry. At the time I took [them], I was in the process of changing bands, and I was with a group called the Styx. We were the house band at JB's, and we started down there in March of 1966, and by this fall here, I was getting some draft notices and things were starting to get iffy with me musically. I didn't know if I was going to be playing in bands or

The Measles facing the old University Commons behind the Engleman Hall dormitory at Kent State in the fall of 1966. *Left to right:* Bobby Sepulveda, Buddy Bennett, Joe Walsh, and Larry Lewis. (Photo by Richard Underwood)

if I was going to be in the service, and in the midst of all that I was also a student at KSU.

After the gigs at JB's and the Fifth Quarter, the different members of the different bands would all meet up for coffee or a sandwich or something and just talk and share ideas. Back then, everybody was doing extremely well. Lots of people went out to hear bands all the time.

So as we're all meeting up on one of these nights, I was talking to Joe Walsh and I had mentioned that I had planned on leaving the Styx. So the Measles were talking about having me come into their band—I remember Joe Basile was kind of like their manager or booker or whatever—he kind of handled the band, and he asked me if I would consider joining. At the time I did really like the Measles, mostly because I really liked Joe Walsh—ya know he was an excellent guitar player. He was one of the best guitarists that I'd seen. Also, the Measles were our competition, so I figured if I joined them there would be no more competition.

So, I was up at this outdoor campus gig to get familiar with some of these songs that they were playing, plus just to get some pictures. The only camera that I had was an Instamatic. It wasn't a really good low-light camera so I figured I could get some nice shots outside. There wasn't even any kind of big crowd there or anything. It was just kids hanging around and stuff like around the lunch hour, and the band was playing. I can remember distinctly that day they

played "Drive My Car" by the Beatles and they probably played "Under My Thumb" by the Rolling Stones, "Good Lovin'" by the Young Rascals, pop songs.

I was asked to join the band because they needed a lead guitar player for when Joe played keyboards. They had Larry [Lewis], who was a great rhythm guitarist, but he wasn't really a lead player. Plus, at that time the Yardbirds were a really big band and there were some songs that we did where we did a similar two-guitar thing.

But like I said, I was out there checking them out to get a grip on what tunes they were playing, plus I wanted to see how they were

The Measles facing the old University Commons behind the Engleman Hall dormitory at Kent State in the fall of 1966. *Left to right:* Bobby Sepulveda, Larry Lewis, and Joe Walsh; *back row:* Buddy Bennett. (Photo by Richard Underwood)

Fall 1966 photo showing Joe Walsh handling his guild Starfire V guitar with the Measles at Kent State (Photo by Richard Underwood)

playing. I was also listening to see how another guitar player could fit in. That's what made the Beatles so great. They really complemented each other on guitars, not just their voices. The Measles were an extremely good harmony band, too. Joe, Larry, and Bobby sang extremely well together. Buddy, the drummer, didn't sing, but when I came in it added another voice to the group.

Joe sang [lead] on some tunes, but he wasn't like a—ya know how Joe's voice is. He was never any kind of great singer, but he made songs fit the style of his voice, which is what made him for years. I think that's what actually brought him out with the James Gang.

[Before I joined] the band, I was really good friends with Joe

Walsh. We used to hang out and play guitar together.

My previous band [the Styx] was just about having fun. The Measles was different. The Measles was pretty much straitlaced—we weren't fooling around, though Joe started to show a little more showmanship. I would change the words to songs and make up stories. For example, we used to play "Gloria" by Them, and I would always change the song so it was about Gloria getting laid. It was after this that Joe added this bit with a story about a king and his daughter's fiancé where he would take a glass of water and pour it on himself because he was told by the king to never drink from the opposite side of the glass.

This period wasn't all fun and games. When we were playing places, there were constant fights. A lot of it you were aware of, and a lot of it you weren't aware of because you were playing. But it was the jocks and the longhairs. [If you] go back to those photos of the band on campus, you don't see long hair on Larry and you don't see long hair on Bobby. Joe has the longest hair. When we were playing, the bands would have the hair a little longer, but the crowd would come in with those buzz cuts.

[By March 1967] the original group broke up. I ended up briefly joining a Cleveland group called the Selective Service, but by the end of May 1967 I had joined the navy. Joe Walsh left the Measles because he wanted to do more like a blues thing, which I thought was weird because the next thing he did was some filling in with the Chancellors, a pop band. It's also during this post-Measles period where you see Joe playing with the Goldthwaites out at the Barn, and when you see me, Joe, Don Goldthwaite, and Gary Slama performing in the Richard Myers film *Akran*.

If you look at my photos [from this event], you can see the Measle van behind them, and you can also see that Joe is playing basically straight through to his amplifier with one of those Maestro Fuzz Tones. That was one of the first Fuzz Tones that came out. Those things were great for songs like "Satisfaction." They give you a great attack, but they had no sustain. The band is basically playing with a wall of amplifiers behind them, which is really pretty amazing for that period.

Later, [when] Joe made it with the James Gang and then with the Eagles, it's like, "Hey man, we played together in this band." It's so cool to have been able to work with somebody who became so famous like that. It was an honor to have played with that guy. When you are talking about this era right here, 1965–75, you're talking to me about one of the best. There were bands everywhere. Every place had live bands, and the best thing was that students supported all of this. A big help, too, was that you could drink and get into these bars when you were eighteen.

We were having a good time, and life was good. I was making steady money; we had crowds every night. It was just a great time period. Plus the musicians that came out of this—like Joe Walsh, Chrissie Hynde, and DEVO. It was probably happening all over the place, but what made Kent different was the exposure here and the venues that were available for people to come to. Kent was just a great place back then, and getting to see so much live music in so many different venues in town is why I enjoyed that era so much.

Larry Lewis, in Ritch Underwood's photos wearing blue jeans and a white striped shirt and playing the Rickenbacker guitar, is originally

The Measles facing the old University Commons behind the Engleman Hall dormitory at Kent State in the fall of 1966. *Left to right:* Bobby Sepulveda, Larry Lewis, Buddy Bennett, and Joe Walsh. (Photo by Richard Underwood)

from the Kent area, but after he joined the navy in 1968, at the age of nineteen, he ended up in Groton, Connecticut, where he has lived ever since. He still remembers that 1966 day on the University Commons and a lot more about playing with the Measles, the old Kent music scene, and Joe Walsh.

At the time of the formation of the group, in late 1965, I would have been in my junior year at Field High School, but when those pictures were taken in the fall of 1966, I was in my senior year, since I graduated in 1967.

I became a part of the Measles [because of] the band that I was in before the Measles, called the Embers, and because of guys going into the military and whatnot, bands were breaking up all the time. So the Embers split up, and one day I got a call from Chas Madonio, and he said a couple guys at Kent State wanted to get a band going, and he knew that I was available. Because I knew Chas, I said sure. So we met at Kent State in the old Student Union in the garbage room just off from the cafeteria, and that's when I met Joe Walsh and Buddy Bennett. They knew one another from school, and I think they had met at maybe some audition for maybe some other band or something and they just decided to start their own band.

So anyway, I met Joe and Buddy there, and of course Chas was there, and Chas was playing bass and I was playing rhythm guitar, and we all hit it off well. We practiced for two or three weeks, and then I believe Chas got an offer from one of the other groups to work five nights a week, and because he was married and he needed the money, he left the group early on. When he left, he recommended or somebody else recommended that we go listen to this bass player in this other band up in Ravenna—so we all went to see this guy, and that's how we got ahold of Bobby Sepulveda.

The Measles was a pretty serious band, though I don't recall any thoughts about being the biggest band in the world. We just wanted to work.

It was clear from the very beginning, though, that we had a very particular sound and we were quite good together. Our harmonies were far better than any we'd heard before, and we just melded together. So, early on we knew that we were quite good, but our ambitions were no more than anybody else's.

After I'd been playing with Joe for about a year or so, I knew that this man was gonna do something, because he had to be the finest guitar player I had ever seen and he had a good business sense as well. I didn't know if the rest of us were gonna make it, but I knew that he would.

I am not sure how this gig [on the KSU Commons] got booked. We didn't really pick up anybody to manage us for a while. It could have just been that this got booked because of word of mouth about us by the organizers. They may have just thought, "Let's get the Measles."

We actually became pretty popular, and one of our biggest achievements was being one of the resident bands playing to big crowds at the Fifth Quarter over on Depeyster Street in Kent. That place was packed all the time when we were there. We really enjoyed that. I also got a taste of being on the road with this band. We did this tour once that was about twenty shows in sixteen different cities over twenty days. The tour was over all Ohio, southern Ohio, and into Pennsylvania a bit. I really didn't like that life. I didn't like it at all. We'd play, then we'd drive through the night, then we'd get a room and we'd sleep till mid-afternoon, and then we'd show up for sound check. Then we'd go and get dinner, and then we'd do the show and break down and do it over again. It was just that, over and over and over, and I just don't know if I was cut out for that. I'm sure for successful groups it's a little bit easier, but still it's a grind to be out on the road and playing.

The Measles was pretty much a Top 40 kind of group. We played what was popular. We played an awful lot of Beatles. We did some Lovin' Spoonful, and we did some Rascals. We did the Beatles' "You're Going to Lose That Girl." That was one that we did very well and that most people requested over and over.

I remember one time we were playing at some big thing and one of the huge radio DJs—Bob Ansell or something like that—I remember him getting up and saying something about our ability to re-create the sounds of the Beatles and the harmonies and being exact. Of course I never played lead guitar, but occasionally Joe would let me play something. We used to do "Mustang Sally," and I would do the little guitar riffs in that. And we did some classical stuff—we did "On Broadway." We also did a couple of Smokey Robinson tunes with nice smooth harmonies. But again, it was mostly Top 40. We played what was popular, and we played it well.

I do remember a conversation that Joe had with the group and we all sat down and discussed [hiring Ritch Underwood]. Joe felt that we needed to expand our sound a little bit, and he was very interested in playing keyboard. He didn't want to always play guitar, but he didn't expect me to jump in and play lead guitar, because I wasn't a lead guitar player. I prided myself on playing excellent rhythm. I remember Joe saying to us, "What do you think about us bringing in another guitar player?" I just went along with it. No big deal to me. But that's about all I remember—because Joe started playing keyboard a bit. And with all the synthesized sounds you could get on a keyboard, it did create a lot more sound for us.

Having grown up in the area, I would say that bands like the Measles and the Styx represented the first generation of any kind of band scene in Kent. I can remember there were no bands locally until the Beatles, and they don't show up till 1964. Before then—the first group that I was in, we just played Ventures—ya know, instrumentals. And then people started forming little groups right after the Beatles invaded America. Man, they just started popping up everywhere in Kent. Everywhere you turned, there was great, great talent. Being a university town, there was certainly plenty of people to play for, and everybody was hopped up on rock and roll. It was a great time to be a young musician, I'll tell you that.

I do not have a single recording or photo from that time, other than what has been put out there on the Internet—like Ritch's Facebook posts and the like. I didn't think that was important to document, and now I regret it very much that I don't have some sort of an arsenal of photos and recordings.

I have a lot of memories of Joe Walsh from those days, and that's because Joe and I were probably the closest. We spent a lot of time together, and Joe started drug use very early on. Some nights we'd be out playing and he was high and he'd go on a guitar riff and just keep goin' and goin' and goin'. I remember very specifically one night coming home from a gig in my car, and he and I were stopped at a railroad crossing, and when I put my parking brake on the little light would flash on my dash. He just leaned over and just got into that light and was goin', "Wow that's great," and he's looking at the flashing lights of the train and the crossing lights going up. And I told him, "Get the hell back over there and sit back and relax." It started early in his life—this drug business. Later in life, he nearly died from drugs, and he's drug-free today.

But I've said it before, and I'll say it again: he's the finest guitar player I had ever seen. His command of the fingerboard is just amazing. Look how big the man's hands are. Seems like he could wrap his fingers around the neck twice. Joe was a good guy; he was talented, I respected him a lot. He had a good head for business. He was a lot of fun, and he was a crazy bastard.

I'll tell you one incident. We were traveling

somewhere, and we stopped at, like, a Denny's or something to have lunch, and he says, "Hey, let's pretend that I'm blind," so he puts on dark sunglasses, and we go into this place, and so for the whole meal he's pretending like he's blind. So the waitresses are bringing him out pudding or something, and he's pounding the table acting like he's trying to find it, and he splats it all over the table. You can read about all the horrible things he did to hotel rooms with chainsaws and stuff like that. But he was a bit of a crazy bastard even way back then, and he was a good guy, and we were good friends. I was really proud when he became successful. He deserved it because of his talent.

Joe has never forgotten me or the Measles, though. Those guys have tried over the years to have a reunion with us, and I remember Buddy or Bobby telling me that Joe always insists that he won't even think about it unless I am going to be there. That's nice for him to say. Maybe someday when I get back to Kent, we can all get back together.

Early 1980s photo showing Joe Walsh and Bobby Sepulveda at a reunion party thrown by Joe Shannon in Twin Lakes (Courtesy of Bobby Sepulveda)

Bobby Sepulveda, playing bass in these photos, has actually never stopped performing live music since his days with the Measles and as of this writing can be heard singing with Danjo Jazz Orchestra. He's quite the firecracker and one of the most enthusiastic persons I have ever met. This is what he told me about those photos and about his days playing with Joe Walsh and the Measles.

I've been singing for over fifty years—since 1958. For a very long time, my philosophy for live performance was to play the Top 40. Play what the kids wanna hear—what the kids listen to on the radio—keep current. I've done that ever since about 1964, which was when the Beatles really hit. That's really when I started in a band. I was always lucky that I always played dance music, and everyone enjoyed that. I did that all the way up to the mid-90s, which was when things fizzled out completely for my band, so since then I've just been jamming with different people and doing recordings at my house.

The way I came about being in the Measles was that back in September–October of 1965, I was playing with a group on a Saturday night at this party on South Water Street for one of the freshman classes or something, and there were a lot of kids around—I was playing bass and singing, too. Back then, I didn't know any bass players that could sing and play at the same time. It was just a gift I had. So we were playing our first set, and in about the middle I looked out and I could see these two guys watching. It was Joe Walsh and Buddy Bennett. Joe was kneeling down, and Buddy was standing behind him, and they both had long hair, and they were just watching me.

So I'm playing and playing, and these guys are staring at me, so I didn't think anything of it. But then came a break, and when I went to sit down with my girlfriend, Joe and Buddy came over and said, "Wow, we really like the way you play, would you be interested in starting a band?" And I said, "No, I don't think so" [laughs]. And Joe said, "Ya know, I'm from New Jersey." Both Buddy and Joe were Jersey boys, and they were telling me that they were freshmen and all that and they wanted to put a band together, and I said, "Yeah, yeah, I'm in a band. Leave me alone."

So then I went up to play for the second set—and I look down, and there's Joe and Buddy again, and they stand and stare at me that whole set—and I'm just playing. I remember them saying [when I finished], "What can we do to get you to come over and just listen to us? We swear to God if you come—" And I was thinking, "Man, I don't know these guys; I could get mugged." So they said, "We'll meet you on a Sunday up at Kent State at Eastway Center at 12:00 P.M., and there will be people around. You don't have to worry, we're not going to mug you, we're not going to beat you up, we're not going to steal your guitar." And I said, "Okay."

So I went that Sunday and—I met Larry. Joe, Larry, and Buddy got their stuff together, and they looked at me and said, "Can you sing 'You're Going to Lose That Girl' by the Beatles?" And I said, "Yeah." I was asked to take the lead, and the rest of the band would come in with the harmonies. Buddy then snapped his fingers four times, and I started singing "You're going

to lose that girl." Then Walsh and Buddy came in with the harmonies, and then when it came to the middle part, "I'll make a point of taking her away from you," the three-part harmonies blended absolutely perfect. Our voices were perfect. When we finished singing the song, I was like, "I'M IN!" And that was it. That was the beginning of the Measles!

When I joined the group, we didn't have a name. Someone mentioned "Robin Hood and the Merry Men," and I said, "I'm not going to be a Merry Man." And then everyone else said, "Well, I'm not going to be Robin Hood." Then I think it was the janitor who suggested the name "the Measles." So that one was going around, but I don't know who made the final decision. I've heard people say the Measles was started before I was there. That may be true, but the name didn't come till after I joined.

I do remember this day that the photos [on the KSU Commons] were taken. There weren't too many people out there to see us. We were kind of playing, and that's about it. That was so long ago. There was a bit of a mystery to one of these pics. This one. You can see Joe and Larry looking at each other, and I was wondering what they were saying.

We were probably just asked to play out there for like $20 apiece. I was just getting out of high school and those guys were freshmen in college, so we could do things like that.

[In] fall 1966, we were doing so much with [Measles manager] Joe Shannon—he's the one who really helped us a lot. The college kids did this poll, and the No. 1 group in the area was the Counterpoints, who had been around for years. We came in second place, and because of this we were the backup band for all these big acts, like the Shirelles, the Vogues, and even Freddy "Boom Boom" Cannon.

I remember one trip we went to Manny's Music in New York—it was me, Joe, Buddy, and the drummer from the Counterpoints—we took that van you see behind us in that photo. We had just played a gig the night before, and that kid from the Counterpoints wanted to drive, but he couldn't drive stick. So while we were going down the turnpike on our way to New York, we just switched drivers without even stopping the car—got out, stood up, and he just went in the driver's seat. So he's driving, and me, Joe, and Buddy are sleeping on the floor in the back of the van, and then I hear, "Hey guys, hey guys." And I keep hearing, "Hey guys, hey guys," and none of us wanted to get up because we were all tired. And I hear from the front seat, "We're coming to a tunnel." I say, "So what?" and he says, "And the traffic is stopped, and I don't know how to stop this thing." Man we jumped up and we whipped him out of there, and I think Joe jumped in the driver's seat and stopped the van. That was it. We were awake after that. We were actually on our way to Joe's parents' house. We spent the night there, and we met his mom and his brother.

At the time these photos were taken, the Beatles were really big and we were playing a lot of their stuff, as well as music by the Young Rascals. We did a lot of Rolling Stones, the Mamas and the Papas. On this day, we probably would have played "19th Nervous Breakdown" and "Satisfaction." We would have done some Yardbirds. We would have played a lot of Beatles, because there were a lot of fancy guitar parts that the Beatles did that nobody but Joe could do. We did "And Your Bird Can Sing," and Joe would purposely turn around so you couldn't see what he was doing, because all the guitarists would come around and try to see how Joe played. We were doing things that other bands just couldn't do. Joe and Larry would just start putting things together, and they would call me and tell me they were doing this, and then I would learn the part.

One time we played at Chippewa Lake Park, and there were twenty thousand people there. Big concert.

So later we got up to sing after the Young Rascals and we did the Mamas and the Papas' "Dedicated to the One I Love." Joe was singing the lead, and we did our own version. Joe just started out with, "Each night before you go." And everyone is looking at us like, "That's kind of corny, Mamas and Papas coming out of a rock band?" And then, all of a sudden, Larry and I come in with the three-part harmony, "Each night before," and our voices were so perfect—the place went *crazy.*

I do not remember any specifics about Ritch joining the band, nor do I remember him taking these pictures, but I definitely knew Ritch back in those days with the Styx. We all knew each other—the Turnkeys, the Majestics—everybody knew everybody back then. Ritch came in there toward the end, and we had another guy come in at the very end because Larry got drafted, but then I think Ritch quit—and then the next thing you know I got drafted, and then that was the end of it.

Joe was always a nice guy. He used to always push me—I wasn't into the music as much as Joe was. Joe was really into it, 100 percent. Us guys were maybe 80 percent, because we had other things that we were gonna do. I remember one time Joe and I sat together—I was working on my guitar, so he sat down beside me and he grabbed his guitar and he ripped it all apart, and he said, "This is how you do it," so I ripped mine all apart—all the electric wires and everything—and we rewired both guitars, and he helped me do it.

The Measles playing at the Fifth Quarter in Kent. *Front:* Buddy Bennett; *back, left to right:* Bobby Sepulveda, Richard Underwood, and Larry Lewis. Joe Walsh is out of frame on the right playing organ. (Courtesy of Richard Underwood)

What I remember about the Fifth Quarter is the stage was really high. And I'm not that tall of a person. Joe and Larry were taller than me. Their heads were almost hitting the ceiling. And there was this odd telephone at the entrance of the club that you could get on that would broadcast through the whole PA system. And one day, we were doing the Lovin' Spoonful's "Daydream" and Joe's singing and then Joe gets ready to do the whistling part, and the police officer, Bob Diss—he was way on the other side at the entrance of the club and he picked up that telephone and he pushed the button and started whistling. And we are all looking around like, "Who in the hell is doing that?" And it was Bob! He was over there whistling, so from then on, every time we did that song, we had the police officer do that.

The crowds were so big because we were playing dance music. You could dance to us. See, that was our thing. We were doing the Who, the Guess Who, Paul Revere and the Raiders . . . stuff that was on the radio. WHLO was the number one station back then, and Uncle Joe Cunningham and so many of those disc jockeys they had there—the songs were hot back in the '60s. Bands were big, the Turnkeys, the Styx, everybody—we were just good musicians. Kent had a lot of good musicians back then.

One time, I was at the Fifth Quarter and the guy who had WHLO—one of the radio announcers that was interested in us—he had a convertible, and I remember he pulled into the driveway in the front of the Fifth Quarter, and he had those amplifiers [shown in the 1966 campus photos] sticking out of his car and another car. And I'm going, "What's going on? Is this for a different band or something?" And as I walked up, he said to me, "We got you a new amplifier." And I said, "You do?" And he said, "Yeah," and I said, "Oh, how am I going to pay for that?" And he said, "We're just going to take $40 a week out of your check," and I said, "Okay" [laughs]. I had two of those bottoms and that big top. I had probably the biggest system in Northeast Ohio.

The Counterpoints were the only really known group that predates this era, and they go back to the late '50s, early '60s. They were older than us. But yeah, the Counterpoints was the band from back then; they had the big equipment. They had a big Hammond B-3 organ, which was so expensive back then. I remember them doing the Beach Boys and stuff like that. They were good. They were hot in the late '50s and going all through the '60s, up until about

maybe 1966 because then the Turnkeys, the Styx, and us—once we came around, we were the new kids on the block and that was a scene. That was a real scene with rival bands and big audiences. And we were part of what would be the first scene of bands in Kent. We were the ones that started it all. Any place they could put a band they were sticking bands in back then.

I could tell you stories—one time we were playing at the Thunderball in Canton with Freddy "Boom Boom" Cannon. So we got there, and we walked into the club and I forgot the cord to my guitar. Well, we didn't have any backup cords or any kind of backups on anything—except for the snare drum. Buddy always had another one because he would always break them. So I said—and this is in Canton—"I'm gonna go home and I'll be back in twenty minutes or so" [laughs]. So I got in my car and I came down Route 44 going ninety miles per hour through all those towns, and I had a '57 Chevy—I mean I was flying. And I came home to Ravenna, went in and picked up my cord, flew back at a hundred miles an hour. I think I did the whole trip in less than thirty-five minutes, or something like that. By the time I got back, it was time to start—because when we initially arrived I had about an hour before we started. I used to do some crazy things.

One time we did *Ghoulardi*, in the studio up in Cleveland. We played songs all night long in that studio while he was broadcasting—we were live on television with him. I remember he sat in front of us, and we played behind him. For one part of the show, Ghoulardi turns around to us and he looks at Buddy, and he says, "Hit that snare," and Buddy goes, "No." And me, Joe, and Larry just look at each other. And then Ghoulardi says again, "Hit that snare!" And Buddy goes, "NO!" And Ghoulardi responds, "Well kids, I cannot believe—k'niff this and k'niff that," and then he says, "We'll be right back in about twenty minutes." When he goes on break, he jumps up, looks at Buddy, and yells, "NEXT TIME I SAY YOU HIT THAT SNARE, YOU HIT THAT SNARE OR YOU GUYS ARE OUTTA HERE." So Joe and I look at Buddy like, "You should really do what he says." And Buddy indicates to us, "Okay." So we come back on the air, and we play a couple songs, and then Ghoulardi comes back on talking like he was doing. And then he goes, "HIT THAT SNARE," and Buddy again comes back with "NO!"—and I remember thinking, "Oooh, shit, we'll never be asked back on this show." And our agents are out there sitting in their lounge chairs, and they're looking through the glass at me, and I'm like, "I don't know," and then Ghoulardi again says, "COME ON, HIT THAT SNARE!" And once again Buddy goes, "NO!" So then he starts something else, and then we do a song, and then when the break comes, he says, "YOU GUYS ARE FIRED. YOU'RE NEVER COMING BACK HERE." He was piiiisssed. And he walked out.

I was really sad to see everything fall apart, but, ya know, there was nothing I could do about it. When you've got the military calling you, you're gone. If I remember right, Joe was trying to get me out of the military obligations. I kept getting letters from Joe even when I was in Vietnam, and then finally I got a letter saying, "There's nothing more that we can do. We've already spent $6,000. We're just going to let it go." So that was it. And then I never heard from Joe anymore, Buddy, Larry—I didn't hear from anybody till I got out in October of 1969, and then I saw Buddy, who was still playing. He was the only one that was around, and I think Joe had started with the James Gang then.

I caught a couple of those early James Gang shows, and we talked and all that. I actually used to run into them at the City Bank around that time. Then the next thing I knew, the James Gang started really taking off.

The last time I saw Joe was—there's a picture I have upstairs—Joe Shannon had a party in the '80s, and we went over, and Joe and I talked and I brought a couple people that we knew. We weren't supposed to bring any people, but these were musicians who had played with him in California and stuff like that. So he was glad to see Mary Delaney, who sang with him on "Midnight Man."

As far as what I took away from my experience with the Measles—well, number one, I got to play with Joe Walsh. Not too many people can say that. We knew each other real well. We played very good together. I enjoyed that time, the memories of that group and those people. Like Buddy—Buddy and I are still very close and he lives in Cape Coral, Florida. He's got a business—a restaurant. He's got a couple restaurants. We're still friends, and I still talk to Larry. I have a house in Florida, and Larry comes down in the wintertime and visits.

We were lucky. When the four of us got together—that was the best Measles right there. The four of us that you see in these pictures. Our biggest crowds and our loudest crowds were a later version of the Measles from when after I got home from Vietnam. Buddy kept the name, and I sang as a part of that later version of the band, which finally ended in 1977—but the original four that you see in these photos. That was the best.

Today, on nice fall days bands will sometimes perform on Kent State's Risman Plaza at the Student Center over the lunch hour. Back in

1966, the Student Union was in what is now Oscar Ritchie Hall, and on nice days students would spend their lunch hours on the University Commons, just behind that building.

Even almost fifty years later, Ritch, Larry, and Bobby vividly recall their experiences with Joe Walsh. How cool it must have been to have been a part of this first band scene in Kent, and how amazing it must have been to follow the Measles!

[The interview in the following *Daily Kent Stater* article was conducted before Joe Walsh's March 13, 1975, performance in the Kent State University Memorial Gym.]

Walsh Recalls "Crazy Days" in Kent
Daily Kent Stater
March 14, 1975

"Basically I'm the same dude," said Joe Walsh, reminiscing about the "old crazy days" of living and playing in Kent.

"I lived in Manchester Hall in '65 and I got a band together." That's probably what started him on his way, Walsh said.

"I just want to play and have people come and have a good time and *So what* about everything else."

This is a "homecoming" of sorts, he said, remembering his "bar days" in Kent at J.B.'s and with the James Gang. "I wish I was here for more than one day. I know all I can do is barely scratch the surface" in getting together with old friends and being back in Kent.

A very quiet person, Walsh said he was very nervous about playing the Kent concert.

Walsh said he has always "dug music" but he said he does not feel he is tremendously talented. "It's very frustrating not to be more talented than I am. I do the best with what I have but I hate my voice.

A line outside of the Kent Kove at 256 North Water Street, circa 1966 (Photo by Gerry Simon)

The Fifth Quarter at 206 South Depeyster Street, circa 1966 (Photo by Richard Underwood)

Circa 1966 photo of Bobby Sepulveda of the Measles in his 1957 Chevy Bel-Air in front of the Fifth Quarter (Photo by Richard Underwood)

Joe Walsh (*Daily Kent Stater* photo by Kathy Siemon)

"Friends tell me it's unique, but I can't stand the way I sing. I make music and I don't care. Everybody says 'you're great.' You can't let yourself get into your ego. My friends are what brought me back down," he added.

"There's a softer side of me that not too many people know. Tonight I think I may sit down with an acoustic guitar. I'm kind of nervous about that because it's a huge hall," he said, hours before the show.

"I've done that, and people just be screaming and yelling for 'Funk 49.'

"Let it rest in peace!

"It bums me out when I play shitty and the audience goes crazy. I would love one night to get booed off the stage for playing really bad," he said, explaining that this would show him people were sensitive to his music.

"One of the things that makes musicians create is some kind of pain or self-sacrifice," Walsh said, adding that a lot of his material has stemmed from experiences in his past.

"I'm whatever people make me," he said sarcastically. "I mean really I'm just *me*. People try to make me something I'm not."

"I don't want to paint feathers on my eyes and glitter. Kids, because they respect me, write me letters or call me up and ask questions about what they should do with their lives and stuff—like I should know. Kids want to know what kind of guitar to buy!" he said.

"*So what?* That's where it's at."

The Lovin' Spoonful played on Saturday April 8, 1967, as part of the KSU Student Activities Board's Spring Fling Concert.

7 Minutes of "Spoonful"
"Open Your Mouth Real Wide, Zally"
By David Bieber
Daily Kent Stater
April 11, 1967

The requests included "Open your mouth real wide, Zally, come on just for one picture, Zally." Following the flapping jaw pose, questions as inane as "John, where'd ya get the idea for 'Summer in the City'" were forthcoming. One can now concur with the Lovin' Spoonful and understand why they granted the press corps only seven minutes during the intermission of Saturday evening's Major Events—SAB Spring Fling concert.

Off-stage, the four Spoonful, John Sebastian, Joe Butler, Zal Yanovsky and Steven Boone, seemed subdued and more than once feigned ignorance of their business interests in the music industry.

"We don't know too much ahead of time what's being planned for us in either appearances or record releases," Butler remarked. However, with thousands of dollars riding on their every professional activity, the drummer and his three musical cohorts cannot help but maintain more than an impassive interest.

He noted that the Kent concert was the final performance of the group's concert tour and that "for the next few days, I'm just going to relax."

However, to assume that the four minstrels have been on an exhaustive three-month crossing of the country is incorrect.

The "current tour" began the previous night when the versatile vagabonds infectiously fused

The Lovin' Spoonful played on Saturday April 8, 1967, in the Kent State Memorial Gym. (Photos by Richard Underwood)

country, rock, blues, folk and you-name-it into a musical experience for students at Purdue University. Next weekend, the Spoonful will play three college dates in Texas and then return north to begin a tour emphasizing concert hall appearances.

Buoyed by the success of eight consecutive single records which have all hit the Top 20 nationally and three albums currently scattered among "Billboard Magazine's" Top 150 sellers, the contemporary aggregate is widely sought for in-person performances.

Yanovsky casually contorted his rubber jowls and proclaimed "I already am a star" when queried about acting intentions.

Sebastian attributed much of the group's preeminence in contemporary American music to the huge publicity campaign focused on the Spoonful last year.

"We were everything from 'Time' to 'Teen' with 'Newsweek,' 'Gentleman's Quarterly' and a dozen other scattered in," the lead singer listed.

This nationally featured promotion in such diverse publications "played a major part in putting us on top," reed-shaped bassist Steve Boone stated.

Not only do they often make the printed media, but Sebastian and Yanovsky are also mentioned in the Mama's and Papa's semi-biographical single record, "Creeque Alley."

"That reference dates back to a couple years ago when Zally and I were playing with Cass and Denny, of the Mama's and the Papa's, in a group known as the Mugwumps," the Civil War-era sideburned Sebastian recalled.

He played straight folk for awhile, experimented with the autoharp, electric piano and "Appalachian music." He later reunited with Yanovsky, and together with Boone and Butler, had their first hit in September, 1965, with "Do You Believe in Magic."

Within recent weeks, there has been a rumor circulating in the entertainment underground that the sartorially deceptive Boone and Yanovsky have been informing the FBI of the drug activities of former friends.

While the Spoonful songmakers had no comments on this subject, one of the members of their road entourage said that "while Zally and Steve were busted on the Coast for possession, they were later released."

"But five other people, including a dealer, were held, and they've been quite perturbed that the performers got off but they didn't," he continued.

The four Spoonful function well together, and as John Sebastian has said many times before, "As a whole, we equal one reasonably efficient human being."

Ray Charles and Louis Armstrong, 1967 Homecoming Extravaganza

October 21, 1967

In what must have been one of the finest evenings Kent State ever hosted, on Saturday, October 21, 1967, Ray Charles and Louis Armstrong coheadlined in the Kent State University Memorial Gym (now the MAC Center). Soul music titan Ray Charles played first, followed by jazz legend Louis Armstrong leading a free dance.

Just a few months before the show at Kent State, Ray had a single in the charts, "Here We Go Again," and he had released a full-length album, *Ray Charles Invites You to Listen.* Just six weeks after Ray's Kent State performance, he appeared on *The Ed Sullivan Show,* with likely the exact same group of musicians who accompanied him at Kent State.

Then senior Kent State journalism student David Bieber reviewed the event and interviewed Ray Charles; his story was published in the October 24, 1967, *Daily Kent Stater.*

Ray Charles: "I Try to Stay in Tune with the Times"
By David L. Bieber

He could easily be heralded as the soldier of sound or the musical amalgamator, but he's known simply as Ray Charles, the Genius, and justifiably so.

When Charles and his retinue of nearly 30 supporting entertainers blended jazz with rhythm and blues, country and western with contemporary pop, the capacity crowd at Memorial Gymnasium realized that Kent State University's Homecoming '67 was indeed a Happening.

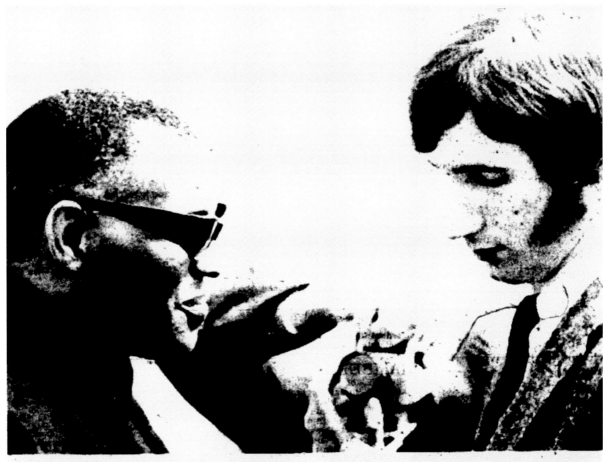

FOCUSSING ON rhythm and bluesman Ray Charles, who entertained KSU homecomers Saturday night is David Bieber, senior journalism student at Kent State. Bieber interviewed Charles following his concert. Louis (Satchmo) Armstrong and his orchestra entertained during the dance.

Kent State journalism student David Bieber and Ray Charles (Courtesy of the *Record-Courier*)

Charles, a master instrumentalist and vocalist, proved his artistry and demonstrated a distinctive ability to successfully transcend musical boundaries in Saturday night's concert.

Although the first half of the evening's entertainment featured only the billing-in-small-letters members of the blind performer's aggregate, the pace was pitched to pacify even the most talent-starved college audience.

The Ray Charles Band's instrumentals ranged from "Walk on By" to "Willow Weep for Me." Interspersing the band's selections were numbers like "Agent Double O Soul" and "Shotgun" by the electrifying gyrating Billy Preston, and "Respect" featuring the Raelettes, Charles' soul-sensitizing quartet of female vocalists.

However, following intermission, the emergence of the Genius provided the focal and vocal lead for the audience to travel even further on the road of musical diversification.

The Ray Charles pop bag of the past was well represented with "Georgia," "Hit the Road Jack" and "I Can't Stop Loving You." Throughout the performance, he reiterated his unchallenged position as a musical magician who can personally adapt and stylize any sort of song to his own "grits and soul" specifications.

Growls of glee intermittently were emitted during "Premium Stuff," a contemporary jazz arrangement, while his country-flavored interpretations of "Cryin' Time" and "Here We Go Again" would have satisfied even Buck Owens.

Perhaps the full spectrum of Charles' vocal variances was revealed in the Beatle-popularized song, "Yesterday." Almost effortlessly, the singer transformed a velvety whisper to an agonizing falsetto, as he melodically crescendoed and cascaded with his muted band in the lyrical, expressive ballad.

The lengthy applause which followed was acknowledged by the performer's comments, "Go ahead! I appreciate it. Ain't no harm to it!"

No harm was seen in a post-performance interview either, and thus, Charles spoke freely about his career and current music.

His personal guideline for maintaining popularity in the ever-evolving American musical scene is simple.

"My theory has been the same for years. I try to stay in touch with the times and attempt to please the people. I've experimented with different types of music and will continue to do so, but the real determination of what I sing depends on public acceptance or rejection," Charles explained.

He claimed that "much of the jazz and blues so popular today has been around for quite a while. Ever since I can remember, this country's had the option of accepting rhythm and blues with a driving beat."

"Actually, some of the blues of the 1930's sound much the same as today's material. But for many years, blues songs unfortunately were categorized as 'race music' and nobody paid any attention to it," the musician noted.

He credited early rock and rollers such as Carl Perkins ("Blue Suede Shoes") and Elvis Presley (several successes) in particular and rockabilly singers in general for bringing "race music" to the masses.

His recording of the Quincy Jones-penned title song of the movie, "In the Heat of the Night," led to the speculation that the versatile artist might himself turn to movie scoring.

"Right now, I have no plans for scoring. I've always believed that to write other than an occasional song, the composer must devote all his time to developing his material. With my schedule of engagements, and club and concert performances, it's simply far too hard to compose in depth," the multi-faceted performer continued.

Meanwhile, although personal appearances demand much of his time and energy, Charles must also maintain his stable of entertainment-related enterprises.

Since he considers Los Angeles his home base, it's understandable that the West Coast City is also the business address of Tangerine Recording company, RPM Recording Studios and Tangerine Productions.

At the current plateau of his career, Charles could well afford relaxation and a respite from the rigors of extensive touring, but the pace goes on.

Truly, it's been a long time and an even lengthier travel from the era of the late 1940's and early 1950's. During that period, the then-younger

Major Events

All big campus events fall under the thumbs of MAJOR EVENTS COMMITTEE. Organized five years ago, the committee plans Campus Day, Homecoming, Winter Weekend and other special concerts. For these festivities, top-name entertainment is imported. During the past year, Major Events has scored a major success with their line-up of Sammy Davis, Jr. for Campus Day '67, a super double-header of Ray Charles and Louis Armstrong for Homecoming, Johnny "Tonight Show" Carson for Winter Weekend and a special concert with The Temptations.

On Saturday, October 21, 1967, Ray Charles and Louis Armstrong coheadlined in the Kent State University Memorial Gym. (Courtesy of the *Chestnut Burr*).

Facing page: Daily Kent Stater ad. (Courtesy of the *Daily Kent Stater*)

artist-composer was writing and recording "I Got a Woman" and "Hallelujah, I Love Her So," and struggling to exit the "race music" syndrome.

The scene's more satisfying now, for the world has recognized that this total concept of a musician.

And it's an added credit to the man that the satisfaction has not become tainted by smugness and/or complacency.

Rich Phoenix, who was a twenty-one-year-old WKSU-FM DJ on Saturday, October 21, 1967, interviewed Ray and Louis backstage in the Kent State University Memorial Gym that night.

I was "chosen" [to interview Louis Armstrong and Ray Charles] because I thought the world of both jazz giants and was not intimidated being close to them. To my knowledge, I was not in competition with anyone else from WKSU-FM and had a weekly jazz show in place at the station for years.

A HAPPENING!!
HOMECOMING '67
RAY CHARLES
Queens
MITCH RYDER
Fireworks
LOUIS ARMSTRONG

Concert: RAY CHARLES   Concert: MITCH RYDER   Dance: LOUIS ARMSTRONG
$2.00, $2.50 $1.50 all seats

OCTOBER 20th & 21st

All Tickets Available at University Ticket Office
Student Union

23

The concert took place in the main field house and interviews were just outside their dressing rooms in the lower level of the building following their performances. Both were coming down from emotional "highs" that follow such a performance. The two interviews were separate, and both performers were very much attuned to where their careers were heading at that moment.

Louis was still very high on the boost his career received from *Hello, Dolly* a couple of years earlier. He was sixty-six years young at the time; once you're in your sixties, time compresses, and his powerful jazz appeal had gone mainstream.

Louis, in the Cold War days of the 1950s and 1960s, had become an American international goodwill ambassador and was beloved in Africa and both eastern and western Europe, including the then Soviet Union. We spoke about that, and he was very philosophical, saying how indebted he was to his fans, wherever they lived and whatever language they spoke. He had truly penetrated the Iron Curtain via the Voice of America and Radio Free Europe and "Hello, Dolly" was a breakout monster. He never anticipated that "Dolly" would turn out to be the hit and career-changer that it became for him.

Stories had circulated that when *Dolly* was still on Broadway, attendees were crushed to discover that Louis could neither be heard nor seen in the production. That was, perhaps, another reason why Hollywood made sure to include him in the lavish film production of *Dolly*.

Louis was a portrait in humility, a humble man whose prodigious talent and career, after much hard work, had made his life turn a 180 from his poverty-stricken youth in the south. In short, Louis was the antithesis of what we think of as pop stars in the twenty-first century!

Ray had a major album project in the works and spoke about that. Both gentlemen were tremendously accommodating and patient with me. Remember, 1967 was a watershed year for pop music, and they were both very impressed with Lennon and McCartney as songwriters in particular. Neither harbored any bitterness about the history of bad U.S. race relations. One thing to keep in mind—they performed separately and had their own backup musicians. It was a remarkable show—a mostly college-age rock-and-roll audience who were quite impressed but had no idea of the gravity of these two individuals that they were experiencing up close and personal.

I am sorry to report that my recorded interviews went with a 1997 house fire. That annoys and depresses me. If WKSU-FM had archived [materials] during its long student-run tenure, they should be able to come up with it, although it's been my observation that they preserved very little from those halcyon days.

The interviews were not broadcast live, and that is a real shame. As far as a live broadcast of the concert itself, that would have been preferable, but rights to such things, for years, have remained a major snarl which keeps these wonderful occasions off the air—and these were in the decidedly pre-Internet days! The record companies and talent management typically had these rights locked up tight and would generally only authorize a broadcast if and only if they could tie it in with a specific promotion, such as a new album.

Looking back at his discography, it confirms that in this relative twilight of the great man's career, [Louis Armstrong] was exceedingly successful with mainstream middle-of-the-road pop music, such as "Hello, Dolly," which had blown the Beatles off the singles charts in 1964. It became a must-play staple at every single gig of the rest of the man's life. I recall his sidemen as being a mix of young cats and some of his contemporaries who had worked with him since his days as a jazz pioneer, going back into the 1920s. This, then, was three years after "Dolly," and the great man seemed to still be bowled over by the international success of the tune, which was virtually unknown when he cut it.

As for the set, I remember it as a mixture of the current and the tried and true. Current—of course he did "Dolly," and I believe that he also performed "What a Wonderful World," which probably became the biggest moneymaker of his posthumous career. Back then, ABC Records, his then U.S. label, would not get behind it and promote it properly, likely a reaction to the politics of the times. The song topped the charts in Europe in the late 1960s. As far as tunes from his earlier days, of course there was some energetic Dixieland music, featuring some of his wonderful acrobatics on the horn. In short, Louie was very philosophical about where music and jazz had taken him—or, had he not been such a modest man, more correctly where he had taken music and jazz. He was a great man and icon, modest to a fault, and never given the credit he deserved in his lifetime for his musical accomplishments, his leadership, or his frequent encouragement to young musicians.

[And] Ray Charles—wow! He was a man constantly in motion. For this show, he had assembled a powerful set of sidemen and, of course, the Raelettes, the all-female backing singers who had started out as an independent hit-making rock-and-roll girl group. He was promoting his recent *Listen* album release, which was positively excellent. If you can find it, you will have some brilliant, slick but vintage Ray Charles added to your music library.

The set, of course, featured the Ray Charles monster hits and crowd-pleasers "Georgia,"

"What'd I Say," "I Got News for You," and many more, including some of the tasty highlights from his magnificent crossover album of country music, of which I believe there were two separate volumes. He also had a "live" album that had been doing very well at the time, with the feature cut being "Makin' Whoopee," then a monster radio hit featuring Ray on his own on solo piano with the live audience egging him on to improvise on the suggestive lyrics—that one's a gem if you can find it, and was a prominent playlist item on WCUY-FM, then Cleveland Heights' pioneering all-jazz station which did frequent promotions with Cleveland's leading jazz club, Leo's Casino.

Of course, I made sure that "Whoopee" got a few plays on my *Jazz in America* on WKSU-FM. Yes, Ray, like Louis, was an icon of a somewhat later era in jazz and pop music and a prodigious talent who, history has told us, was often victimized by his own goodwill and generosity. Again, another humble man who experienced grinding poverty in his youth. He was trusting of his management to a fault and, although he enjoyed the great success which he richly earned and deserved, was allowed to take home only a fraction of the money he had earned for the publishers, promoters, and record companies. His two major labels of the time were ABC Paramount and Atlantic. When we spoke, Ray was very forthcoming and ready to talk music—all forms of pop and, of course, jazz. He was in awe of Louis, certainly! Ray was greatly impressed by the quality of songwriters of the time: Lennon and McCartney, Bacharach and David, and Jimmy Webb, amongst others, as well as the Motown stable in particular. He was an advocate for pop and jazz music to be taken much more seriously as the music of the people that would endure and said so.

He took special pains on stage to introduce the various musicians accompanying him. Ray sat stage left while Billy Preston sat far stage right. Billy came up with some very tasty keyboard licks whenever he got a break and was up and dancing whenever the music permitted. He had all the intensity and moves of Jerry Lee Lewis without using his feet on the keys. Of course, the Genius gave Billy and his talents a big boost on stage; and, within two years' time, Billy became the fifth Beatle on the roof of the band's London townhouse/office in their *Let It Be* feature film.

In the interview, Ray waxed very philosophical about the music business, taking pains to eschew the limiting effects of labels on music, whether it be termed rock and roll, country, jazz, or R&B. He was a purist for the quality of the melody in the music and for its being played tunefully and accurately with respect. Once again, Ray was all about taking the spotlight away from himself and diverting attention to the young musicians and composers on the scene just trying to get their careers up and running. After our too brief encounter after the concert, I knew that I had truly been in the presence of genius, or more precisely—two of 'em in one evening!

This was always something in my KSU experience that came and went too quickly—like the morning after a too vivid dream in blazing color, with smells and sound to match—things you reached out and touched. Of course, the morning after, you turn things over in your head, saying, "Did this really happen?"

The Temptations played at Kent State on Sunday, November 12, 1967.

The Temptations
Their Concert Souled Out
By David L. Bieber
Daily Kent Stater
November 14, 1967

Mighty Motown descended upon Kent State Sunday evening with synchronization and a co-ordination of efforts befitting a Detroit new car assembly line.

A momentary closing of the eyes would have convinced the listener that he had transcended the Memorial Gymnasium confines and rather, was part of a soul show and revue at either New York's Apollo Theatre or the Regal Theatre in Chicago.

Soul is a term too often loosely applied to many Negro and a few white musical performers. The on-top-of-the-market musical entrepreneur will explain in simplistic terms the reason for the expansion of the world of soul. Stated simply, soul sells, whether the word is applied to the blues in the raw of Howlin' Wolf and John Lee Hooker or the chicken-rock sound of Peaches and Herb.

Somewhere in the midst of this broadening musical culture is "The Sound of Young America," or Motown. The Temptations, the Elgins and, yes, even ventriloquist Willie Tyler and his lifelike cohort, Lester, fused the worlds of blues, rhythm and blues and pop and catapulted a handclapping, often vocally encouraging audience into a land bordering on Harlem and Hough; Soulsville.

The Elgins, one of the lesser-known aggregates in the Berry Gordy Jr. Hitsville groove stable, provided a more than adequate prelude

By Popular demand Major Events Presents:
THE TEMPTATIONS -- In concert

November 12, 1967
8:00 p.m. Memorial Gym

Tickets sold at University Ticket Office
$2.50 - $2.00 -- $1.50

The Temptations played at Kent State on Sunday, November 12, 1967. (Courtesy of the *Daily Kent Stater*)

to the second half concert appearance of the Temptations.

Functioning with the clocklike precision implied by their collective name, the Elgins stylishly revamped and revitalized several rhythm and blues classics, such as "Midnight Hour," "It's a Man's World," and "Beechwood 4-5789."

Also introduced to the Memorial audience were several of the group's own R&B chart toppers, including powerhouse vocal treatments of "Put Yourself in My Place" and "Heaven Must Have Sent You."

Bridging the musical respite between Elgins and Temptations was Willie Tyler and Lester. Ventriloquist Tyler utilized his 20 minutes in a series of skillfully manipulated comedy exchanges with Lester, his affable and witty (pardon the term) dummy.

Smokey Robinson and the Miracles filled the Memorial Gymnasium on Sunday, October 13, 1968. (Courtesy of the *Chestnut Burr*)

The two parlayed colloquialisms like "say what" into a session of soulful sneezes, before concluding with a Motownized version of "I'm a Believer," leaving little doubt that the Monkees have touched us all in one way or another.

Enter the Temptations. Bedecked in black tuxedos, crimson-lined and double-breasted, the five showmen grabbed from several sound bags to effortlessly and effectively convey good vibrations from the Motor City.

Leading with a medley of their vintage hits, including "Girl, Why You Wanna Make Me Blue" and "The Girl's Alright," David Ruffin and crew progressed on their path of musical successes. Throughout the performance, they reiterated that while their roots may have been planted in R&B their shoots now have emerged full bloomed and custom-tailored to the pop market as well.

Visual plus vocal excitement reigned, and while primarily renowned as singers, the addition of their frenetic choreography certainly enhanced the continuous musical movement.

Although the crowd clearly favored the rapid-paced presentation of top ten selections like "Beauty's Only Skin Deep" "My Girl," and "Ain't Too Proud to Beg," the Temptations did on occasion successfully depart from their chart material. "Hello, Young Lovers" was a precision production, meshing singing and dancing which would have pleased not only Rodgers and Hammerstein, but the Rockettes as well.

Flexibility came to be the keynote of the evening, as the group showcased its diverse abilities by rhythmically blending "Yesterday" with "What Now My Love." In this combination, the bass voice of Melvin Franklin extracted the last ounce of sound from the lower scale, and the audience reaction was heavy.

An inventive interpretation of "Swanee" further amplified the Temptations' vocal dexterity and was neatly augmented by steamboat sound effects by the band. Sans musical accompaniment, the five singers deftly carried a stanza of "Way Down upon the Swanee River" before concluding the number.

Moving with mercurial fluidity, the acrobatic quintet solidified their Kent popularity with versions of their most recent singles skyrockets, "You're My Everything" and "It's You That I Need."

The spotlight ceased after "I'm Losing You" and the group packed up their talents and headed for Cleveland.

However, as the pre-concert ticket rush in the sub-Hub indicated, the Temptations KSU concert was definitely "souled out."

Smokey Robinson and the Miracles filled the Memorial Gymnasium on Sunday, October 13, 1968.

Smokey Fires Up Greek Week
By Saul Daniels and Harold L. Greenberg
Daily Kent Stater
October 15, 1968

Motown sound—lots of it filled Memorial Gym Sunday night as the Greek Week '68 activities came to a close with a concert starring recording artists Smokey Robinson and The Miracles.

The brassy, jazzy sounds of Bohannon and the Motown Sound, followed by a swingin' quartet The Monitors—filled in the evening's measure of talented entertainment.

The Bohannon men, featuring three saxophones, two trumpets, double guitars and drums, opened the show with several popular songs, including a hot, brassy upbeat version of "The Look of Love," and a fine rendition of "Uptight," which featured alto saxophone and drum solos which drew modest applause from the attentive audience.

The octet, dressed in black tuxedos and white turtleneck shirts, also provided the music for The Monitors and Smokey.

Bohannon and the Motown Sound did their thing, a combination of the smoothness of Lawrence Welk with the brashness of the Tijuana Brass and a good hunk of Motown thrown in.

Smokey Robinson and the Miracles in Kent State's Memorial Gymnasium on Sunday, October 13, 1968 (Courtesy of the *Daily Kent Stater*)

To the music "Looking for Love," the four Monitors moved onstage and drew immediate audience reaction with the purple suits worn by the three men. White piping along the jacket edge combined with white shoes, turtlenecks and handkerchiefs provided a contrast to the purple, while the female member wore a white, tiered chiffon mini-dress.

The group proved to be a crowd-pleaser as it mixed good singing with appropriate choreography and occasional pantomime.

The Monitors were rewarded with heavy applause for an old standard designed especially for sweethearts, "I Only Have Eyes for You."

Their version was slow and heavy with the Motown beat.

The four then took part in a mime version of "Frankie and Johnny," as lead singer Richard Street intoned the tragic story of the girl "who shot her man in the middle of his big affair."

For men between 21 and 26, the quartet brought forth laughter with "Greetings, This Is Uncle Sam, and I Need You," a sharp satire in which the group displayed its excellent overall talents. The group then went into a number of skits about Army life.

"We gonna make a man out of you, we hope," said one.

"No," said the other in a fragile, lisping voice.

The Monitors ushered in the interval with a soul-session sing-along. And all that was left was for Smokey and his Miracles to appear. Finally, after a brief intermission, the moment the audience had really been waiting for arrived. Smokey Robinson and The Miracles jogged into the spotlights.

The quartet wore powder-blue velvet double-breasted jackets, white satin shirts and bow ties, contrasted by red carnations provided by Phi Sigma Kappa fraternity.

They easily slipped into their polished version of "I Second That Emotion," for an opener, and then Smokey got the audience involved by asking them to say "yeah" or "no" in response to the questions "Do you want to be loved?" and "Do you want somebody to hurt you?"

The group's choreography and form was excellent, which is no wonder considering the four have been together since 1955, when Smokey was still in junior high school. He is now 28.

On the love theme, Smokey and his Miracles sang "More Love" and "Yesterlove," both of which brought rounds of applause from the receptive crowd. Moving in and out of the blue spotlight beam, they began "Tracks of My Tears," a recent favorite.

They showed beautiful voice control and artistic choreography in their rendition of The Fifth Dimension's "Up, Up and Away." They followed this with "Special Occasion," another favorite of the audience.

The soft, slow, Grammy Award–winning song, "Theme from the Valley of the Dolls," got a moving interpretation from the versatile foursome.

The crowd clapped in time with the music as the group jumped into "Just Give Me Some Kind of Sign." It was about this time that ties and jackets worn by the performers came off. They were really in the groove now and the audience was loving every minute of it.

The crowd oohed and aahed as The Miracles did a few bumps and grinds and began a soft harmonizing version of "Flamingo" in which they sounded somewhat similar to the Four Freshmen vocal group.

After that, Smokey got a little more personal with his admirers and, in prefacing his next song, "You've got your arms around your girl or you're holding close someone you love very much, like those two guys up there . . ." and pointed vaguely toward the bleachers. The audience burst forth with laughter and applause at his antics.

And then, inevitably, the group sang its last song of the show, a rousing version of "Going to a Go-Go," after which it headed for the dressing room while the audience showed its appreciation for the evening's fare with a standing ovation.

The eighth annual Greek Week was finished. It was possibly the biggest and best bash the Greeks have ever thrown for themselves and the university. All that was left was the cleaning up.

· · ·

For members of the press, the evening wasn't quite complete. A 10-minute press conference with Smokey, while he underwent a quick change of clothing, followed the concert. A very frank and personable fellow, Smokey proved to be easy to talk to and well aware of the environment in which he has become a star.

The four *Stater* staffers and *Burr* editor Jeff Sallott all had questions for Smokey.

"This is a wild year, politically . . . " Saul Daniels, Stater managing editor started to say, to be interrupted by Smokey's comment, "It's a complete farce . . . like in the vaudeville days when you saw plays about politicians going around; everybody's running, kissing the babies and smoking cigars. This is ridiculous."

When asked about the candidacy of George Wallace, Smokey replied, "He's ridiculous! That's my reaction to him. He's ridiculous. He is one of the million people who makes the campaign ridiculous.

When Harold Greenberg, *Stater* editor, asked him if he would vote this year or boycott the election, he said, "I won't let it go by. I haven't made up my mind exactly what I'm going to do yet. They killed my man, ya dig? I was for Robert Kennedy and he's dead. It's ridiculous. It's a fanfare. I know you must have to admit that to yourself. Have you ever seen anything like this in your life?"

Playing three concerts a week, Smokey said that he has felt some repercussion from the fact that he and the members of his group are black. He said that he is sure that he and other black performers would have gone much farther in their careers if they were white. "Take for instance a group such as The Supremes. If they were white, they'd all have TV shows each one of them!"

As quickly as it had started, the conference came to an end. Smokey and his Miracle men had a plane to catch for a return trip to Detroit.

Eric Burdon and the Animals played at Kent State on Monday, October 21, 1968.

KSU's First
An Experience in Sound
By George Markell
Daily Kent Stater
October 23, 1968

It was a long wait for Eric Burdon and the Animals. Since the concert was sponsored by the Homecoming people, we were treated to a little march of the Queen candidates to start the program. Then Bert Mason did a coffeehouse type thing, playing a folk guitar and singing blues, right down to "When the Saints Go Marching In." His spoken routine had some subtle humor to it, but a bristling barrier of uneasiness between him and his audience killed his act. Maybe he assumed too much sophistication on the part of the audience, but the Wills Gym floor was none too comfortable for his hour and a half act when the people came to hear the Animals.

The Animals immediately commanded the sharpest attention from the half-numb, wandering minds. They were loud, exciting, and beautifully electric. Eric Burdon did a lot of jumping and screaming and shaking, playing the tambourine and throwing his microphone into the air. Flashing colored lights and strobe lights made the walls and ceiling respond to the music, adding another dimension to the total-environment effect. Did you say psychedelic?

They started with some new things: "Gemini," "White Houses," and "Colored Rain" took up the first 45 minutes, and by that time the lights were finally working properly. The music was overpowering, rousing, and the effect was very physical. They made everyone's head an echo chamber, with prolonged crescendos and

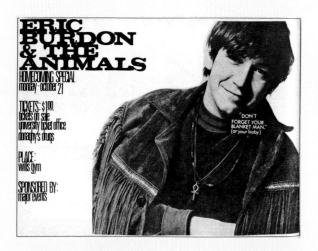

Eric Burdon seemed to "freak out" during his performance of "Monterey" in which he jumped and crawled all over the stage.

Eric Burdon and the Animals played at Kent State on Monday, October 21, 1968. (Courtesy of the *Daily Kent Stater*)

cymbal rolls like musical orgasms. The whole gym vibrated, and the audience was carried off into electronic euphoria.

They played "To Love Somebody," an old Bee Gees' number, and then reached their highest pitch with "Monterey." The crowd began clamoring for "Sky Pilot," and the Animals were prepared to oblige.

This, their final number, was a spectacular finishing touch. A cloud of smoke and a searchlight from the stage, with sirens in the background simulated the conditions of an air raid. The crowd edged closer to the stage, and as the smoke cleared the excitement grew. Soon Eric was rolling on the stage, fighting with his organ player, and as spectators mounted the platform for a better look, the Animals dropped everything and were out the back door.

Every minute of the performance was exciting. The frenzied action on the stage never let up and no one could guess what extremes Eric would be carried to next. They began with ten amplifiers, but blew two of them out by the third song. Six songs lasted an hour and a half, and only rarely did they tone it down to catch a breath.

As musicians, on records, you can take them or leave them, but at the in-person performance, there was no choice. It was their trip, and they took everyone with them.

On Sunday, January 26, 1969, B. B. King drew a crowd in the University School gym.

1969 Creative Arts Festival
The King—B.B.
By Dave Pack
Daily Kent Stater
January 28, 1969

The King of Blues, B.B. entered Kent. The crowd, after the concert, left shaking their heads. It was a time well spent.

Applause was in the air long before the concert had begun. B.B. entered at 7:30 in a classy pink overcoat and immediately was greeted with clapping hands from what was then a gathering of about 100. At concert time there were 500, as B.B. came to the stage, he received a standing ovation. All this occurred before he had touched Lucille. So much more was to come.

The show, given before a devoted audience, began with B.B.'s back up group, Sonny Freeman and the Unusuals. After two jump jazz numbers, which had heads bobbing, they went into "Up, Up and Away," a song less moving, but definitely symbolic of B.B.

As B.B. entered, the crowd was up and clapping enthusiastically. Then B.B. went for Lucille. She didn't respond. No sound. A bad chord.

Enthusiasm became submerged, tenseness filled the air. B.B. attempted to gab it with the audience, but as he was to say later, "Without my guitar, I feel undressed." Indeed, he was naked, embarrassed and groping.

But—from the audience came a chord. And from B.B. came a sound. And B.B. began to play and all became so good.

With Lucille in his hands, B.B. took command. Using a whining feedback technique, he virtually wound a note round the audience. He then fed them a one-hand guitar riff. It was fast, and executed well by the master. Most of all it typified B.B.'s musical desire. "I work hard 'cause I want to be wanted. Yes, I study quite a bit."

B.B.'s class and study brought him through. Now the crowd really wanted "Him!"

Guitar notes began darting through the audience. Piercing, stabbing. B.B. was a painless needle freely shooting impassioned blues. Veins were surfacing and hearts began beating wildly.

Heaving bodies and the painfully sweet fingerwork of B.B. manifested multiple orgasms.

B.B. was extremely climactic throughout the night. He would begin playing so, so softly. So soft, yet so magical was he. Geometry was all around, for B.B. was twisting people in right

On Sunday, January 26, 1969, B. B. King drew a crowd in the University School gym. (Courtesy of the *Daily Kent Stater*)

33

angles. With his chick-a-chick, jab-a-stab, whine-awhile guitar, he would first bring the people into him.

But not all was in B.B.'s guitar. He, too, has a voice. With it he began an expressive and communicative tale of the blues.

B.B. sang with unrivaled enthusiasm, always striving to become a part of his surroundings. His barrelhouse delivery and sometimes bawdy lyrics were quick to draw nods as well as laughter.

Admiration and respect were in all faces. This was especially evident when B.B. took time out to introduce his backup group. Upon introduction, they all received subdued but appreciative applause. But his final introduction phrase, "and Lucille," brought not subdued applause but rather spirited cheering and thunderous applause. Such was the scene in the first half of the show.

Intermission.

Elmo Morris, "No. 1 Soul Brother," began the second half. He didn't do any show-stealing, but then again he had neither the intention nor the power. Singing "Knock on Wood," and a slow and soulful "Tobacco Road," he was a contrasting element, rather than an outright talent. He served his purpose—anxiety was in the crowd. They wanted to hear B.B. Minds had definitely been working in the King camp when Elmo was put on stage, for the crowd was wanting King more than ever. Enter B.B. and yet another standing ovation.

He ripped off three successive instrumentals. The crowd, composed of blues gluttons, was devouring every damn note. Every eye was on this man King, it was all so good that it couldn't have gotten better, yet it did. B.B. went to his voice and began singing "Someday." Tinged with vulgarity, it was the lyrical work of a genius, for he placed bawdiness so perfectly, so artistically, that it came out as a truly beautiful

love song. After all was said and done B.B. received four standing ovations, and a block of mass love. Words can never express what was felt for this great, great, blues man. He was so good, so good, oh, so good.

On Sunday, October 5, 1969, Sly and the Family Stone played at the Memorial Gym for Greek Week.

Audience Gets "High" on Sly

By T. P. Waterhouse
Daily Kent Stater
October 7, 1969.

Sly and the Family Stone, featured musical group of the Greek Week concert, exploded Sunday night in Memorial Gym before a capacity audience. The musical explosion was approached gradually, with the music becoming heavier as the night progressed.

The crowd enjoyed hit songs played by the group, such as "Stand," and "Everyday People," but the audience really began to go wild when the Family Stone sang "Take Me Higher." During that number the group made the sign of peace toward the crowd. The audience then displayed the peace sign in return, meanwhile standing and dancing and shouting back "Higher!"

When it seemed as though the crowd couldn't be taken any higher, Sly and the Family Stone ran off the stage. The still-standing and clapping audience applauded, screamed, whistled and shouted for more.

The group then returned to the stage to do the seemingly impossible: Encoring with "Hot Fun in the Summertime," they took the gym full of people even higher! Hallelujah, brother!

The Liverpool Scene, who preceded The Fam-

On Sunday, October 5, 1969, Sly and the Family Stone played at the Memorial Gym for Greek Week. (Courtesy of the *Chestnut Burr*)

ily Stone, began their set with some entertaining and original material. Their freeform, eerie jazz piece, "Tramcar to Frankenstein," was exciting and musically tight, featuring the lead guitar player and saxophonist.

The Reverend Gary Davis headlined the Fourth Annual Folk Festival on Friday night, February 13, 1970.

Rev. Davis

"The Sweetest of Melodies"
By David Pack
Daily Kent Stater
February 17, 1970

About 300 lucky people attended the Ohio Folk Festival staged in the University Auditorium Friday night. The "lucky ones" were pumped country blues, music of the Appalachians, Dylanism, Simon music, Rush, Lightfoot and Bevan.

Daily Kent Stater cartoon by Chuck Ayers, fall 1969 (Courtesy of the *Daily Kent Stater*)

▶ 35

The Rev. Gary Davis in the University Auditorium Friday, February 13, 1970 (Courtesy of the *Chestnut Burr*)

The Reverend Gary Davis headlined the Fourth Annual Folk Festival on Friday night, February 13, 1970. (Courtesy of the *Daily Kent Stater*)

The Rev. Gary Davis in the University Auditorium Friday, February 13, 1970 (*Daily Kent Stater* photo by Howard Ruffner)

Playing the country blues, the Rev. Gary Davis took his audience back to the days of house rent parties. If the audience couldn't visualize the hog maws and chittlings on the table, hear the shouts of "shake 'em on down," the whine of bullets in the air which happened when people got to feeling good; at least the audience had the opportunity to feel the scene through this blind man.

Led by one of the performers, the Rev. Mr. Davis came tottering to the microphone and said, "I ain't gonna do like these folks was doin' before I came. I ain't gonna cause I can't." But Davis' statement was one of unconscious irony.

Not only could no one on the stage recapitulate his guitar phrasing but with the previous feats of men like Blind Blake and Bill Broonzy, it remains to be seen if anyone in the world can play like the Rev. Gary Davis.

From within his bent, 73-year-old frame came a voice of amazing vitality, and from the fingertips poured the sweetest of melodies. From his lips came the well-known sermon on the game of the he versus she.

Before the concert the Rev. Mr. Davis was asked what numbers he'd be doing. He answered, "It depends on the way I feel." Evidently the Rev. Mr. Davis was in a happy mood, for a great part of his one-hour concert was, in his words, "happy music."

He began with two spirituals, "Keep your Lamb" and "If I Had My Way," then switched to a lighter, "easygoin'" form with "She's Funny That Way," and instrumentals interspersed with "de da da do do's" and shouts of joy.

The country blues singer has remained untouched by flux and fads of society, and by remaining unchanged, he has isolated himself from his audience. Therefore, he will never become rich. "I played more guitar for a nickel than I did for a dollar," said the Rev. Mr. Davis. Yet despite blindness and old age, he is the freest man I have ever seen,

"Blues ain't nothing but a 'gutbucket' crowd of people," said Gary Davis. Not many people would like that adjective used to describe them, but the people at the concert would, I am sure, consider it a compliment.

Seven acts preceded Davis' and, for the most part, they got progressively better. The S & R Housing Development, from Lorain Community College, began the show.

Sunni Light from Lake Erie College followed with "Cathy's Song," by Paul Simon, and two songs of her own, which were, in her words "a nameless song" and "a little ditty." Sunni had a fine voice and could pick the guitar rather well.

Larry Lamovsky, from Kent State, appeared next and was the first performer to draw extended applause.

"The Wine Song," "Four in the Morning," and "A Song for my Guitar" were done by Al Bevan from Akron University and Rolly Brown from Kent State as they combined vocal and guitar talents to emerge as the finest folk duo of the night.

With the advent of Terry Singleton from Cleveland State and accompanist Bill Bloom, one had a rare combination of Dylanesque vocalizing and Castillian guitar.

Howard Cory Hobbes from Kent State took

me back to the days of such famed musicians as Charlie Poole and Hobart Smith.

Rob Reide, a self-styled humorist, singer and guitarist from the University of Cincinnati, closed out the show of Ohio talent.

Then came Davis and a series of non-toxic highs.

On Sunday, October 11, 1970, as part of the Homecoming festivities, Sha Na Na opened for Jefferson Airplane in the Memorial Gym.

Sha Na Na Outshines Airplane

By Doreen Sapir
Daily Kent Stater
October 13, 1970

To the surprise of many in the capacity-filled Memorial Gymnasium Sunday evening, Sha Na Na outshone the performance of the highly acclaimed Jefferson Airplane at Kent State's 1970–1971 Homecoming Concert.

Introduced as "a group of grease," Sha Na Na's dozen-plus members harmoniously performed popular rock 'n' roll hits of the 1950's via both singing and choreography.

Advertisement for Sha Na Na and Jefferson Airplane during Homecoming (Courtesy of the *Daily Kent Stater*)

Jefferson Airplane performing in the Kent State University Memorial Gym (Photos courtesy of the *Chestnut Burr*)

The performers' garb included white socks, athletic t-shirts, high-topped black leather jackets, faded Levis, skin-tight sleeveless jerseys and dark sunglasses. The three major choreographers sported shimmery light-colored slacks and open jackets with no shirts. Slicked back hair and thick sideburns were prevalent among the group's members.

Each "golden oldie" hit Sha Na Na performed was a brief act in itself, complete with expressions of emotion through both gestures and voice. Never, though, did the group lose its tongue-in-cheek atmosphere.

Hit tunes revived from the 1950's include "Chantilly Lace," "Let's Go to the Hop" and "Why Do Fools Fall in Love?" The audience wildly cheered and clapped along to "Rock 'n' Roll Is Here to Stay."

Receiving several well-deserved standing ovations, Sha Na Na returned to the stage for three encores. The incessant, demanding rhythmic clapping and shouts of "We want more!" from the audience were only ended after the final encore when the lights were turned on for intermission.

Unfortunately, the last half of the show featuring the Jefferson Airplane was a letdown from the first part of the concert. In the 9 P.M. show most of the songs performed by Grace Slick, sounded the same, with the exception of "Somebody to Love," "White Rabbit" and "Volunteers of America."

Miss Slick, adorned in a striking purple maxidress and wearing her dark hair long and curly, addressed several comments to the audience which were inaudible to the majority of her listeners in the gymnasium.

At first the light show which was flashed on a screen across the back of the stage by Glenn McKay's Headlights was hypnotically captivating, and the audience appeared to be on a natural, non-drug-induced "trip."

Throughout the Airplane's performance, projectors flashed both abstract and realistic images on the screen in a psychedelic blaze of color.

Parliament-Funkadelic headlined a show in the Memorial Gym on Saturday, November 14, 1970.

Black Concert
"Beautiful and Moving"
By Wayne Moyer
Daily Kent Stater
November 17, 1970

What can a white "doper" with a suburban middleclass background get out of a black concert? The answer is light entertainment as well as a heavy learning experience—particularly if he

Advertisement for the Parliament-Funkadelic show in Kent (Courtesy of the *Daily Kent Stater*)

attended Saturday night's black concert in Memorial Gym.

The concert was one of many events during the "First Annual Black Togetherness," Black Homecoming. The evening was both beautiful and moving, with philosopher-comic James Reston Jackson, the Parli-Funkadelics and Watts 103rd Street Band.

Arriving early, I was first moved to review only the audience, forget the music. Dressed in their brilliant plumage, I was aware of the high degree of sophistication and individualism with which they dressed.

I sensed how dull the white freak culture was by comparison—the "Airplane" audience as an example—how desperate for entertainment. This audience, however, was able to enjoy themselves and their night, be it proud or just good fun.

Jackson, the comic, began the night's show with a social commentary and "life-message" that was truly beautiful. Unfortunately, most of the message was lost to a bad sound system. His idea, "free your funky minds and your ass will follow," I will remember. For this and other thoughts, I thanked Jackson after the show. I now thank BUS for engaging Jackson.

It had been said that Jackson was there to prepare the audience for the Parli-Funkadelics. I soon found this was necessary—they were

Parliament-Funkadelic headlined a show in the Memorial Gym on Saturday, November 14, 1970. (*Daily Kent Stater* photo by Frank Schwelik)

immediately hypnotizing. I lost my mind temporarily, but they returned it to me. I appreciate that because they didn't have to give it back, I know. Thanks guys.

The Funkadelics played what sounded to be two songs, each at least a half hour long, each consisting of three or four movements. Three instrumentalists and four singers, all blasting away, down on their knees, dramatically acting out their lyrics and images. Sweat soaked the lead singer's army camouflage suit and, at times, pain or ecstasy contorted his body.

Not being a single-record group, they did not present songs as such. Instead they gave the audience something more positive, an experience. They closed their act with a stage packed with

a dancing audience, caught up in the music and chanting repeatedly a melodic passage lasting an additional 10 minutes.

A half hour break preceded the Watts Band. Some man came on and told us someone had "accidentally" broken into the Funkadelics' dressing room while they were on stage and had stolen all their clothes. Unfortunate.

So was the Watts band. They've made drastic changes in their style in their three years. Now it's big band, lots of brass and top 40. It was a light way to come off a heavy night. The hits were played and so the crash was easy. A little too easy perhaps, but nothing could have torn down the good solid evening.

Chrissie Hynde

Fall 1971

For a long time any stories about Chrissie Hynde in Kent were pretty vague. What was known was that she went to Kent State in the late '60s and early '70s, but that was many years before her music career would even start. When a photo of her along with two others posing as greasers on a Kent street corner popped up on Facebook around 2011, I had to know more about what I was looking at. Through asking around I found out the photo was taken in the fall of 1971 by a man named Stephen Buck for an old underground Kent newspaper called *Stump City* (a play on Tree City). Through some acquaintances I was able to identify the two folks on the left and right of Chrissie as Bill Rubenstein and Jim Greco (respectively). Jim Greco, who was a passionate activist living in Kent at the time the picture was taken, agreed to talk to me on the record about it. This is what he told me about *Stump City*, Chrissie Hynde, and that photo taken on the corner of West Main and South Mantua Streets in Kent:

I went to Kent State starting as a freshman in 1968, and I lived in town on and off through those years. I was really caught up in the times and the whole movement. By the fall of 1971, which is when that photo was taken, I was at the point where if we believed all those things we really believed in, we really shouldn't be in school, and I still believe that. I had dropped out of school after the fall trimester after the 1970 shootings, and then I went back for one more semester, and I realized that staying in school didn't make much sense to me.

Left to right: Bill Rubenstein, Chrissie Hynde, and Jim Greco, fall 1971. Originally printed in *Stump City*. (Photo by Stephen Buck)

Page from *Stump City* (Photo by Michael Pacifico)

Early on, I was very active in SDS [Students for a Democratic Society], and I just remained active after leaving and then coming back to Kent in 1971. By 1971, the political climate at Kent State had become pretty dissipated compared to just a couple years earlier. There were some liberal dorm hippie kind of politics going on, though nothing really heavy, and SDS was completely dispersed.

There was a political Kent paper, the *Dragonfire.* I believe it came out in the winter of 1970, more of a straight political paper. Later on, we decided to do *Stump City,* which was a commentary on the fact that Kent was pretty much being torn down to accommodate the large number of students and the people who were starting to come into the area.

We all had multiple roles. We all did everything. Steve Buck was responsible for the photography, but other than that, it was more or less everybody did everything. It wasn't like things we had done before, where you had an ideological push behind you. This was more or less people in a particular place and we were making commentary.

Chrissie Hynde wasn't necessarily part of the circle I traveled in, but there were people who knew me who were part of another circle who knew her. I wasn't particularly close to her. She was just someone I'd say hi to in the dorms, and it just so happened that we were going to take this picture, and she was willing to come down. I mean she wasn't "Chrissie Hynde" back then. There was nothing special about that photo coming together; I think it was just happenstance.

You wanna know what that photoshoot with the car was about? It was about attitude. What attitude? Just that we were doing whatever we wanted to do. We saw this hip car, and we thought we'd do something with it. It's a great

The present-day southwest corner of Mantua and West Main Streets where Bill Rubenstein, Chrissie Hynde, and Jim Greco were photographed in fall 1971 (Photo by Jason Prufer)

shot though, isn't it? And the photo throws across an attitude.

We were all dressed as greasers because in 1971, that was a relevant icon. We were part of a generation that was really young in the '50s and the early '60s, and those people were all around us. I saw it that way, and I am sure Bill Rubenstein would say that. It was iconic. It was a cool shot.

I pulled my hair back and I'm smoking. Bill looks good. Chrissie to my right. Look at her face, how she's looking off the other way and she's smoking and her legs are split open. Also, I'm looking at one side and Bill is looking through those sunglasses with a pack of cigarettes rolled up in his sleeve. There's a lot of pretense there, but the shot works.

And with Chrissie—I mean who in the hell knew who she was back then? She wasn't doing

any music or anything. I mean, it's not like we were hanging out with *the* Chrissie Hynde, it was just—she was just Chris Hynde.

Stump City didn't really go that far. It wasn't like we had a publications committee or an editorial committee—that kind of stuff wasn't really happening with the paper. It was just something that happened for a very short amount of time, and it was something that still sort of had a connection to the earlier days. *Stump City* was more of an attitude, and I think the picture says that. In fact I think the picture is the best thing that was done for the entire run of the paper. If there's anything which brings back any part that was left after the shootings, it's probably that picture.

It's a great picture, and it has an attitude, and it makes me remember Bill, and it makes me remember that close group that we had.

Sly and the Family Stone played at Kent State on Friday, February 19, 1972. (*Right*: Courtesy of the *Daily Kent Stater*; *below*: courtesy of the *Chestnut Burr*)

This Friday!
Memorial Gym

TICKETS NOW ON SALE
AT THE
UNIVERSITY TICKET OFFICE
STUDENT UNION
672-2010 FOR INFORMATION

A watch and three free lessons from Mickey Mouse to Sly and his Family Stone for punctuality above and beyond the call of duty and contract. Along with it, an accountant to Belkin Productions, which had about 5,300 paid admissions and about 7,000 persons at the concert.

Sly and the Family Stone played at Kent State on Friday, February 19, 1972.

Out-of-Tune Sly Not Worth 4-Hour Wait

Charles Hupcey
Daily Kent Stater
February 22, 1972

I'm writing this letter to express my feelings about the Sly concert last Friday. I've two basic complaints about it, though.

First I arrived with my date at 9 P.M. Friday, and when I got to the gym there were already about 200 people at the Bowman-side entrance. It was fairly cold outside, but most people felt they could stand it until the doors opened at 9:30—only the doors didn't open at 9:30! By 10 the crowd was cold and very restless, but who could blame them? By 10:30, they started to let people through the gates, too late for one girl, who had gotten physically ill due to the squeezing of the crowd for the past hour and a half. Finally by 10:45 my date and I were seated.

Now comes my second and most serious complaint. Where was Sly? Records were played and played and played; finally a girl came on with her group—I never caught her name—but as it turned out, she was the best part of the show.

Where was Sly? Then one of the emcees came to the mike and said Sly would be on in five minutes; he was dressing. Forty minutes later, Sly appeared. It was now 12:50! It wouldn't have been quite as bad a show if Sly had been in tune and on key, but he wasn't!

My date and I were miserable, after all this and now Sly sounded terrible! It was just too much to take. We left after two songs, it was all our ears could stand.

In conclusion, I have a few words of advice for the Community Action Council. First, I hope they've noticed the kind of respect Sly has for his viewers and listeners and never ask him to appear here again! Second, I hope whoever was in charge of admitting the audience into the gym reads the letter and realizes the contempt I have for their actions of last Friday. I'm sure my feelings are shared by many others.

Finally I hope the CAC can get themselves together—I've seen great concerts in the past; I hope I can see them in the future.

Ravi Shankar played at Kent State on Sunday, April 16, 1972.

Shankar
Dual Musical Role: Traditional, Experimental
By Bob von Sternberg
Daily Kent Stater
April 18, 1972

Ravi Shankar speaking backstage to the press before his performance in the University Auditorium at Kent State on Sunday, April 16, 1972 (*Daily Kent Stater* photo by Diana McNees)

"We believe the spiritual aspect of our music is so very important—that is why it is standing like a rock." Ravi Shankar is in his dressing room, just before his concert Saturday evening—explaining his music.

Shankar is the commanding presence in the room. His large, liquid brown eyes rivet on those with whom he is speaking, and his hands, delicately orchestrating the conversation, command the listener's attention. Staunchly defending his work, he explains a dualism in his music:

"I have a dual role in my music. I first offer the traditional orthodox music; but I'm not afraid to experiment outside the tradition. And I've been trying to make Westerners understand the truths of our music—not to merely listen to it in terms of Coltrane or because I'm a friend of George Harrison's."

He tries to explain an apparent dichotomy between Western and Indian music: "In our country we have a constant rapport with out audiences. The Indian is familiar with the raga—here that is impossible; the rapport is missing.

"Western audiences try to understand, even though they may not be able to feel as sentimental as the Indian may feel," he explains in his high, singsong voice, smilingly looking around the incense-clouded room to where Alla Rakham, the tabla player, is standing, nervously eyeing the clock and dabbing perfume all over his body.

Ravi Shankar speaking backstage to the press before his performance in the University Auditorium at Kent State on Sunday, April 16, 1972 (*Daily Kent Stater* photo by Diana McNees)

ficial aspects. I've been trying—I think I've been successful by working on the solid basis of my music."

Finally, in regard to the recent assimilation of Indian music into Western modes, Shankar says, "I work with musicians, like Yehudi Menuhin and the London Symphony, and I have always tried to keep the Indianness. Many people have tried our way—Coltrane, even those in the classical field."

But, for Shankar, a moot question remains: "How much of this activity is a gimmick," he asks, "and how much of it is truly creative? I have found after years of work that anything beautiful and true will stand the test of time."

Explaining that he has to prepare for the concert, Shankar excused himself with clasped hands and a beatific smile. He seems bottled up, his energy contained; he is waiting for his music to release him, to do his speaking in a far more eloquent way than words.

And so the music. Shankar, with his sitar gently cradled in his lap, educates his audiences. The music itself is beautiful, lilting, frenetic, impassioned. To an ear weaned on the music of the West, his music can only be compared to free-form jazz, with shifting patterns of tone, color, timbre and improvisation.

Shankar: Super Musical Evening
By Mark Kmetzko
Daily Kent Stater
April 18, 1972

It's understandably difficult as a performer of Indian music to get through to a western audience, but Ravi Shankar accomplished the task with ease Saturday night.

Shankar and his two sidemen, brought here by the Artist Lecture Series, played a tight and emo-

In referring to the audience he will face in a few minutes, Shankar says, "I'm offering peace, some kind of cleansing feeling. Young people are looking for something—they may not know what it is, but they are looking—and you MUST go inside yourself."

At the same time, he maintains, "It is insulting to the music and ourselves when people smoke and are necking with their girlfriends."

He is also insulted by the almost automatic association some people make with his music and drugs:

"I am trying to separate all of the irrelevant mixture—like music and hashish. It's ridiculous and very sad to bring in all of these silly, super-

tional two-hour set before a jammed University Auditorium. Instrumentation was tabla, an Indian version of our drums, and tamboura, which could be compared to our bass, in that it provides the main tone on which the melody is built.

The three men played five pieces, ranging in mood from serious to romantic to solemn. Each musician was very competent on his instrument, but the ensemble sound was especially impressive. Their brightness was such that it was hard to believe that three minds were inventing the music and not one.

Individually, Shankar was amazing as his sitar elaborated on the droning of the tamboura. Tabla player Alla Rakha not only provided rhythm but constantly accented and highlighted Shankar's melodies. At one point, Rakha did a tabla solo, explaining beforehand that each sound on his two drums had a verbal equivalent. He then began chanting syllables and imitating them on his instrument.

It is apparent that this music requires tremendous discipline both from man and instrument. For example, the tabla had to be tuned to the other instruments. In our western music, percussion is not usually tuned, with the exception of tympani. Sometimes the tuning procedure took as long as five minutes, but the audience found such waits worthwhile when the next piece began.

Shankar adhered more to the idea of the Artist Lecture Series than have past performers. Before each piece, he not only gave the title but explained the structure and rhythm pattern of each selection. He also told the audience that each raga (or piece) is connected with a certain time of day or season. Thus he acquainted the mostly western-eared crowd with the subtleties of Indian music.

The Artist Lecture Series people did a particularly outstanding job in connection with this. Each member of the audience was given a program which filled out Shankar's explanations and also provided some background on Shankar himself. I hope the people kept those programs, because they would serve as a fine reference source for a basic understanding of Indian music.

In general, it was a super evening of music, the only drawback being that the music came out of FM radio later that night seemed bland and simple. But for most folks, it's a once in a lifetime experience to hear Ravi Shankar in person, and I'm glad I had the chance.

The tabla and sitar interact in fierce solos or blend in quiet, subtle textures.

The audience is his. With music and incense pervading everything, it becomes one person, attuned to the music. The thundering ovations prove that he has won them over. Shankar's most eloquent testimony is not his words, but his music, the art that he has both shaped and been shaped by.

Elton John played in the Memorial Gym on Friday, May 5, 1972.

Elton John a Sellout
By Mark Kmetzko
Daily Kent Stater
May 9, 1972

As one who attended the Elton John sellout concert Friday night in the anti-acoustic Memorial Gym, I can testify to the fact that Kent rock audiences are probably the most immature in Ohio.

First, they are rude. Most of Friday's capacity crowd talked loudly while the first band, The Dillards, played some fine bluegrass tunes. As a result, the audience missed a beautiful ensemble country sound, as well as some exceptional banjo

Elton John played in the Memorial Gym on Friday, May 5, 1972. (*Bottom left: Daily Kent Stater* photo by Greg Santos; *other photos:* courtesy of the *Chestnut Burr*)

picking and beautifully greasy three-part harmony. A fiddle or pedal steel guitar would have been a welcome addition to the band, as either would have provided a droning sound to contrast with the staccato banjo, guitar and mandolin.

The Dillards battled the noisy audience for 35 minutes and were finally awarded a standing ovation. This struck me as funny, as many of the folks never heard a note that was played.

The audience's immaturity further showed when Elton John came on. They applauded loudly for the first half hour, and rightly so, because John's first 30 minutes were very good. His piano, his incredible voice and his band ran through beautiful oldies such as "Border Song" as well as new tunes like "Rocket Man."

After that, the monotony of John's material became evident. But the audience's response increased, especially when John began his piano theatrics on a few up-tempo numbers.

It was amazingly depressing to see an audience give repeated standing ovations to songs in which Davey Johnstone's guitar playing was inaudible because of John's piano.

Soon folks got the idea that they could better observe John's facial expressions and athletic display (which were a blatant rip-off from old rock 'n' roller Jerry Lee Lewis) by standing. More and more people got on their feet, and within five minutes most of the audience was standing on its seats. Thus, those of us who wanted to remain seated couldn't see anything except a lot of denim covered rear ends.

Then as an encore, the very original Elton John furthered his Lewis rip-off by playing one of the Jerry Lee's most famous tunes, "Whole Lotta Shakin' Goin' On." The crowd stood, screamed and clapped along as John became more hysterically anti-musical. I walked out.

So, Kent audiences have come a long way.

They ignore the music half the time, stand so others can't see and give standing ovations to very low degrees of musical quality.

So you want to be a rock 'n' roll fan . . .

Stevie Wonder played in Kent State's Memorial Gym on Sunday, November 12, 1972.

Wonder Hits Great Show to Exhausted Audience
By Bobbie Rust
Daily Kent Stater
November 14, 1972

Three hours after the concert, truly versatile, personal, and dynamic Stevie Wonder appeared

Stevie Wonder played in Kent State's Memorial Gym on Sunday, November 12, 1972. (Courtesy of the *Chestnut Burr*)

Stevie Wonder performance in Kent (Left: courtesy of the *Daily Kent Stater; right and below:* courtesy of the *Chestnut Burr*)

on stage; but most of the audience was too tired to show the enthusiasm they felt.

If anyone could wake up an audience which had sat for three hours, Wonder could, [and he] tried wholeheartedly. He was drenched in sweat by the end of his first number. The audience wanted to show they were enjoying it, too, but except for occasional bursts of energy, the members of the audience sat on their numbed derrieres and wondered if they'd ever walk again.

It all began with the Black Ensemble's ap-

pearance onstage at 8:10 P.M. They featured a remarkable flutist and a strong opening. As the crowd clapped its approval, an attractive couple known as the Syndicate of Sound came on and commenced singing "Where Is the Love?"

As with all their songs, the potential for great harmony was there, but they didn't blend well. The female's soothing voice was always overridden by the powerful voice of her partner. They had a lovely sound, but it wasn't syndicated.

Four vocalists replaced the Syndicate of Sound in the next act. They had much the same problems. Singing "It's Too Late," the effect was one of lost unity within the group. Each singer seemed to get caught in the spirit of performing and forget he was part of a group. Except for the song "Sincerity," which was a pleasure throughout, everyone did nice things, but not together.

During these acts, the Light Fantastic Light Show was projecting a slide of paint smears on the black wall. Very symbolic, I'm sure, but not too fantastic.

After the Black Ensemble's final number came the first of many pauses. As smoke swirled past the No Smoking signs, people watched the clock roll from 9 P.M. to 9:25.

Onstage, the Untamed Band, backup group for the Impressions, was tuning up, then retuning up, then deciding what to play, for all the audience knew. An announcement crept over the mike that the bass player was having trouble. No one knew with what, but it sure took him long enough to get over it.

At long last, the Impressions hit the stage, and the wait seemed worth it all. Facing an audience that had been sitting for one and one-half hours, the groups succeeded in rousing the lull. Dressed in purple, cranberry, orange, and white "zoot" suits, the four singers did a takeoff on the Jackson 5 that would have fooled Mrs. Jackson.

Everything clicked together, from their movements, to their sound, to the snapping of their fingers. The act never lagged, actions were abundant and graceful, and the music had energy.

Most of all, one sensed that the Impressions took pride in their performance. They were having a good time and it was contagious.

By the time they had finished, the audience was wide awake. Their versions of "Backstabbers" and "In the Rain" had put the crowd in the most receptive mood seen all evening. Cheers congratulated the departing group for a fine show, and everyone was "up" for Stevie Wonder. The crowd tensed in anticipation as the announcer, Winston Gragg, stepped up to the mike, smiled, and said, "There will be a 25 minute intermission."

The crowd was not smiling in return. Thirty minutes later, the audience was still waiting for the houselights to dim. They had dimmed once, but the stagehands had ordered them on again.

Sensing the crowd was getting sleepy—probably from the snores he heard—B.U.S. President Duane Cox introduced the Homecoming Queens. Senior Queen Joice Smith made a little speech, which bought the stagehands more time. One spectator was overheard to say, "The Three Stooges would have better organization than this." One tended to agree with him.

At 10:40 P.M., the announcer introduced Wonderlove, Stevie Wonder's backup group. They played jazz, and they played it well, but the crowd was underwhelmed. The crowd was tired. It became 11 P.M. with no Stevie Wonder in sight.

The light show was now flashing a slide that they brought in and out of focus in time to the music. Their act improved during the last half of Wonder's performance, but they never redeemed themselves fully.

Shortly after 11 P.M., Wonder came onstage dressed in a bronze-colored velvet tunic. By the end of the first number, Wonder had played the drums and the organ. Soon after, he played the harmonica during "For Once in My Life," the piano in "You and I," a sweet, bluesy song that proved the highlight of the evening, and the Arp synthesizer.

He sang medleys including songs like "If You Really Love Me," "You Call My Name," and "My Cherie Amour" with that husky, warm, and mellow quality. No doubt about it, this man was a super talent.

He frequently exchanged laughs and comments with the audience and the members of Wonderlove. After one spectator had repeatedly called out, "One more time! One more time!" Wonder stopped the performance and called back good-naturedly, "All right, man!" and one more time it was.

When one of Wonderlove would create an unusual or outstanding sound, Wonder would stop the show to tell them so. He asked one of the male vocalists to repeat a note he'd sung well, and when one of the girls held a perfectly pitched high note for several seconds, Wonder shouted his praise.

The instruments, the audience, and his group members are never beyond his attention. He is aware of every aspect of performing. As a result, the entire performance holds together and keeps the audience involved.

Wonder is no longer a "Motown performer." He has emerged into a jazz artist, a blues man, and a soul singer combined. He has definitely grown musically over the past ten years, while many other artists have faded or stagnated.

His performance was totally satisfying. Unfortunately, the organization around it left him with a drained audience, and he had to work very hard to earn the enthusiasm he deserves.

Yes played at Kent State on Sunday, November 19, 1972. (Photos by J. Ross Baughman)

Yes band members (*left to right*) Steve Howe, Jon Anderson, and Chris Squire (Courtesy of the *Chestnut Burr*)

Yes played at Kent State on Sunday, November 19, 1972.

Capacity Crowd Hears YES
An "Indescribable Group"
by Dave Voelker
Daily Kent Stater
November 21, 1972

> brilliant bits of light on assembly
> music that probes the outer limits
> unnatural and extraordinary
> a thunderous ovation
> the group took possession of the crowd's
>   mind

A capacity crowd in Memorial Gym gave Yes their heads to play with last Sunday night. All were returned in good condition.

All Campus Programming Board produced the show with the help of Belkin Productions in Cleveland. If this concert is any indication, it looks like ACPB has really got it together this year, booking a tremendously popular group and actually having the show start on time for a change.

Lindisfarne played warm-up at the concert: "one of the most misunderstood" British groups. Their music was an easygoing combination of the Byrds and the Irish Rovers, but with its own distinctive blend of harmonic ballads and foot-tapping melodies. They were pleasant, competent, and well-received. Lindisfarne is the kind of group that invites more outside appreciation than gut involvement.

It's groups like Lindisfarne that make you marvel at how rock has become a melting-pot for practically every musical style, welcoming into its ranks everything from country to jazz to classical. But if the ballads of Lindisfarne seemed strange and unfamiliar, the incredible

Yes band members playing at Kent State: Jon Anderson (*top left*); Rick Wakeman (*top right*); Steve Howe and Jon Anderson (*bottom left*); and Alan White (*bottom right*) (Photos by J. Ross Baughman)

phantasmagoria of the Yes sound left everyone with his mouth open.

Yes is a virtually indescribable group. Their music probes the outer limits of the imagination. Just when you think you've got it down, it jumps into another dimension and starts all over again, teasing your mind, making you grin like an idiot when you least expect to, leaving you stunned and inexplicably fulfilled.

You've heard about how psychiatrists are able to induce euphoria in a patient by electrically stimulating the pleasure centers of the brain. That's what Yes does—without wires.

And the immersion was complete. Pulsating rhythms wrought of steel and electrons swum

around the gym. Ingeniously intricate lighting kept tune to the music, accentuating and intensifying. Yes used every means possible to get inside its captive audience's brains.

They let you know they were playing with your head, too. As if the music itself wasn't enough, a revolving reflection wheel strewed brilliant bits of light on the assembly, evoking "Ooh!"'s and "Ah!"'s from the astounded crowd. Keyboard man Rick Wakeman simulated a fire on stage, complete with smoke, sirens, and a beacon.

I must point out that, though the atrocious acoustics of Memorial Gym have always been notorious for chewing up good music and spitting out sound soup, it seemed almost a sacrilege to feed it Yes as a victim. The individual elements of their sound must be perceived separately, with the most discriminating awareness, to get the most out of it.

The concert by Yes wasn't as good as their concert at the Akron Rubber Bowl this summer, but, as a pale and drained Jon Anderson told me after the concert, the boys have been touring off and on for almost a year, and will soon return to England for a well-earned rest. So if they didn't jump around as much as usual, they had good reason.

I hope everyone at the concert noticed that Yes didn't come out in jeans and flannel shirts, as has become the custom of groups trying to look more natural and ordinary. They didn't, because they are unnatural and extraordinary.

They dressed like the wizards they are, in colored suits of silk and satin and flowing capes embellished with stars and moons.

The audience was impressed, if not a little shocked. The group took complete control of their minds while they moved ritualistically back and forth in their seats, agog and dumbfounded. They showed their appreciation with a thunderous ovation, and were rewarded with a powerful encore of "Yours Is No Disgrace."

I confess. Yes brainwashed me, in every sense of the word. But if it feels as good as it did Sunday night, they can do it any time they want.

Santana played at Kent State on Thursday, February 15, 1973.

An "Interesting" Sound
Santana "Still Adjusting"
By Ron Kovach
Daily Kent Stater
February 20, 1973

Santana playing at Kent State (Photos by J. Ross Baughman)

Can an extraordinarily talented and successful group of hot-blooded Latin-rock musicians forsake much of their "old" sound, eliminate anything old that smacks of commercialism, and still remain interesting? Although it's too early to answer that question, "Santana" gave a concert Thursday night that was good but not great, and interesting but, for much of the time, boring.

At the outset, it should be noted that this was a "new" Santana. It was readily apparent that the days of "Evil Ways" and "Black Magic Woman" are long gone. Gone also are the former organist, bass player and conga player—and, I might add, most of Carlos Santana's hair. The partial breakup of the group which began after the third album was released, keyboard

Santana played at Kent State on Thursday, February 15, 1973. (*Daily Kent Stater* photo by Diana McNees)

player Rich Hermode told me, was a reflection of the change in their music that was so apparent Thursday night.

Not all was different however. The exceptional percussion section was still there. The new addition of two keyboard players to the group kept the keyboards, as before, a significant part of the group's sound. The hard-cooking Latin rhythms and the almost overwhelming full, layered potent sound was still there. And, needless to say, the wailing guitar and quick hands of Carlos Santana were still present.

But the group was, for much of the concert, monotonous, and became increasingly so as the evening wore on. With their vocal work now, unfortunately, almost completely abandoned as well as most of the group's more "popular" cuts, "Santana" now relies almost totally on their instrumental work and "jamming."

And the result wore thin Thursday night. Most of the songs "Santana" played eventually turned into the same thing—a brew of Latin-rock, screaming guitar, driving percussion, and improvised keyboard work.

This is not to say that "Santana" and some of

the new directions they showed were not exciting and interesting. The keyboard solos—especially on the electric piano—of Rich Hermode and Tom Coster added a dimension that is largely new to the "Santana" sound—namely, jazz played over Latin rhythms. Indeed, the group is approaching an almost avant-garde jazz sound in some of their work.

The sheer energy and power of these musicians, as was evidenced in the concert, is awesome. And the fact that they feel and can get into their music more than many groups is unquestionable.

"Santana"'s development and total mastery of a sound completely their own shows an originality many bands could only wish they had. But power and energy and feeling and originality go just so far by themselves.

Perhaps "Santana" is still adjusting to their new direction. Perhaps they haven't yet gotten where they'd like to be, musically speaking. Certainly the evolution of a group's music is important and vital. But perhaps also, "Santana" right now is a little too much into their own musical trip at the expense of the listener.

Pink Floyd's Dark Side of Kent

March 10, 1973

One legendary Kent show that seemed to have been lost to time is a performance by Pink Floyd, in what is now Kent State's Memorial Athletic and Convocation Center. Through some sleuthing, I found great information from folks directly involved with this event.

It's impossible to discuss this show without talking about Pink Floyd's landmark LP *The Dark Side of the Moon,* because the Kent State performance occurred at the apex of the Dark Side of the Moon Tour and everyone kept referring to that album when talking about the show. It's also impossible to write about Pink Floyd's *Dark Side of the Moon* without going over much covered ground. In brief, it's one of the top-selling albums of all time, and it spent 741 weeks on *Billboard*'s top LPs and tape chart between 1973 and 1988. The band had been performing *The Dark Side of the Moon* as part of its live set for just over a year by the time it came to town.

The *Daily Kent Stater* did some limited reporting on the show, though I found only one advance ad, and since the concert occurred during spring break, a week in which the *Stater* wasn't printed, there was no review.

Michael Solomon, the All Campus Programming Board Concert Committee chairman from 1972 through 1974, was the chief promoter on this concert. Michael, who turned twenty-one years old on the day of this event, remembered the show well many years later.

It was unbelievable. They did the show in quadraphonic. There were speakers at the back of the gym, and there were speakers all the way up on the right and left side above the bleachers. They brought in the most equipment that I had ever dealt with. They brought in this forklift, and when they started rolling it across the gym floor, you could see the floor buckle. I happened to be standing right there with Keith Raymond, who I worked with, and we looked at each other, and I just said, "Stop! Please stop! We can't bring equipment in this way." So then Keith and I looked at each other, and I said, "Find the money and go find twenty kids that we can pay $20 apiece and get them to hand carry all this equipment, otherwise we can't do this show." And we did! So we moved all the equipment into the gym by hand.

We were worried that there might be some drug overdose that night, so we worked with the local hospital and the local police and everybody else to set up like a care unit down the hall from the performance. It was a good thing that we did that, because it was unbelievable how many kids were in there hallucinating, just having out-of-body experiences, out-of-mind experiences—it was kind of fun to walk through there and overhearing what people were saying. Nobody died, and nobody was actually having any serious problems, but it was wild. I remember someone saying, "I saw God, I saw God out there."

The other thing was that this was the Dark Side of the Moon Tour, and ya know where there's that giant explosion on the album? For that part of the concert, they did this really amazing thing where they caused this big crash at the back of the stage off to the side, and there were a couple of us standing in that general vicinity and right on cue there was an actual giant explosion that was so powerful that it left all of our ears ringing for days. Their show was the most technically brilliantly production I had ever witnessed. Being able to bring that to the gym—it was an amazing event.

J. Ross Baughman, who took the never-before-published black-and-white photos that accompany this piece, was the nineteen-year-old editor of Kent State University's yearbook, the *Chestnut Burr.* He arrived at the gym early that evening to get in place to take some all-access photos.

You wanna know what the mood of that place was? Roger scorned me. Roger Waters personally scorned me from being able to be up on stage, when every other major act I'd worked with had no problem with this.

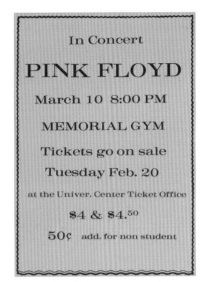

Original *Daily Kent Stater* ad for Pink Floyd's Kent State performance (Courtesy of the *Daily Kent Stater*)

Ticket stub from Pink Floyd's March 10, 1973, performance in Kent State's Memorial Gym (Author's collection)

Roger Waters and Richard Wright of Pink Floyd in Kent State's Memorial Gym on March 10, 1973 (Photo by J. Ross Baughman)

When they were ready to come out and do their sound check, I was out there right on the wings of the stage, and Roger looked towards me and said, "What's this guy up here for?" And I said, "Well I'm part of the furniture, I'm part of the woodwork, I'm Kent State here." I introduced myself in a friendly way. I was trying to be ingratiating, but he wasn't having any of it, and he said, "You're finished." So I just kind of looked around, and all the other people running security and running the concert just looked at me and gave me that smiling shrug, like, "Hey, Roger Waters has spoken." I wanted to reason with him, but he wasn't having it.

So to shoot my photos I had to squeeze into a scrum of annoyed photographers crouching in front of the stage. They had already staked out their turf. The band was snarling at the crowd. Roger was literally insulting the audience. Someone would shout out a request, and Roger would come back with something like, "Shut up, we're trying to do something more important up here." I was just trying to take some decent pictures—and I was impressed with the music, and I loved the band, and I loved that

David Gilmour of Pink Floyd in Kent State's Memorial Gym on March 10, 1973. Does his shirt say "Kent State"? (Photo by J. Ross Baughman)

album—and I was really excited about this, but they were feeling incredible pressure to be in total 100 percent anal compulsive control over that concert.

Oh, and you know what the other thing was? They wouldn't even let us shoot the entire concert. We were limited to the first few songs—and this was the first time I had ever heard of this. To me it was outrageous. I remember thinking, "What? They are telling us we can only shoot the first twenty-five minutes of the concert?" Which is absolutely normal now. I think that—as a veteran concert photographer, having shot photos with carte blanche red-carpet treatment, this was the first time I had ever known this to happen. Not long after this, I covered both Paul McCartney and Wings and the Rolling Stones for a couple of cities, and both bands embraced me as one of the guys.

A handful of these Pink Floyd photos turned out okay, though not compared to all the other concerts I shot where you see I'm right next to these guys. For Pink Floyd I was there for only enough time to take maybe twenty or thirty frames for the whole concert, and only just a few photos even turned out, compared to other concerts where I would have had, like, fifty pictures that I really liked.

I think that concert was more important to them than people realize. That shirt David Gilmour is wearing—I think it's a red and blue shirt and the star is yellow. I think it was a Viet Cong shirt, but it may well have been that he added "Kent State" to it. I am pretty sure his shirt says "Kent State," and you know what that tells us? They knew that Kent State was the closest you could get to the Viet Cong here in America.

You could not find a revolutionary red and blue shirt with a big yellow star on it in the campus bookshop, because that was just too darn left, anti–Vietnam War revolutionary, so he must have made it. What I think you are seeing here is Pink Floyd celebrating Kent as something they cared about. What I find ironic about this is that they couldn't have been less congenial. They were alienating the audience because they were such *artistes.*

Is David Gilmour in fact wearing a customized "Kent State" T-shirt? It certainly looks like it. A quick online search reveals some other photos of David Gilmour wearing the same shirt from what looks like different dates on this same tour, and in all the photos that shirt appears to say "Kent State."

Kent native and premier guitarist Bruce Fulper was nineteen years old on March 10, 1973, when he had a whirlwind Pink Floyd experience.

On Friday March 9, I woke up in Fort Sill, Oklahoma, having just completed my AIT [Advanced Individual Training]. I was damn lucky that I was not chosen to go to Vietnam, as a few of us had been held over for two weeks until Uncle Sam made up his mind. I got to go to Germany instead. So, Friday was it. Two weeks' leave until I had to go overseas. I had bought a real clean 1955 Ford four-door and decided to drive it back to Kent.

Neatly enough, a few guys who lived along the way helped with gas and driving. We left at noon that Friday and deadheaded straight through. I rolled into my parents' driveway on Fairchild Ave. at 11:30 A.M. sharp on the morning of Saturday, March 10. After the typical "Hi, Mom and Dad" stuff, I called my pal Rob Ginther.

The first thing Rob said to me was, "Aw man, I wish you would have told me you'd be home because Pink Floyd is playing the gym tonight!" Of course, tickets had long been sold out. So with nothing else to do, and the show being the biggest thing to ever hit Kent (as far as we were concerned), we decided to just go up and sit at the north end of the gym, because we knew the stage was at that part of the building.

So, there we sat, watching the crowd go by, listening to people asking for tickets. *Lots* of people asking for tickets. Just forget it. No one was selling tickets. So we were killing time, glad we got a spot where we hoped to hear the show, and then a guy walked off the sidewalk and came over to us, without us even motioning that we wanted tickets. He saw us sitting over there by the building, and he walks up to us and asks, "You guys want to buy some tickets?"

"Really???"

"YES."

"How much?"

"Oh, just face value. $4.50 each. They're pretty good seats, too."

You know the part where life hands you *crap* too often, but every once in a while you get lucky? Well, certainly I've had my split of super

Roger Waters and Richard Wright
of Pink Floyd in Kent State's
Memorial Gym on March 10, 1973
(Photo by J. Ross Baughman)

highs and super lows, but this day—wow. We were freaking out that *now* we're sitting in the fifth row, center section.

So—the show. It's the first time I got to see Pink Floyd, and, by the way, I had just been turned on to them the previous Christmas, so I had only known of them for three months. My initiation to them was through a pal's headphones as he put on "Meddle" and said, "Sit back." So I thought I was ready.

Ha! *Not.* The first half of the show was stuff off *Ummagumma,* and they ended [it] with "Careful with That Ax, Eugene." Now that was the first stunner. For that song Roger had a tiny black light on his mic that they turned on and it lit up his teeth—creepy cool.

During that song, a monster half sphere rose up from behind the drummer. It was covered with tiny mirrors. When it got to full height, it slowly began to rotate. On each side of the stage were five red lasers. Ten total. As this mirrored half sphere turned clockwise, the lasers started firing at what looked like five-foot-long beams of light, filling the entire place with what looked like red snow. You could see the lengths of the beams just screaming by every which way.

Nick Mason of Pink Floyd in Kent State's Memorial Gym on March 10, 1973 (Photo by J. Ross Baughman)

If you're familiar with the song, you know it builds to an incredible climax, and at the moment of that climax they set off a fireball explosion from behind the sphere that was so huge we felt the heat from the blast. It was later reported that one or two people fell off the balcony when that happened. It was stunning.

Then, they took a break. Now, not being as hip as I wished I was, I had not heard that they had a new album. They played *The Dark Side of the Moon* in its entirety. I remember the three black backing vocalists—stunning—and of course the sound system. The first ever quadraphonic live sound system.

Hearing the cash register in "Money" ping-ponging four ways from stack to stack was incredible. A future roommate of mine was an electrician for KSU and told me he worked three full days helping them set up those speakers in the rafters.

There were troubles, though. The stage-right speaker column went out three or four times, and it nearly killed the show. You know what it's like to unplug a guitar with the live end of the cable—you touch it and it goes "WHOMP!!" Well, imagine a massive speaker rack doing the same thing, at a zillion more DBs. It was brutal. You *know* it bummed out the band. But they kept playing and got through it.

That's it in a nutshell, as much as a nutshell as I can put it in. I went to see them in Pittsburgh a few years later when they had the flying pig, and it was almost a 180. We sat under the model plane at the very top of the stadium. Decent show, but it was no comparison to the fifth row, center section.

It sounds like an incredible night. Whenever I ask locals who were in town around this time about the concerts they used to have in the gym, almost everyone brings up this show. Even though there were many huge events like this in Kent, it still boggles my mind that the legendary Pink Floyd came *here* and played its most famous work when it was brand new.

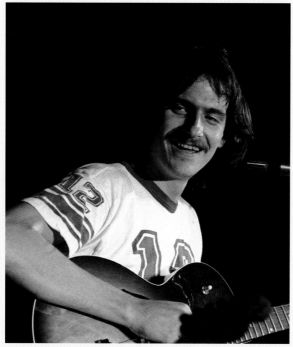

James Taylor played at Kent State on April 17, 1973.
(Photos by J. Ross Baughman)

James Taylor played at Kent State on Tuesday, April 17, 1973.

James Taylor "Entertained All"
By Keith Sinzinger
Daily Kent Stater
April 19, 1973

James Taylor is a performer. When the lanky balladeer appeared Tuesday night, he surprised some and pleased many, but entertained all.

Although the show started an hour late due to transportation problems, the crowd reacted warmly to the smiling, waving Taylor as he opened his first set, appropriately, with "Sweet Baby James."

Possessing a distinctive style of both singing and finger-picked guitar playing, Taylor was soft-spoken and informal on stage, casually sipping gin (?) between songs, yet his stage presence was powerful, almost charismatic.

The emotional feel of each song was reflected in Taylor's face, and a good sound system highlighted his voice and the clean crispness of his acoustic guitar with exceptional clarity.

Singing of sad lonesomeness in songs like "Riding on a Railroad," Taylor was warm yet distant. His ability to project emotion through his voice and instrument was strongly utilized, but he still maintained a mysterious aura of detachment, often closing his eyes or staring out into space.

The versatile Danny "Kootch" Kortchmar, Taylor's sideman since the days of "The Flying Machine," joined him on guitar for a slightly different version of "Lo and Behold," and halfway into his first set, Taylor brought out the rest of his band.

This reviewer, like many others, awaited the band's appearance with fearful apprehension, recalling the over-production present on some of Taylor's recorded work. Comprised of Kootch, a bassist, a piano player and a trio of percussionists, "The Section" was a welcome addition to the Taylor show, providing the adrenaline necessary to carry on the concert with a high degree of excitement.

Perhaps their most important function was to present a variety of accompaniments, working with Taylor as a unit and in two, three and four-man combinations. The songs performed encompassed Taylor's four albums, and led by Kootch, the band achieved a subtle Latin undertone.

Old Taylor standards like "Country Road" gained a new flavor as the band cooked with high energy and volume, although sometimes obscuring the vocals, especially in the first set. Tight and precise, they tottered between strict arrangement and jamming, yet unfortunately cut their solos to a minimum. Kootch demonstrated a number of techniques on acoustic and electric guitar, showing hints of jazz influence in his melodic complements to Taylor's singing.

In the jamming aspect, Taylor himself displayed continual improvisation, using his voice as a most effective instrument. Competent and in control, Taylor showcased his vocal range in some "a capella" riffs of the bluesy "Steamroller."

In all, the second set resembled the first, with a pleasing blend of ballads, love songs, and favorites. The band helped to provide a well-balanced and entertaining show, and the evening never dragged (as many folk/rock concerts do) thanks to the continuously changing moods and music.

Taylor replied to an inquiry from the curious and request-calling audience that his wife, singer Carly Simon, was home in New York. Judging from the completeness of his show, it didn't seem that she was missed.

The Mahavishnu Orchestra and Frank Zappa played at the Memorial Gym on Tuesday, May 1, 1973.

"One of the Strongest Concerts"
An Extraordinary Evening of Music
By Bob von Sternberg
Daily Kent Stater
May 3, 1973

In what should rank as one of the strongest concerts ever presented at Kent State, the Mahavishnu Orchestra and the Mothers of Invention gave a KSU audience an extraordinary evening of music Tuesday.

Bathed in blue light, guitarist John McLaughlin began the Mahavishnu Orchestra's set with what he called "a few bars of really beautiful quiet." A virtually silent Memorial Gym then was greeted with an unrelenting barrage of musical virtuosity that continued unabated for more than 90 minutes.

The music of the Mahavishnu Orchestra is an awesome combination of technical pyrotechnics and pure musical communication. The band's five musicians left the audience literally dumbfounded at the conclusion of their performance.

The Mahavishnu Orchestra does not rely on "songs" as such in concert. Rather, they present a theme—a motif—and then proceed to tear it to shreds through soloing and improvisation. Once each piece has been reduced (or expanded) to its absolute limit, layer upon layer is reconstructed to reform the original musical theme.

As elementary as this sounds, in the hands of these five musicians—the process forms a dazzling, amazing spiral that winds its way through the entire performance.

Perched amidst a forest of microphones, drummer Billy Cobham set a frenetic, rapid-fire

John McLaughlin of the Mahavishnu Orchestra, Memorial Gym (Courtesy of the *Daily Kent Stater*)

Frank Zappa, Memorial Gym (Courtesy of the *Chestnut Burr*)

pace for the rest of the band. A blur of movement, he carried the band through esoteric time signatures and ever-increasing tempos effortlessly. Bassist Rick Laird was a powerful counterpoint to Cobham, laying an immense, punching bottom throughout the band's compositions.

McLaughlin, violinist Jerry Goodman and keyboardist Jan Hammer continually swirled solos among one another, trading dialogue through their instruments or sending one instrument soaring above the rest of the band.

Both Hammer and McLaughlin stood out; Hammer's lyric/frantic moog work alternately battling or synthesizing McLaughlin's speed and imagination on the guitar.

Beyond the individual proficiency of the members of the Mahavishnu Orchestra, the most overwhelming aspect of the music is the total communication between the musicians— they merge into one instrument, not five; each of the musicians directed toward a single, unified sound. McLaughlin calls his music "spiritual." After experiencing it and witnessing its effect on a crowd, he could very well be right.

As strong a musical aggregation as Frank Zappa had in his newest version of the Mothers, to these ears, it simply could not surmount the emotional and visceral effect left by the Mahavishnu Orchestra.

On a different level, the Mothers were outstanding, but they should not have played after an act virtually impossible to follow.

In the midst of minor electrical failures, pseudo-comic lyrics ("big green hockers in a Greyhound locker . . .") and some general screwing around, the Mothers presented some excellent Zappa material in a straight-ahead jazz format similar to Zappa's recent recorded work.

George Duke on keyboards, Jean-Luc Ponty with a swooping, lyrical solo violin, long-time

Mother Ian Underwood on reeds and Ruth Underwood on vibes and percussion musically stood out in the ten-piece ensemble. Zappa's guitar playing seemed fluid and precise, cutting loose in his solos.

The band played a tight, structured, disciplined set with Zappa occasionally conducting.

As an integrated ensemble, the band was impressive. Unfortunately, due to the precise and close-knit structure of many of Zappa's compositions, soloing was relatively minimal throughout the set. When a solo would begin to evolve, the band crept back in, smothering it.

Possibly the strongest composition of the evening were selections from Uncle Meat rearranged somewhat to fit the groups more big-band format.

Tuesday evening presented a close fusion of jazz and rock—it was not an evening of mindless heavy-metal "boogie" dronings. Rather, it was full of subtleties and imaginations of jazz combined with the raw power and energy of rock and roll. In all, a most impressive evening.

Zappa
His Music, Himself
By Bob Datz
Daily Kent Stater
May 3, 1973

A Winston barely clinging to his lips, Frank Zappa relaxed after Tuesday's concert in Memorial Gym and discussed a variety of topics.

Stater: The Mothers have seen a lot of musicians come and go. When you write, are you writing for the person you're playing with or do you just let your own trends develop?

Zappa: Well, it's a little bit of both. You get a better performance if you write for the idiosyncrasies of the players.

Stater: How do you adapt the older materials to the players?

Zappa: The first thing you do is to gauge the playing ability of the new musicians and figure out whether or not the equivalent part held by the last guy who held that position is insulting to his intelligence. In other words, if the new guy has more technique, you make the old part harder. If it's the other way around, you simplify the part.

Stater: Do you notice a change in your audience as your group evolves?

Zappa: I don't believe that there are more than, say, 5,000 people in the United States who have any idea of the continuity and growth of the group. Most of the people in the new generation of audience we have started listening to us about the time "Hot Rats" was released. They never saw the group in its early days and can't appreciate how radical it was at the time it was formed.

Stater: What's happened to the more scorching social lyric that was common on your earlier work?

Zappa: Well, what's the percentage in presenting scorching social lyric to an audience that wishes merely to be entertained?

Stater: Can that be attributed to the death of the "counter-culture," if there ever was one?

Zappa: Yes, if there ever was one. Maybe it's not dead, it just smells funny . . .

Stater: Are the comments that you've done on "groupies" a sort of overall reflection of American womanhood?

Zappa: Well, I have an opinion of American womanhood, but that's not to single out groupies as being any specific example of the whole spectrum. . . . You classify a groupie by her occupation, not by her personality.

Stater: Were you satisfied with "200 Motels," and do you have any plans to do any more cinema?

Zappa: I'm probably going to do another at the end of the year. There were a number of things in "200 Motels" I wasn't too thrilled about, but all of that could have been corrected with more time and money. Seeing how none of that was available I'd just have to say ——.

Stater: How did you come to be thrown off the stage in London?

Zappa: I was attacked by a mentally unbalanced person from the audience who came on stage at a point where the security guards were getting loaded on the side. He ran up just as we were finishing the encore, and the next thing I know I woke up in the orchestra pit with a broken leg, a broken rib, a hole in my head, my neck was twisted to the side and somebody saying, "Is there a doctor in the house?" I spent the next month in the hospital over there and then nine months in a wheelchair.

Stater: What are your perspectives on higher education?

Zappa: I spent one semester at junior college. I went to college for one reason—to get laid. And I got laid and I got out . . .

Stater: You've lampooned the Holiday Inn scene. Are you staying at the Holiday Inn while you are in Kent?

Zappa: What's it to ya?

Bring Him Home, Mother to Mom
Take Frank Zappa Home, Anybody's Mother Would Like Him
by Cindy Kudlaty
Scene Magazine
May 10–16, 1973

I am thoroughly convinced that Frank Zappa is the kind of man that you could take home to your mother.

Never having seen a Zappa performance until the May 1 concert at Kent State, I was thoroughly prepared for (and half-ready to forgive) one of those "I am a remote artist and you people don't understand anything" routines. But he just wanted to play his music. He likes to play with it, break it into little pieces and build it up again.

Zappa would probably like it better if he could play a concert without an audience. Audiences are notorious for being drunk and stoned and horny and making demands such as "We want 'Billy the Mountain'!" It's a well-known fact that Zappa has a pronounced aversion to that kind of thing, but after all, audiences are just people who pay outrageous prices to sit on bleachers, risk their lives climbing over one another, and enjoy being entertained.

So Zappa entertained. During a seemingly endless period spent trying to rectify sound problems, he told little stories and jokes. He played bits of Richard Nixon's Watergate speech. He didn't want us to get bored. He even played "Uncle Meat" and "Chunga's Revenge."

And then he played some incredible music. Nothing like "Suzy Creamcheese," "Mud Shark," or any of "that kind of swill," as Zappa referred to his past musical excursions. The sound was powerful, tight, jazzy, and definitely Zappa. The band included Ian Underwood (the sole survivor of the old Mothers) on sax, Ruth Underwood on percussion, Jean-Luc Ponty on the electric violin (whose amp, unfortunately, was not loud enough), and George Duke on keyboards. They are all adequate musicians in their own right, as evidenced by their solo work. And Frank Zappa is no half-assed guitar player.

Also present in the group are two dude-like individuals who primarily act as vocalists. They do a lot of soulful yelling, absurd dancing and spinning about, and they get wound up in their microphone cords a lot. I'm convinced that they are on stage only because Zappa is amused by their antics.

Often under attack is Frank Zappa's insistence upon absolute control and dogmatic direction of his musicians, allowing them no artistic license of their own. The band does seem to rely heavily on Zappa's direction and follow his every whim, but it is difficult to tell how much of his direction is legitimate and how much is show. Whichever is the case, his directing is artfully executed, brilliantly timed, and amazingly funny. And the music, the end result, stands on its own merit.

Frank Zappa is an incredible person. He's all bones, with a nose, and some fuzzy hair, like some kind of bird. He doesn't want anyone to get hurt, or be unhappy. He just likes to play music.

Anybody's mother would like him.

Paul Simon's 1973 Homecoming in Kent State's Memorial Gym

October 20, 1973

For as well documented as it was, Paul Simon's Homecoming concert at KSU was very soon forgotten. This performance occurred during one of those great nights or weekends at Kent State where everything came together perfectly. From the Homecoming football game, which saw the Kent State Golden Flashes beat Eastern Michigan 34–20, to Paul Simon's jam-packed concert in the Memorial Gym and the official dedication of the brand-new Student Center, Kent State burned bright.

Paul Simon's spectacular performance in the Kent State University Memorial Gym was a well-publicized and well-attended stop on the tour for his album *There Goes Rhymin' Simon.* The show, like the album, featured some of his finest and well-known solo recordings, including "Kodachrome," "American Tune," "Loves Me Like a Rock," and "Something So Right."

The *Daily Kent Stater* documented the entire weekend—with several preview pieces, a detailed review, and then an additional piece by *Stater* reporter Jan Clark getting an exclusive interview following the show—complete with an exclusive *Kent Stater* photo showing a bearded Paul Simon. The *Chestnut Burr* yearbook also covered the event.

Kent State's All Campus Programming Board was responsible the concert. Then twenty-one years old, Michael Solomon, ACPB Concert Committee chairman from 1972 to 1974, was the show's chief promoter.

Paul Simon was awesome. Great show, packed the Memorial Gym. I got into a huge argument with one of Paul's managers be-

cause we had a deal with Paul Simon that he would get a percentage of the gate as opposed to just a flat fee, and as it turned out
we had about a hundred unsold tickets. Well, if you know how
that gym seating is laid out, you know that the upper area is just
filled with long permanent benches instead of actual seats, and at
times it can just turn into a general admission free-for-all. So if the
gym held seven thousand, and we only sold six thousand tickets,
you would never be able to tell, because everything just fills out
up there. So it was *so packed* that the manager didn't believe me
that we didn't sell the last hundred tickets, and he wanted his
money. And I tried to explain the *real* situation.

Paul Simon was great. The show was great. I remember afterwards in his dressing room, I went back there and I was near the
door. Paul's brother Ed was there touring with him, and they look
so much alike that I remember asking him a question thinking
he was Paul Simon. [And] he says, "Why don't you ask Paul?"
And I'm just like, "Oh, okay." And I ask Paul Simon, "What did
you mean in that song by the lyrics 'loves me like a rock'?" He
just looked at me funny, and he didn't answer. He was answer-

Paul Simon performed in Kent
State's Memorial Gym on October
20, 1973. (Photo by J. Ross
Baughman)

Paul Simon, Kent State Memorial Gym (Photos by J. Ross Baughman)

ing other questions, and he turned back to me five minutes later and said, "That song was about Richard Nixon and he felt like he could do anything he wanted, and I just attributed it to the fact that his mother really loved him."

"Loves Me Like a Rock" was Simon's big chart-topping hit when he performed here on campus, so it makes sense that it was the song on Michael's mind.

Another major player that night was future Pulitzer Prize–winning journalist J. Ross Baughman, the 1974 *Chestnut Burr* editor re-

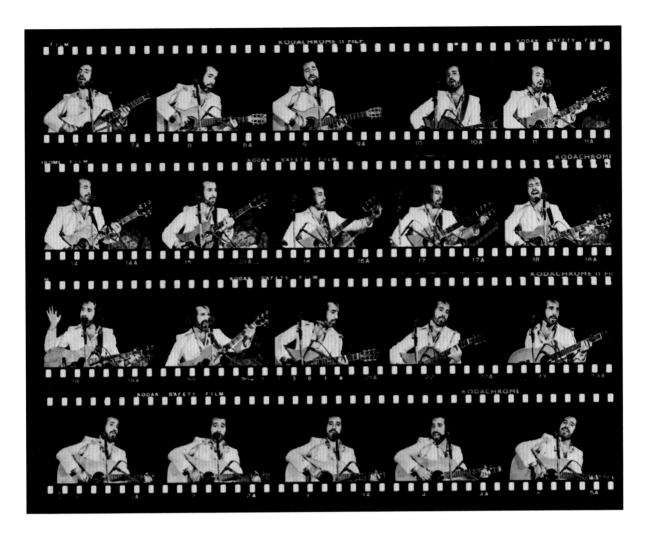

sponsible for the Paul Simon Kodachrome photo collage published in the *Burr.*

Paul Simon Kodachrome photo collage published in the *Chestnut Burr,* by future Pulitzer Prize–winning journalist J. Ross Baughman (Courtesy of the *Chestnut Burr*)

Back in 1973, my neck of the woods at Kent State was student publications, as I had become the editor of the school yearbook, the *Chestnut Burr,* and if I recall this correctly, we fell under the same parent group as the All Campus Programming Board, the ones who put on all these big concerts and other student events at the university. So there was a great deal of friendly coordination between the yearbook, the *Daily Kent Stater,* and the All Campus Programming Board. In fact, my friend and fellow staffer Mark Greenberg happened to have been roommates in an off-campus house with a guy who had some kind of close relationship with the Belkin Brothers, who the All Campus Programming

Board collaborated with to bring in all those huge national acts. Mark Greenberg was also my chief photographer at the yearbook, so this afforded us very comfortable freedom and access to these events.

So with just about every concert that came to Kent State, we would get this opportunity to shoot photos close-up, in front of and behind the stage. Several times, we volunteered to escort the visiting talent down to the old Student Union Rathskeller in what is now Oscar Ritchie Hall. We got to hang out for a little while with the likes of Frank Zappa and others, and Mark Greenberg even got to get some more candid pictures of these people while they were in town.

Mark Greenberg made a point of posing for kind of crazy, hand-shaking grip-and-grin—that's what we called it—photos. And then he would get an autograph from each visiting performer.

That night at the show, Paul Simon came off as more of a kind of nervous thoroughbred. He was a bit of a hypochondriac. He would use this as a way of saying, "Well I can't really do my best, so please don't hold me to whatever built-up preconception you have about me."

So after Paul's concert, Mark Greenberg, Jan Clark [*Stater* and *Burr* reporter], and I were just hanging out backstage at the Memorial Gym with Paul's brother Eddie, and Eddie invited us to go back to the University Inn on South Water Street, and that's where that *Kent Stater* interview with Paul took place. Paul's room was on the top floor of the inn, far left-hand corner as we face the building, but on the back. We spent quite a few hours up there just hanging out, and at one point it started getting late and everybody was getting hungry, so we wanted to convince Paul to come across the street to Jerry's Diner. It must have been midnight or pretty close to that, but

Paul was doing his kind of hypochondriac "What kind of place is it? What kind of food?" And we were all just kind of rolling our eyes because he was being such a wet blanket.

So eventually Eddie and I went without Paul. Eddie was just so similar in appearance to Paul that many people mistook him for Paul. But over at Jerry's Diner, people kind of might have raised their eyebrows there and said good luck or something, and they certainly were aware of the show that night, but nobody really bothered him. We actually enjoyed our excursion, and we wound up taking food back to Paul.

Baughman mentioned that photographer Mark Greenberg, who is responsible for the *Chestnut Burr* photograph taken at that concert, would have more insight on what happened that night.

At the time that Paul Simon played on campus I was a photographer / photo editor for the *Chestnut Burr* yearbook. We had pretty much unrestricted access to these kinds of events, and photo credentialing and so forth was not like anything you might imagine today or even twenty years ago. If you had a couple cameras around your neck, you probably had carte blanche. The other thing is that we knew the people who handled security, and this allowed us to always be onstage or backstage when there were big concerts at the Memorial Gym.

I remember very little about shooting photos of Paul Simon that night. I remember, however, choosing that frame because it was so early in my photographic career—we were always supposed to be paying attention to foreground and background, which helps give a photograph dimension. I liked the idea that the hands were a part of that photo because really the photo wouldn't have been much, but the hands actu-

ally give the photo an "it takes you there" kind of thing. You are right there with the audience.

In those days, the girls' locker room is where the bands' dressing rooms would be. I remember less about my experiences at the Paul Simon concert than I do the Duke Ellington or Bruce Springsteen shows, but I do remember I was in that main dressing room with another member of the *Chestnut Burr* who was all excited, and I remember Paul Simon being a very quiet guy. There was another guy there who looked just like him, and it turned out to be Paul's brother Eddie.

At one point, Paul had packed up and gone his way, and we were kind of surprised that he and his brother Eddie had split up. Eddie had said to me that he was going back to Cleveland Hopkins Airport, and I just offered him a ride, which I thought would be great fun. I had an Oldsmobile Convertible, and the three of

Paul Simon's 1973 performance, including an audience member's hands (*Chestnut Burr* photo by Mark Greenberg)

us just drove up and chatted. That's really my greatest recollection.

Simon Provides Homecoming Audience with Quiet but Exceptional Performance

By Ron Kovach
Daily Kent Stater
October 22, 1973

Paul Simon overcame a broken guitar string, a broken thumbnail and gave a sterling performance Saturday night for a Homecoming crowd of 5600 in Memorial Gym.

Bearded and attired in a resplendent white suit, Simon exhibited flawless style, both in his singing and acoustic guitar work. While he engaged in some banter between songs and equipment repairs, he was not, nor did he try to be, a memorable showman. When one is a songwriter like Simon, one sings his songs; that is enough.

For the audience, it was largely a night of quiet listening to a true artist who relied on no gimmick except talent, a rarity in today's music scene. Although the actual playing time was a bit on the skinny side—95 minutes and the show began 50 minutes late—Simon brought the crowd to its feet for two encores, "Loves Me Like a Rock" and "America."

Much of the show was Simon's alone. Some additional instrumentation would not have hurt on a few of the tunes he played alone, and though the concert was perhaps a little too laid-back and controlled, Simon rendered his songs perfectly, with feeling and grace, and little else was needed.

However, no singer can captivate an audience forever on just his voice and guitar. In each half of his show, Simon received a little help from his friends, the Jesse Dixon Singers and Urabamba, who provided a needed change of pace.

Urabamba, a group of four South American musicians playing native wind and string instruments, played some refreshingly new sounds for American ears. When they weren't accompanying Simon on "The Boxer," "Duncan" and "El Condor Pasa," they played two South American folk melodies that were striking in their beauty and simplicity.

After a low-pitched and somewhat restrained first set, the Jesse Dixon Singers supplied the surge of power the crowd was waiting for and almost stole the show in the process. The group consists of three gospel singers, a bass player, a drummer, and Jesse Dixon, singer and organist.

With Simon, they did gospel versions of "Sounds of Silence," "Mother and Child Reunion" and "Bridge over Troubled Water." Alone they did a rousing gospel number, "Jesus Is the Answer." All four songs came off well but would have taken off with some decent instrumental support. This might be partly attributed to the sound system equipment, for the concert arrived too late to complete a sound test.

In any case, the drummer, who should have been the driving force, sounded mediocre, the bassist only adequate, and Dixon should have stuck to singing. But, Simon and the other three singers, of course, made the difference.

Fittingly, the concert ended with Simon alone on stage singing "America," which is, in its visionary way, one of the finest and most meaningful songs Paul Simon has written.

Afterwards, Simon was complaining about a sore shoulder, displaying his by-then patched-up fingernail and saying how "my songs are never specifically about me" and how "they just come out."

Someone asked whether he had made enough money in his career to retire.

"Retire?" he said. "I'd go insane if I retired."

Early 1970s postcard showing the University Inn at 540 South Water Street, where on the night of Saturday, October 20, 1973, Paul Simon stayed and was photographed and interviewed by the *Daily Kent Stater.*

Yet the Crowd "Wanted More"

It Was a Bad Day for Simon

By Jan Clark

Daily Kent Stater

October 24, 1973

Saturday was just one of those days for Paul Simon when he appeared for the Homecoming concert in Memorial Gym.

Even rock stars have bad days, especially when their playing fingernail breaks the morning before a concert. Simon said "it would take a month before the nail grows back" to where he can play without a pick.

Not only was Simon's playing finger malfunctioning, but his left hand was acting up as well. Before the concert, he explained that he has visited acupuncture specialists twice in order to relieve a nervous disorder from playing the guitar too much.

"You have to go a few times before acupuncture can be effective," he said.

A bad arm didn't stop a favorable audience response to Simon's performance, according to Michael Solomon, the concert organizer. He said there were three curtain calls for Simon and the crowd "still wanted more."

Other things were also going wrong for the Simon tour group. Simon explained that the sound equipment first went to Canton instead of Kent and then the truck broke down on its way here.

Paul Simon in his hotel room at the University Inn after his October 20, 1973, performance. *Bottom right:* Seated behind him is his brother Ed Simon. (Photos by J. Ross Baughman)

Therefore, rehearsal for Simon was four hours behind schedule, and even then "it didn't sound right," Simon said. It was Paul Simon's brother, Ed, who encouraged Paul not to worry about the day's mishaps.

"My brother Ed is my favorite person in the world," Paul said. Ed, who looks a great deal like his brother, travels with Paul when he can get away from his music school in New York.

After the concert, Ed explained that Paul first composes the music and then sets the lyrics "to the mood of the music."

The original words to "Kodachrome," one of Simon's latest hits, were "going home," but Paul "didn't want to write another song about going home," Ed explained.

After Paul "played around with word arrangements" similar to "going home," Ed said Paul came up with the word "Kodachrome."

According to Ed, the next step in creating "Kodachrome" was that Paul associated Kodachrome color film as an opposite to black and white film.

Paul then further linked the brightness and distortedness of color film as a contrast to the "reality of black and white film," Ed said.

Speaking for himself, Paul said, "No one taught me how to write lyrics. I just sort of experimented and taught myself."

"Any time I can sit quietly somewhere and I can think—I can create," Paul said.

Commenting further on songwriting, Paul said, "Whether a song is technically good or bad doesn't matter." He explained there is "some sort of quality that makes a song good that can't be described."

"I don't have any economic drive to produce albums," he insisted. He said the production of albums is based on "when I feel like making them."

Simon also said he doesn't have a philosophy as a performer. "I perform because I'm a ham," he remarked with a smile.

"Almost never are my songs about myself. Maybe generally about me, but never specifically about me," Simon said.

Simon told students, "No one has to say a message in a song—people can read the important messages."

However, Simon did explain that the song "Like a Rock" was "about people who abuse power—like the Nixon people."

Simon predicted that his music "will become more up-tempo than it ever was with Art Garfunkel.

"I'd really like to put out a live album of the show done at Kent," Simon added.

After the concert at Kent, Simon was approached by a student who wished to pray for him. Simon replied, "Do what you've got to do, but I've got a lot of people praying for me. When I'm ready I'll ask for Him myself."

According to Simon, "Campuses look the way they always have—I see hardly any changes."

Earth, Wind & Fire played at Kent State on Sunday, October 28, 1973.

Michael Solomon Reflects on Earth, Wind & Fire at Kent State in 1973
2011

Earth, Wind & Fire played to a very packed house on Sunday, October 28, 1973. Almost forty-five years later, Michael Solomon, the All Campus Planning Board Concert Committee chairman from 1972 to 1974, remembered the lead-up to the show and the wild night itself.

So by the fall of 1973, as All Campus Programming Board Concert Committee chairman, our whole group and I had begun to develop a reputation for bringing great concerts to Kent State. By this time we had brought Cheech and Chong, James Taylor, Pink Floyd, Yes, Elton John, George Carlin, Paul Simon, and others.

And there was a whole area in the Student Center where ACPB and a lot of the other student organizations existed. So, somewhere along the line, I met the head of the Black United Students. I think his name was Silas Ashley, and Silas said, "Why don't you bring a great black concert? Do Earth, Wind & Fire."

I asked him, "Will we sell it out?" and he said, "Absolutely." So we booked Earth, Wind & Fire into the Student Center Ballroom, and we initially sold only six hundred tickets. In those days we had a capacity of around two thousand for that room.

I said, "Silas, it ain't happening. What's going on?"

He said, "Did you run ads on the radio stations I told you to?" (which were like Canton-Akron, the various soul stations of that time).

In Concert

EARTH, WIND, and FIRE

Sun. Oct. 28, 8pm Ballroom - New Student Center
Tickets 4.00 advance - 4.50 at the door
On Sale at Student Center Ticket Office
An ACPB Production
in conjunction with B.U.S. Homecoming

Earth, Wind & Fire played at the Kent State Ballroom on Sunday, October 28, 1973. (Courtesy of the *Daily Kent Stater*)

And I said, "Yeah, that stuff's been going."

And he said, "Don't worry about it. The black people, they all pay for their tickets the night of the show."

He was making me nervous, so we stepped up the radio ads.

So the night of the concert, an hour before the show, people started showing up. And we're selling tickets—*lots* of tickets. And about half an hour before the show, the hallway was so jammed with people, all pushing forward, that literally the walls of the ticket office were shaking and the guys inside were afraid. There were *so many people*. At some point we all looked at each other and said, "What the hell?" We made the announcement in the hall: "The gates are open for everybody, just go inside."

We have no idea how many people were in the ballroom that night, but at the time we made that announcement, we had sold two-thirds of the tickets. We really couldn't take any more money because we were really afraid somebody was going to get trampled so we just opened the doors. Earth, Wind & Fire put on an *unbelievable* concert. Twenty-five hundred people? Three thousand people? It was just wild.

The fire marshal and that crew, they were SO pissed at us, and we said, "Well, what are we supposed to do?" Nobody was happy except the people in the crowd and the band. Silas Ashley said to me at some point, "You are the best, can I just say." I was just lucky to be alive after that show.

It was really one of those shows where, once it started, all of us looked at each other and we didn't want to be there. It was frightening because there were so many people there. I just know that the people loved it, though. Those guys were just so good.

Hallway on the second floor of the Kent State Student Center, which became so overwhelmed with Earth, Wind & Fire concertgoers trying to get tickets that the promoter had to turn the event into a free concert. The original ticket booth was at the very end of this hallway and is now closed off by a wall. (Photo by Jason Prufer)

Bruce Springsteen's 1974 Party in Kent

January 19, 1974

One of the great rock-and-roll Kent stories I'd heard since I was a kid was that in the mid-1970s Bruce Springsteen played in the Kent State University Student Center Ballroom as the opening act for southern rock band Black Oak Arkansas. And purportedly, a bootleg recording of this performance had been widely circulating among Springsteen collectors for years.

On the night Springsteen played at Kent State, he was not yet a superstar; however, the real music connoisseurs of the day knew all about him. Bruce wouldn't get his first dose of major stardom until he released his breakout album *Born to Run* in August a year later. That night in Kent, he was out supporting only his second major label album, *The Wild, the Innocent & the E Street Shuffle.*

Michael Solomon, the 1972–74 All Campus Programming Board Concert Committee chairman, was the chief promoter on this concert. Years later, Michael remembered:

An agent at William Morris who I developed a good relationship with over the phone named Sam McKeith said, "I'm gonna send you an album and I want you to listen to it," and it was by a brand-new artist named Bruce Springsteen. Over that Christmas break at the end of 1972, I was at home in Columbus and saw Springsteen open for Sha Na Na, and I was blown away.

I thought, "This guy is fabulous." And then later I listened to *The Wild, the Innocent & the E Street Shuffle* album more times than I can remember. I got ahold of the agent and said, "Let's create a show where I can get him in here in the Student Center Ballroom."

He said, "Book this band Black Oak Arkansas for January 19;

they did this song 'Jim Dandy to the Rescue.' You'll fill a couple thousand seats, and we can bring in Springsteen to open for them and we'll charge you $750."

Black Oak Arkansas may have cost a couple thousand dollars—maybe $5000, but Springsteen was $750. And that included Springsteen having to pay for his own transportation. They drove in from Jersey!

So the Black Oak guys told me before the show, "We don't know who this guy is who is opening up for us, but he gets 45 minutes and not a minute longer. If his show goes more than 45 minutes then we are not performing." They were total pricks.

And I was like, wait a minute, this guy came all the way here. I'm all upset, and I explained this to Springsteen and the band, and Bruce said, "Don't worry about it." They were all together, backstage in the Student Center. There wasn't much backstage. It was a pretty small area. We found a different area for the Black Oak guys.

During the opening set, one of the Black Oak guys was standing next to me and looked over and said, "Who is that guy?" They were stunned at Springsteen's performance, as was everybody that heard him. He was spectacular, amazing.

And so then later that night, as was typically the case, we had a party at this house I lived in. We had lots of people over, and Springsteen is there sitting on the floor in a torn leather jacket, boots with a hole in 'em, saying to a friend of mine, "Man we've been at this a long time. I just hope we can keep the band together a little while longer; I think we are getting close." Those were his exact words. I lived in a little house on North Depeyster Street. It was 403, corner of Brady Street. Bruce was sitting on the floor in that place talking to people. I remember Clarence Clemons

Advertisement for Bruce Springsteen and Black Oak Arkansas in the Kent State University Student Center Ballroom (Courtesy of the *Daily Kent Stater*)

A present-day photo of the house on the northeast corner of Brady and Depeyster Streets where Bruce Springsteen and members of the E Street Band attended a party on Saturday, January 19, 1974 (Photo by Jason Prufer)

was there. I don't remember who else. It was just lots of people in and out. I had a lot of friends and friends of friends who always would know that there would be something going on back at the house after concerts. That is a night etched in my memory. A couple of years later when he was on the cover of *Time* and *Newsweek* the same week [October 27, 1975], lots of people called me to remind me of that concert and that night. These are the best of memories.

The *Daily Kent Stater* reviewed the show, and the reviewer seems to have been traumatized by the entire experience.

Some Kind of Zoo in Hell

By Clyde Hadlock

January 22, 1974

I used to hate people that went to concerts and praised the warm-up band over and over and over and then hatcheted the "stars." So go ahead and hate me, but then I'm not going to go off the deep end about Bruce Springsteen either.

His set had all the usual drawbacks one has come to expect from any concert. A good 40 percent of it was totally inaudible, as were a few members of his band from time to time. If the echo had been any more delayed, we could have heard the show twice.

The fragments that I was able to catch from time to time convinced me he was one hell of a poet and probably an excellent singer but had been burned savagely by being asked to appear at a zoo like that.

My biggest complaint was that he brutally marred their big show-closing piece, "Rosalita," by whipping into Junior Walker's "Shotgun" and taking about ten minutes to introduce the band.

It was like slapping a bumper sticker on a Dali painting.

If you get a chance, go see them in a small club somewhere, but hurry, they probably won't be playing them much longer, if they do at all.

Well, end of the entertainment. Like they say, "tragedy tomorrow, comedy tonight."

Black Oak Arkansas was a downright scream the night of the show, but looking back on it the next morning it was kind of tragic.

Not just because they were deadly serious in their "git high, git nekkid, git down" campaign but because the whole audience bought it. Bought it and, hell yes, *identified* with it.

B.O.A. are what everybody in the U.S. would be like if the south had won the Civil War: a bunch of backward, noodling crackers. They are to music what the roller derby is to TV.

I'm mildly surprised they didn't have the audience divided up according to race.

Think I'm kidding? Listen to some of leader Dandy Jim Mangrum's sexraps and tell me he isn't capable of such outrages.

These, by the way, are all delivered in his best sub–Mason/Dixon Line intonations, much resembling the voice of a man who has just gargled with a lit sparkler:

"You shore got a nice campus aroun' here; lotta fine lookin' women, too. Well, it gets me horny, just like any man that sees a fine lookin' woman with a nice rear-end gets horny."

And: "There's a lot heat in here an' you know where it's coming from? Between our legs."

And: "This song's called 'Hot Rod' an' it ain't about no car."

And so on.

Swallow *that*, libbers.

When they got around to making music (assuming they did), it all sounded a lot like chains in a blender set for liquify.

If they'd done the same song eleven times or eleven different songs, it wouldn't have mattered anyhow, the audience reaction would have been the same and everyone would have gone home just as ecstatic.

So, why shouldn't bands like B.O.A. be big

stars, and why shouldn't people keep using wall-of-cough syrup sound systems in their hall of public herding as long as the masses keep flocking in happily like they're going to a party as some kind of zoo in Hell?

You answer me that.

On June 1, 1974, a little over four months later, Springsteen came back to Kent State and headlined a multiband concert in the Memorial Gym.

Bruce Springsteen
Equally a Poet and Rock and Roller
By Clyde Hadlock
Daily Kent Stater
June 4, 1974

The concert Saturday night was close to six hours long, owing to a couple of acts that were sandwiched in between Michael Stanley and Bruce Springsteen. One was 15-60-75, a band you can see at your favorite bar every other day. The other offering was "The Banky Brothers," two guys you could probably see in someone's basement for about 19 cents.

Michael Stanley did a fine set of new, yet-to-be-released material, coupled with tunes from his last two albums. Standouts were "Rosewood Bitters" and "Poet's Day." His bassist was Dan Pecchio, formerly of Glass Harp.

Now we'll talk about Bruce Springsteen. A lot of people have been calling him "the next Dylan," mainly because he's the finest rock 'n' roll poet to come along since Dylan and probably because he looks a little like him. Well, Bob Dylan was the "next Dylan." Bruce Springsteen is the next Bruce Springsteen, and that's fine with me.

Springsteen is a very rare and talented performer, being divided equally between poet and rock 'n' roller. He's fun to watch, as he momentarily lets his guitar land idle while he uses both hands to weave pictures of his scenic New Jersey street imagery for you, or acting out lines of songs, like "banging them pleasure machines" in the arcade. He reminds me of a young Gregory Corso, a street brawler with visions of heaven.

His songs are hot-blooded and romantic, yet sexy without being sexist. His guitar playing is clean, piercing, and never overdone. His voice is an incredible mixture of equal parts Lowell George, Van Morrison, Andy Devine and Gregg Allman.

His five-member band, the E Street Band, is excellent, knowing when not to play, and also being able to put out enough energy to tear the place apart without being obnoxious about it. Standouts are Clarence Clemons on sax and David Sancious on keyboards. Springsteen is a very lucky man to have a band like that with him, and it looks like he knows it and enjoys every minute of it.

I was worried about some of the incredible hype a lot of critics and reviewers had been giving him, since nothing ruins a new performer faster than trying to live up to what is written about him. Bruce Springsteen has nothing to live up to, he simply is what he was born to be, and no amount of hype or critical great expectations can alter that.

Michael Solomon, 1972–74 All Campus Planning Board Concert Committee chairman, reflected years later on his experience bringing Duke Ellington to play at the Student Center Ballroom on Friday, February 1, 1974.

Duke Ellington played at the Student Center Ballroom on February 1, 1974. (Courtesy of the *Chestnut Burr*)

Recollections of Duke Ellington

We had been doing these concerts, and we had always kind of been pushing the envelope of the university's patience, like with the Pink Floyd thing and almost wrecking the gym floor.

So I thought it would be nice if we did something that was nice for the university. And I happened to like Duke Ellington. He's obviously a legendary musician. I contacted the agent; I found out we could get him.

We gave free tickets to like twenty people from the City of Kent Mayor's Office and to the top people in the university administration. We allowed them to have a cocktail reception where Ellington dropped in, which I think was in the Schwebel Room on the third floor. And all my people in my little group, we all rented tuxes and had our girlfriends get formal gowns, and we had all the students who we had hired to be ushers looking great. It was a wonderful event.

The black fraternity that I guess he was in [Alpha Phi Alpha] when he was in school presented him with a special award that night. It was really, really nice.

Ellington was pretty feeble. He came out onstage, I think I shook his hand, I introduced him. But I mean, he died four months later. The concert itself was *phenomenal.* That was some of the best music I have ever heard.

And then at the end of the night these guys in Ellington's orchestra looked over to us and said,

"Hey, we want to go jam somewhere. Where can we go?" And we took them right downtown to North Water Street and they walked right into the Kent Kove and heard 15-60-75 [the Numbers Band] playing. They put down their cases, opened them up, grabbed their instruments, stepped up onstage with those guys, and played until two or three in the morning.

Duke Ellington—
"We Love You Madly"
By Mary King
Daily Kent Stater
February 5, 1974

I suppose that when a reviewer attends a superb jazz concert given by a man 74 years of age and his band, some of whose ages touch that altitude also, that reviewer's first impulse is to ramble on about something called a generation gap being bridged and to commend the performers in an "even though" fashion, as if musical ability were suddenly cut off at a certain age and senility allowed to creep in.

I believe that when one's life and love is something as immortal as music, there is no time for the critic to commend or criticize using age as a major premise.

Duke Ellington and his orchestra began their concert last Friday evening with "C Jam Blues," a rocking instrumental which woke the audience out of its pre-concert annoyances and ennui and had it clapping and stomping to each succeeding song.

When the music turned sweet and soft, as when veteran sax man Paul Gonsalves played the soothing "In the Sentimental Mood" while walking among the audience, we listened in silence and admiration.

The orchestra performed songs of many moods and backgrounds, interpreting in both the improvisational and memorized sections. The soloists (and each member is a soloist at one time or another) did not divide the songs into segments as "take your turn" jazz bands often seem to do, but played every solo fitting to the mood of the piece.

And "mood" is an important word in Ellington's musical vocabulary, because in the fifty-odd years he's been composing he has written with the varying temperaments and nuances of his band members first in his mind. Ellington's late co-composer and friend, Billy Strayhorn, remarked once, "Duke plays the piano. But, his real instrument is his orchestra."

The musicians who really shined Friday evening were Gonsalves, who plays so smoothly that the sax seems almost a part of him; Harry Carney, another Ellington veteran, who played baritone sax solos which were interrupted more than once by spontaneous applause; trumpeter Ronnie Johnson, who won over the crowd with a tremendous Satchmo imitation and whose piercing trumpet solos must be among the most imaginative in jazz today; and Harold Ashby, who added the Eastern flavor to "Afro-Eurasian Eclipse" so well.

But the greatest—it was the Duke himself. His piano work, guiding the orchestra through each song, was so delicate, so confident, that one readily felt the intimacy between the man and the instrument. His deep, sophisticated, seductive voice when he introduced songs, when he informed us that he "loved us madly"—there we felt the intimacy between the man and his audience.

Some who would assert that Ellington's music belongs to a certain generation, that it is a thing of the past, are pitifully in error. Just as Ellington's jazz evolved from influences like European and classical music, African dance and American Negro field hollering and blues, the music of the seventies evolved from men like Ellington who together shaped what is now the American music image.

Duke Ellington, at whatever age, belongs to every generation, to all those he professes to love madly. And Duke, we love you madly too.

Dizzy Gillespie and the KSU Jazz Lab Band played at Kent State on Tuesday, April 30, 1974

Gillespie and Lab Band
"Inspiration in Jazz"
Daily Kent Stater
May 2, 1974

Dizzy Gillespie's appearance Tuesday night with the KSU Jazz Lab Band was a great success, for both Gillespie and the Lab Band.

The Lab Band performed alone during the

Advertisement for the Dizzy Gillespie show in Kent
(Courtesy of the *Daily Kent Stater*)

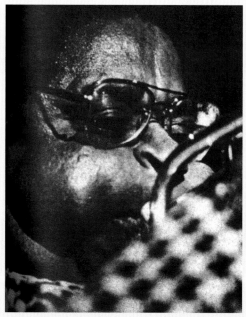

Dizzy Gillespie shows the form that made him
great. (*Daily Kent Stater* photo by Steve Stroud)

first half of the show. In the sections when they all played together, they sounded unified, really enthusiastic about the jazz.

However, they were quite weak in the improvisational sections; some of the soloists were not free enough with their instruments to perform good, improvisational jazz. They tended to fall back upon the simple runs rather than let themselves go and experiment.

I was very impressed with Tom First and Bernard Watt, who each soloed on sax. Tom First has a very clear tone which made Sammy Nestico's "All My Life" a favorite with the audience. Watt's tone is a little more subtle, but he has real gift for improvisation: the kind of soloist you can depend on not to expire in the middle of his solo.

When Dizzy Gillespie appeared, there was an incredible change in the atmosphere on stage. The Lab Band loosened up, developed a better sense of dynamics, and their solos had more meaning.

Dizzy himself captured the attention of both the Lab Band and the audience. His tendency to ramble on in his verbal introductions and his clumsiness on stage disappeared soon after he began to play. He has tremendous agility with high notes—there was no cracking, no note-slipping.

He is probably most remarkable on his muted solos. With them, he can make his notes waver and can drift from sharp to flat with ease. In many cases, the Lab Band would stare and laugh in amazement at some of Gillespie's seemingly impossible solos.

He may be getting older; he may not be able to play well into the night as he did once with Charlie Parker in the birth of be-bop. But he is still a major source of inspiration in jazz, as was seen clearly in the delicate, profound communication he formed with the Lab Band Tuesday.

On Friday, February 21, 1975, Herbie Hancock played at Kent State.

Hancock Electrifies Ballroom Audience
Daily Kent Stater
February 25, 1975

"Right on!" exclaimed the head-swaying, hand-clapping, foot-tapping, sold-out audience that heard the electrifying Herbie Hancock jazz concert Friday in the Student Center Ballroom.

Hancock proved to be a master of jazz. His universal, modern interpretation excited everyone—from intellectuals to the hip dudes in the corner.

At times, the acoustics were not up to par and Hancock seemed slightly irritated, delaying the performance until the sound equipment measured up to standards.

Hancock brought a classical approach to the piano, beginning his jam session with the popular "Maiden Voyage." It had the soft and beautiful texture of an African violet.

Following the opening number, Hancock went backstage, leaving the talented Headhunters to give a warm-up performance worthy of their standing ovation.

The Headhunters, members of Hancock's band, sang and played a variety of instruments that had a funky, danceable beat. They were uninhibited, singing a number of hits: "If You Got It, You Get it," "Daffy's Dance," "God Make Me Funky," and others.

The musicians were a concert in themselves. They include Paul Jackson, electric bass; Benny Maupin, tenor sax and bass clarinet; Mike Clark, drums, and percussionist Bill Summers, who had the audience eating from his hands when he played a solo on shakere (an African gourd with beads).

On Friday, February 25, 1975, Herbie Hancock played at Kent State. (*Chestnut Burr* photo by B. Jones)

After intermission Hancock returned—it was hard to believe that you were not in Harlem's Apollo Theatre or Carnegie Hall. In black English, "Herbie got down! The brother was outta-sight!"

Hancock played his fingers to the knuckles. His frenzied fans could have been the emcees of the show.

The highlight of the evening was "Butterfly," which Hancock dedicated to the ladies in the house. It was soft as a kiss and rich in piano arpeggios.

Many of the events that make up Kent's rich musical history took place off campus, as this excerpt from a Stater article illustrates, in a snapshot of Kent's 1970s social scene. The downtown bars, from the Water Street Saloon and its countrified house band Good Company to 15-60-75 (the Numbers Band) playing at the Kove.

Kent Bar Scene
From Glitter to Football Jerseys
By Joe Kullman
Daily Kent Stater
May 22, 1974

Friar Tuck's hosts a variety of rock 'n' roll bands three nights a week. The Krazy Horse has a band only one night a week, but on that night women wearing halter-tops pay only one-third the usual admission charged.

Security for the bar owner is establishing a regular crowd.

Friar Tuck's was one bar that had a unique problem. They took over the old Robin Hood, which was like a second home to many students. When Robin Hood rode gallantly away, and Friar Tuck took over his quaint tudor-style home, many old customers rebelled and stayed away.

"Whenever you change, you wipe out a lot of old memories," Scott Howett says. "But you have to get the old people back, as well as get new ones in."

Harassment is an element of the bar scene Jim Harmon would like to spare his female customers in the Town House.

"Gentlemen," the sign outside the bar reads, "must be 21." The reason for this, Harmon says, is "to keep the place nice." For although other Kent bars, like the Krazy Horse, may not be a place to wear your best suit and bring your date, Harmon wants the Town House, with its upstairs balcony bar and soft red lantern lights, to be the place where this is possible.

"We get a very strange crowd. We get everyone from the hippies to the glitter people. But everyone gets along," he adds.

The "glitter people," as Harmon calls them, provide the ultimate in offbeat *Clockwork Orange*–type costuming for Kent's downtown night-lifers. All the way from one's Top Hat or feathered cap to striped socks and six-inch platform shoes.

If the "glitter people" at the Town House offer a futuristic look at Kent's night-life, another bar on the "outskirts" of downtown perhaps offers a view of what the "bar scene" in past times looked like.

A large building on West College Street that was once an automobile showroom has been The Dome since 1966, a bar that is more than twice the size of other Kent bars. On weekends crowds of over 600 people, most of them from Akron, will provide this bar with a scene reminiscent of a rollicking old-time dance hall.

"The band is so loud, I have cotton in my ears," says one Dome bartender. "Sometimes we get seven or eight hundred people and this place looks like it's in the middle of a mass fight."

"I keep a bouncer," says manager Nancy Cameron. "But 90 percent of the time I don't need him. Most of the kids with fake I.D.s. We don't prosecute them; we just call their parents.

"We do keep the younger crowd," Cameron admits. "The kids are just out to have fun. They're not rowdies."

"This is the only big dance hall left," says Measles band drummer Buddy Bennett. "We play a five-hour gig. We keep the same songs unless people don't like one of them, then we drop it. We work like machinists in a factory."

"We are just a dance place," Cameron continues. "Kids may change the way they dance, but they will always dance."

Ritch Underwood of the band Monopoly calls many people in the bars today "sit downs." They are the ones, says Ritch, who stand in the corners with their eyes shut, rolling their heads around while the band is "playing their asses off" trying to get a response or to get them to dance.

"I think it would be good self-expression," Ritch says. "People don't respond as well as they used to."

According to one person who apparently liked the bar scene so much that he once lived in a back room at the Kove, "It's depressing to go downtown now and see everyone on downers, bumping into walls and not knowing what's going on. Actually, people were friendlier when they were just drinking and dancing."

For another Water Street bar, it might be incorrect to say that the house band, Good Company plays at the Water Street Saloon. It might be more accurate to say that Good Company is the Water Street Saloon. At least that is how the band members see it.

"We created the crowd in here." says rhythm guitar player Perry Bocci. "People don't come here just to hang out; they come here to see us."

The band draws in as many as 300 people on Friday and Saturday nights to listen and dance to their spicy country and western music, complete with fiddle and pedal steel guitar.

Good Company has created a rather unique scene for a Kent bar. People dance and prance in hoe-down style to the whines of Mary DuShane's electric fiddle and Charlie Palace's slick, country-styled lead guitar.

Walter's Cafe stands as the elder statesmen

15-60-75 (the Numbers Band) playing at the Kent Kove early 1975 (Photo by Richard Underwood)

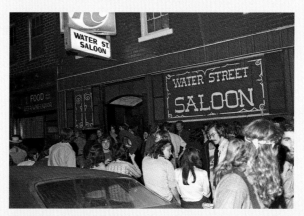

The Water Street Saloon, Kent, November 1974 (Photo by J. Ross Baughman)

among Water Street's honky-tonk bars, decorated with lighted beer displays, neon signs, old-style whiskey bottle taps and other trinkets and miscellaneous items collected over some 27 years since it first opened after World War II as Seaver's Tavern.

The bar came to be known more affectionately by Seaver's first as "Orville's." Orville died in 1968, and a man he hired as night manager in 1952, Walter Horvath, 65, is now the owner.

Walter has since turned the night manager job over to Jake Marx, 32, who once taught at the university and has an M.A. in English.

"Orville's idea of a bar was to have eight old men as regular customers and that was it," says

Marx. "But Walter really digs the kids, even though he never stays around to see what goes on at night. I think one time he fell asleep here and woke up at ten that night. The place was full of people, and Walter got up and practically ran out the door," he says.

Walter's opens at six o'clock in the morning and serves as the halfway house of Water Street for many faithful customers. Ages range from about 21 to 75 and the jukebox selections range from Mott the Hoople to "I'm Getting Sentimental over You" by Tommy Dorsey.

"It's like a movie in here," says Marx. "There is something about Orville's (he uses the old name) that keeps the people coming back even though the place never changes. I don't know what it is."

Just before 2 A.M. most bartenders and band members are putting their bars back together and gathering their equipment, ready to pack up and go home.

But at the Kove, the dance floor is swarming and jerking, swaying bodies. While the rest of Water Street begins to quiet, 15-60-75 is performing a sultry version of "Sea Cruise," then blast out "Voodoo Love."

The dancers are not just "customers" or "fans." These are the hard-core worshipers of the "back-to-the-roots" blues played by 15-60-75, which has been the Kove's house band for over three years.

Bob Kidney, playing guitar, is the maestro of the band. He stands stoically on stage, cueing the other four musicians with pointed glances. He thinks the band's music is good, but he doubts that it is the only thing that brings multitudes to the Kove.

"People come to the Kove because they can get high there. And our music sounds good to people who are high," he says.

"I don't think a band creates a crowd," he continues. "I think a band is blessed with a crowd. I know because I've had crowds and then lost them. And I've had good bands that nobody came to see."

"Why do people keep coming to the Kove? I don't know," he adds. "I can tell what people are thinking, but I can't tell why they are thinking that way."

"Our music may sound like basic rock 'n' roll, but rock 'n' roll is just blues slicked up. And blues is rhythm is what everyone understands no matter what kind of music you play. Maybe that is the one thing all these people have in common that moves them."

Sun-Ra played at Kent State on Thursday, February 13, 1975.

Sun-Ra "Fiery, Powerful"
By Roland Forte
February 18, 1975

It was the year 2000. Astro-jazz had a delightful discordant sound.

"The Universe sent me to converse with you. Now it's time to leave this planet with me," Sun-Ra invited the enthusiastic standing-room-only crowd Thursday in the Mbari Mbayo Theatre.

Wearing glittery, African-inspired "solar system costumes," Sun-Ra and his multi-talented troupe-consisting of five musicians and two dancers—provided an awesome performance.

The concert was enhanced by a multi-media array of psychedelic stage lighting, slides and a movie projector running simultaneously. The movie screen danced—flashing scenes of the ancient Egyptian pyramids and the sphinx juxtaposed with pictures of outer space.

The pair of chanting dancers, decked in silver hats and dashikis, moved with the precision of the U.S. space program. At times it seemed as if their toes would touch the stars!

There was a lot of audience participation. When Sun-Ra removed himself from producing odd sounds on an electric keyboard, he moved into the audience delivering poetic and powerful sermons.

Like a faith healer, he touched his responsive white and black congregation and preached, "Don't give up your life for me, give up your death!

"There's no future in this world. The world ended 2,000 years ago. Why do you prefer to stay on one planet? Come out into the greater universe," he pleaded.

The astro-jazz musicians possessed the energy of the sun. Their performance was a prime example of super-progressive jazz, and the concert as a whole was a tour de force in sound, dance, fiery poetry and psychedelic lighting.

Sun-Ra backstage at the Mbari Mbayo Theatre in Kent State's Oscar Ritchie Hall (Courtesy of Kent State University Libraries. Special Collections and Archives.)

Sun-Ra performing at the Mbari Mbayo Theatre in Kent State's Oscar Ritchie Hall (Courtesy of Kent State University Libararies. Special Collections and Archives.)

DEVO's Seminal 1975 Night on Kent State's Front Campus

April 4, 1975

As I was doing some initial research on Kent's music history, I came across a very mysterious yet stunning three-quarter-page 1975 *Daily Kent Stater* advertisement for a couple of DEVO performances where they would be opening for two showings of John Waters's *Pink Flamingos* in the old University Auditorium up on front campus. It stunned me, for so many reasons. Why had I never heard of this event? Who set it up? Who was there? What was the show like?

Some months after first spotting the old advert, I received an e-mail from a buddy who told me that DEVO cofounder Mark Mothersbaugh would be having his artwork featured at an exhibit at his sister Amy Mothersbaugh's Studio 2091, on Front Street in Cuyahoga Falls. Mark would host a live question-and-answer session at the reception. Indeed, I had a question! So, I went to the reception and presented him with the original 1975 *Daily Kent Stater* advertisement. I asked him what he remembered about that night.

Yeah, we opened up for *Pink Flamingos* [film]. I think the band at the time was my brother Jim, my brother Bob, Gerald Casale, and myself. It was just the four of us, and, um, there are some really bad recordings that Chuck Statler made that night on one of those old video cameras where it ends up looking like old black-and-white surveillance film when you are done. But Jim was kind of ahead of things, and he was into what now is called "circuit bending." He was working on an invention of one of the first electronic drum kits, and in preparing for that show he tried this thing where

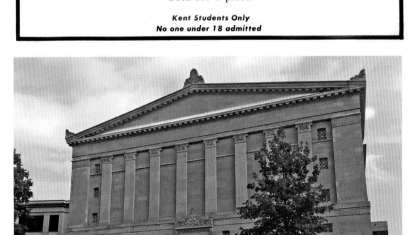

he took acoustic drums and he attached acoustic guitar pickups to the drum set and then ran those into wah-wah pedals and Fuzz Tones and finally an amplifier onstage. It was a godawful sound. It was amazing. Nothing that we've ever done sounded like that again. Nobody would ever go for that sound on purpose, because it was too difficult to do and it was uncontrollable, but now there's a whole movement of people that do circuit bending, where they take toys and electronic instruments and make them do things that they weren't supposed to do.

I'll tell you why I remember this night specifically. It's one of the only times that I was Boogie Boy [later called "Booji Boy"] all night. Leaving the mask on just suffocates you to wear it for more than a couple songs. It was a full head mask that closed off underneath, at least the original version did. The other reason I remember it is because I found something at a Salvation Army store called an Optigan—something that Sears had tried to put out in the '70s. It was like a home organ that was on a totally different system than any of the other home organs. It had optical discs that actually were quite interesting sounding. We used the Optigan on the last song of the set. It was like a $20 purchase. But you could take these discs and turn them upside down so drum kits and guitar sounds would play in reverse but in perfect time. Years later, I found out that the Beatles used an Optigan on *Revolution #9.*

Yeah, back in those days if there wasn't a physical confrontation, we felt pretty good about a show. It wasn't a full house, I can tell you that. We had about ten die-hard fans, and there would be the unsuspecting thirty or forty people who accidently would wander in and slowly filter out before the set was over. Gerry was Chinaman that night. He had these un-PC

glasses that had plastic Oriental eyes inside the black frame. We kind of borrowed them a little bit. We poked out the Oriental eye parts and I just wore the frames—they were the same glasses I wore on the cover of our album *Oh, No! It's DEVO.* Bob Mothersbaugh was a clown back then, and Jim was Jungle Jim, and we all wore matching one-piece "fireman leisure suits" of a janitorial mid-blue coloring. We were characters the whole night.

I would say the *Pink Flamingos* show very much represented "when DEVO created DEVO." At this show, for an encore, the band played and Boogie Boy dropped his drawers and did a scarf dance to the tune of "The Girl Cant Help It" as an homage to the song appearing in the movie *Pink Flamingos.* In my opinion, that show was DEVO at its highest state of artistic purity and sounded the closest to the original band seen in the Chuck Statler film *The Truth about De-Evolution.*

A reference to this event on a database of all live DEVO performances referred to DEVO collaborator Gary "General" Jackett as having been there. Jackett recalled the event:

Dick Myers brought the film *Pink Flamingos* in to show in the University Auditorium, and it was quite avant garde, even for Kent at that time. This was when Mark's brother [Jim] was playing drums for DEVO. In this era, Gerry had a tampon coat, where he took, like, a doctor's white coat and either glued or soaked tampons in paint and then attached them [all over the coat] using safety pins or something like that.

That night would have been just at the beginning of DEVO as a musical band where they were trying to present a familiar sound, like where people would begin to recognize that

DEVO performing at JB's in Kent in 1977 (Photo by Bobbie Watson Whitaker)

what they were doing was music. They were really born of that Captain Beefheartish, real angular school of music. The whole concept of course was they weren't trying to make pleasant music, they were trying to make offensive music basically.

It was a good crowd, and it was mostly probably film students and art students. I was there with the girl I was seeing at the time, and all of DEVO's girlfriends were there, too. But as I remember it was a pretty good crowd—pretty raucous. But then when DEVO came on, of course, people didn't really get it. It wasn't really the sound of what was happening at that time. We were still at the tail end of the Crosby, Stills and Nash kind of thing, so everybody was aghast. I can't remember if there was a mass walkout or not. All I remember were people saying, "What's this?" or "This isn't music."

Since it was one of those early shows, they were probably as stiff as they ever were. They hadn't developed their stage show at that point. It was a fun night for all of us who were DEVO-tees, and that's because they were finally doing it. It was in a legitimate nice setting, just being in the old University Auditorium like that. In the early days, there was nothing musical about what they were trying to do. Gerry was trying to get as far away from pleasant music as possible. It was really an art thing, too. In a sense it was just like *Pink Flamingos,* in that the intent was to assault the viewer. And it wasn't till they got to Hollywood and wanted to make it that they had to change their direction a little.

I wasn't in school at that time. I don't think any of them were in school, either. Gerry might have been in grad school, I don't know. But he still had a link with Dick Myers, because, of course, without Richard Myers the night wouldn't have happened, and it was kind of like the art school was starting to feel the effects of May 4 in the sense that there was all that loss of all that energy that had been created up until May 4 in the artistic, musical community, which was thriving in Kent at that time. So Myers was probably one of the last vestiges of that late '60s, beginning '70s art scene, music scene. Gerry knew him, although a lot of people knew Dick Myers.

Richard "Dick" Myers is a retired film professor; maybe he knew more about this night. According to the advertisement, Tuesday Cinema, Richard's long-running film series, sponsored the event. The series was Richard's brainchild, and he oversaw its various incarnations from the 1960s through the 1980s. I asked him about Tuesday Cinema and his relationship with DEVO.

I started teaching at Kent State in 1964, and I am pretty sure we started showing films as Tuesday Cinema around 1966–67. We started in Van Deusen Hall, which is where the art department used to be. There was an auditorium in the back, and we started showing films there on Tuesday nights. Tuesday night was one of the nights that nobody was showing films; ACPB [All Campus Programming Board] was always showing them on weekends and I think International were showing them on Thursday nights. We charged 50 cents to get in.

It was interesting, it was kind of a hippie crowd, art crowd, English department crowd. They used to bring a soup kitchen every Tuesday night, also a big pot of soup, and they would put it up front for anybody who wanted a bowl of soup. We were always afraid to eat it, because we kept thinking they were bringing the same pot of the same soup every week, but some of the kids didn't have any money and so they would partake of the soup kitchen. I'm sure they meant well. They would take this pot of soup around to various groups on certain nights, and they called themselves "the soup kitchen."

So we started off with the films of the '30s, experiments by the French surrealists, and then little by little we started adding schlock, because we weren't getting that big of a crowd for just experimental films. So we started showing more contemporary experimental from the '40s, plus films from James Broughton, and then we were showing the California filmmakers and the New York crowd, you know, short films.

Little by little we started showing the kind of films that we recognize as cult films today—*Pink Flamingos* was one of the first we showed. We were also trying to make money to buy equipment for the film program for the university, so whatever we made at the door went to ordering the next batch of films as well as buying cameras and tripods and all that kind of stuff. And then later we got some money from the Ohio Arts Council, and then we got money from the National Endowment for the Arts.

By 1975 we had Tuesday Cinema in Oscar Ritchie Hall, but we would occasionally hold a show like *Pink Flamingos, Reefer Madness,* or the old black-and-white *King Kong* in the University Auditorium if we thought we were going to get a big crowd.

In fall 2010, the Kent State University School of Art brought DEVO's Gerald Casale in to lecture on a host of subjects, among them directing music videos, the history of DEVO, his Theodore

Roosevelt High School days, and his time as a Kent State undergrad and grad student. At one point while he was discussing DEVO's early days, he paused, peered deep into the audience, and asked, "Is Richard Myers here today?" A number of people pointed to him, sitting with his wife, Pat, at the back of the auditorium.

Gerry asked, "Didn't we open for *Pink Flamingos?*"

Richard responded, "Yes, I believe you did."

Gerry paused again, as if reflecting, and addressed Richard once more: "Richard, you helped change my life."

Gerry then spoke to the rest of the room: "I mean, Richard was a singlehanded film department. He brought in all the greatest underground films to Kent State University."

During Gerry's undergraduate days, he was Richard's student. Richard told me that in the early 1970s, Gerry contributed to his films *Confrontation at Kent State* and *Deathstyles.* Some time later, I asked Richard what he thought about his former student making such a public statement, and he responded:

I think it was great that he said it. I don't think he was talking just about my films. I think he was talking in general just about the films we were showing. But he also liked my films, and we would have talks and discussions here and there about it. But he was in the music scene by then. DEVO did a couple of shows for us back in those days of Tuesday Cinema, and I don't think we even paid them a dime. I think they just did it because they were just starting to get popular.

Can you imagine that spectacular 1975 Tuesday Cinema event? Two showings of *Pink Flamingos,* two performances by DEVO, an Optigan, circuit bending, Boogie Boy, the Clown,

and a horrifying sound created by acoustic guitar pickups running through wah-wah pedals, Fuzz Tones, and an amplifier. Talk about jumping off the aesthetic cliff and diving straight into the abyss. And in Kent, Ohio! This was a homegrown, original performance, before DEVO was well known or famous. The people who attended this show on Friday, April 4, 1975, must still have some sort of trauma from the experience. Viva Kent's underground and viva DEVO.

Stater "Jocko Homo" Classified

This image is an artifact of one of the most incredible and original artistic projects to come out of Kent State University and the city of Kent itself. This tiny advertisement ran in the *Daily Kent Stater* for four days straight, between Tuesday, May 11, and Friday, May 14, 1976.

This ad, buried among the mundane Kent State classifieds, is asking anyone who reads it to show up at the Governance Chambers in the Kent State Student Center on Monday, May 17, 1976, to be an extra in what would become DEVO's career-changing short film *The Truth about De-Evolution.*

Those who showed up for the filming actually walked into what would be a visual construction

Pin out be a star major filming Re Devolution noon Monday May 17 Governance Chambers N.S.C. See Devo!!!!!!!!!!

This ad, buried among the mundane Kent State classifieds, is asking anyone who reads it to show up at the Governance Chambers in the Kent State Student Center on Monday, May 17, 1976, to be an extra in what would become DEVO's groundbreaking short film *The Truth about De-Evolution*. (Courtesy of the *Daily Kent Stater*)

for DEVO's manifesto. A manifesto that they would ride for their entire career. This would be a music video (before proper music videos existed) for "Jocko Homo," which introduced the now-infamous call-and-response: "Are we not men?" / "We are DEVO!"

The actual "Jocko Homo" sequence in the film shows Mark Mothersbaugh as a mad professor addressing the mini–United Nations–looking Governance Chamber. His audience (who showed up in part because of this *Daily Kent Stater* ad) is a disturbing group of inept-nerd-pseudosurgeons that look to have just left the asylum.

While the short film is not for everyone, it's incredibly inventive and entirely exceptional. Completely home-produced, it pushed the very edge of music, art, and film.

Gerald Casale spoke at Kent State on Friday, October 1, 2010.

DEVO Co-Founder Stresses the Importance of Keeping Artistic Relevance
By Sarah Lack
Daily Kent Stater
October 4, 2010

Gerald Casale, co-founder of DEVO and a Kent State alumnus, spoke Friday as a part of the Centennial Alumni: Firsts exhibit in the School of Art Gallery.

Casale discussed his time at Kent State, as well as the progression of his creative career from high school to DEVO and his experience directing music videos and television spots.

He shared several examples of his work in the form of video clips, including the music videos for DEVO's "Whip It" and Soundgarden's "Blow Up the Outside World," both of which he directed. He also shared several TV spots, including commercials for Miller Lite and PBS.

Above all, Casale stressed the continued need for artists and creative minds in today's world.

"Art is intended to make people think or make people feel better," Casale said. "Artistic expression is the enemy of mediocrity."

He pointed out that in a corporate-dominated culture that reduces artists to "content providers," it's becoming more difficult for artists to break through and stay relevant.

"I think more than any other craft, being creative is not a choice as much as some kind of destiny," Casale said. "The artist is driven, and you have to be considering the odds of failure."

And although Casale's continued success has taken him away from Ohio and Kent State, he maintains that this is the place where everything began.

"Ivy League schools like Berkeley had nothing on this place," he said. "The artistic and philosophic aesthetics that I used the rest of my life were formed right here."

The Eagles played at Kent State on Saturday, May 3, 1975.

Eagles Concert "Superb" Despite Amplifier Woes

By Alex Hudson

Daily Kent Stater

May 6, 1975

On Saturday, May 3, 1975, the Eagles played in the Kent State University Memorial Gym. (*Daily Kent Stater* photo by Dan Young)

Despite a rowdy and an obnoxious sound system, the Eagles did a superb job Saturday night.

Dan Fogelberg opened the show with some very traditional country material. Fogelberg broke from this tradition, however, with "For What It's Worth."

His solo rendition of this Buffalo Springfield classic was excellent, his coarse voice providing a gruff contrast to the original version.

It was not until after 9 P.M. that the Eagles—Glenn Frey, Don Henley, Bernie Leadon, Randy Meisner and Don Feldman—entered the gym.

Frey and Feldman led off with a blistering guitar duet on "Already Gone." There are few groups that can claim even one accomplished guitarist, and the Eagles have three.

"Outlaw Man" gave Leadon the chance to offer his musical contributions.

The mellower Eagles sound was then given its moment to shine in a set featuring material from the group's soon-to-be-released album.

The set concluded with "Desperado" and Don Henley doing the excellent vocals for this number. This was also the set where the speaker troubles began, however.

The entire stage-left side of the amplification system quit, cutting off Feldman's mandolin solo.

"Lady Luck" and "Midnight Flyer" snapped the mellow, slow tempo, winding up with another impressive solo by Feldman. He is most rapid and could be the next guitarist superstar of the rock domain.

Then came the song the crowd had anticipated. "Ohio" brought back five years of memories in only five minutes of song. It was an emotionally draining performance for everyone in the gym.

When the Eagles finished the Neil Young tune, it felt as if a great weight had been lifted, and a nearly audible sigh of relief came from somewhere in the front bleachers.

"Take It Easy" followed as the planned finish for the show, and the three guitar virtuosos all "got down" (à la WMMS's Murray Saul) and the group left the screams from the crowd and angry hums from the address system.

The Eagles encored with "James Dean" and "Tequila Sunrise" but declined to continue playing, out of respect for the Candlelight Vigil.

Linda Ronstadt played at Kent State on Sunday, May 11, 1975.

Ronstadt Delivers Full Deck

By T. J. Elliot
Daily Kent Stater
May 13, 1975

Linda Ronstadt was refreshing in both voice and appearance Sunday evening in Memorial Gym as she provided the swan song to a beautiful weekend.

Dressed in a sleeveless white summer dress with a purple sash, the 28-year-old queen of hearts turned in a golden-throated effort that alternately rocked and flowed.

Fighting fatigue, flat tires and echoes, the queen enlisted the help of an ace guitarist and a pair of pedal steelists in playing a full hand of old favorites.

"Colorado," "Love Has No Pride," and "Desperado" were early showcases for the power and beauty of Ronstadt's voice, while "Silver Threads and Golden Needles" lived up to Ronstadt's advanced billing, and pedal steel guitarists Eddie Black and Dan Dugmore proved to be "twice as good playing at the same time."

Despite a broken string, guitarist Andrew Gold added some excellent licks, most notably in "When Will I Be Loved?" "You're No Good," and "Heat Wave." In between, Eddie Black pedal steeled a string of love songs, including "Keep Me from Blowing Away," "Tracks of My Tears," "I Can't Help It If I'm Still in Love with You" and "Long Long Time."

Through it all, the lady with the broken heart giggled and smiled warm appreciation of the crowd's enthusiasm. At the end, she thanked the audience for coming, waved goodbye and walked off the stage.

Above: Linda Ronstadt played in the Kent State University Memorial Gym on Sunday, May 11, 1975. (Courtesy of the *Chestnut Burr*)

Left: Ad for Linda Ronstadt's Kent show (Courtesy of the *Daily Kent Stater*)

SPECIAL GUEST: **AL STEWART**
SUN., MAY 11—8 p.m.
KSU MEMORIAL GYM
$5 gen. adm. / $5.50 reserved
ON SALE NOW: Public Hall Box Office, AKRON — Mayflower Ticket, Akron Tux (Summit), Kent Community Store; CANTON — Cleveland Tux.
PRESENTED BY: KSU ALL CAMPUS PLANNING BOARD & WMMS
BELKIN PRODUCTIONS

North Water Street High and Lows: Emmylou Harris and the December 1975 Fire
July 9, 1975, and December 3, 1975

This is one of my very favorite Kent stories. It has every element of a great historical tale: an international icon in her prime, a long-gone local saloon, long-forgotten photographs, a fabled recording, and vivid memories from several folks who participated. On Wednesday, July 9, 1975, rising country music superstar Emmylou Harris and her Hot Band did a short, impromptu performance at the Water Street Saloon, on Kent's vibrant North Water Street strip, where local country rock band-in-residence Good Company was playing to its regular crowd.

When I first heard about this story I had so many questions. Why was Emmylou Harris in town? Why did she play a free show? How did she get here? What and where was the Water Street Saloon, and whatever happened to it? What was the band Good Company? Are there photos? Did anyone record it?

One of the more intriguing elements of this story is that it took place in the summer of 1975, the tail end of the legendary days of the North Water Street bar strip. On December 3, 1975, just six months after Emmylou Harris performed at the Water Street Saloon, a raging fire would destroy half of that strip, including the Water Street Saloon, the Kove, and Pirate's Alley—punching a giant hole into a thriving downtown nightlife.

But on this night, all of the excitement and energy focused on Emmylou Harris. In the mid-1970s, her career was on the rise—in the summer of 1975, she was on tour supporting her fantastic major-label debut album *Pieces of the Sky.*

Also, since Emmylou was at the Water Street Saloon on Wednesday, July 9, 1975, she played and was recorded there just

Emmylou Harris and Rodney Crowell with the Hot Band plus Steve Downey at the Water Street Saloon on North Water Street in Kent on Wednesday, July 9, 1975 (Photo by Richard Underwood)

three weeks before she cut tracks for Bob Dylan's phenomenal album *Desire,* on July 28–30. The reel-to-reel recording made that night, which had been buried in a local archive for decades, clocks in at only eleven minutes and twenty-eight seconds, but its three songs provide a portrait of country rock roots mastery. The performance started with "That's All It Took" from George Jones and Gene Pitney's 1965 album *For the First Time.* Next on the recording is Gram Parsons's "Sin City," from the 1969 Flying Burrito Brothers' *The Gilded Palace of Sin.* The final song of the set is the 1952 Hank Williams classic "Jambalaya (On the Bayou)." The bootleg recording still floats around on the Internet, and if you poke around there you are likely to find it.

That evening, local artist, archivist, and entertainer Richard Underwood slyly, and without authorization, maneuvered himself into the backstage area at Blossom Music Center in Cuyahoga Falls during an Emmylou Harris and James Taylor show. He managed to get Emmylou to stop at the Water Street Saloon in Kent later that night. He recalled:

1975 *Daily Kent Stater* advertisement for Good Company at the Water Street Saloon (Courtesy of the *Daily Kent Stater*)

The way I ended up backstage at so many of those Blossom Music Center shows in the 1970s was I would literally just BS my way back there, and I also knew some of the people at Blossom. A lot of those people who worked there had seen me around numerous times, and I think a lot of [them] just thought I was somebody because I would always be seen with a lot of celebrities—hanging out with them, taking pictures, and stuff like that. I would make it a point to be friendly with the staff and the likes.

On the night of that James Taylor/Emmylou Harris show—I really don't remember exactly how I got back there. I imagine it was because I would park in the VIP section and then somebody would recognize me and I would just get let through.

I remember being backstage and talking to Emmylou's band members. I had heard the name Emmylou Harris, and I knew who she was, and I had heard some of her music, but I wasn't really totally familiar with her.

My biggest reason to be back there was James Taylor, and I was finding him to be kind of an a——hole. We talked a bit, but

Advertisement showing a pair of July 1975 performances of James Taylor and Emmylou Harris at Blossom Music Center (Courtesy of the *Akron Beacon Journal*)

Perry Bocci, Emmylou Harris, Bob Smith, Mary DuShane, R. T. Mansfield, and Steve Downey at the old Water Street Saloon on North Water Street in Kent on Wednesday, July 9, 1975 (Photo by Richard Underwood)

he was kind of standoffish and wasn't real open or friendly. Usually when I am around celebrities like that, I watch how they are around other people before I even approach them, and if I see someone being standoffish with others I am not even going to bother.

But anyway, I was talking to Emmylou's band members, and they were talking about possibly going out some place after the performance, and they were wondering about any clubs around where they could go check out a band or hang out. I told them about the Water Street Saloon in Kent, and I was mentioning that these friends of mine are in a band called Good Company and that the Water Street Saloon is really a cool place. It's one of these bars where the stage kind of looks like a living room and they have these old lamps in there and you'll even see a dog walk through every once in a while. I was basically telling them how laid-back it was and that it wasn't any kind of place you would have to dress up to be in. Plus, the house band played country rock stuff.

Emmylou's band was being real receptive to what I was saying. As it turned out, they were up to it, and they were wondering how to get out there, so I wrote down the directions from Blossom to Kent, though I had no clue they would actually come to Kent and bring Emmylou with them.

At some point after the show, I ended up giving a ride to this guy who had his car at the Holiday Inn on Route 8 [near the Turnpike]. There were actually two major hotels out there, and that was where most of the Blossom acts would stay. I don't remember who he was, but he must have been a friend of somebody's or one of the crew members. So I remember dropping this guy off at the hotel and telling him what was going on in Kent, and he said he was going to come by afterwards—but I have no idea if he ever did. So, after that, I headed to Kent, and that is when Emmylou and the band showed up.

I remember telling Emmylou's people earlier in the evening that there was this girl who would be there, Mary DuShane, who plays fiddle in Good Company, and she's gonna flip 'cause she's a big fan. Later, I found out that all those members of Good Company were so close to that music of Emmylou's and Gram Parsons's.

I remember when I got to the Saloon walking up to those guys in Good Company and mentioning that there were some people in the room from the Emmylou Harris band, and Emmylou

is with them, and then Emmylou comes walking in, and Mary just had this look on her face and she was in shock. She was just amazed that Emmylou was even in the Water Street Saloon. Emmylou was really cool, and the whole thing was really cool.

I also remember taking those photos, and I just knew that this was someone that people were really fond of, though I did not know to what degree. I mean, I was thinking that this person just performed at Blossom and she was famous, and I was trying to capture this moment of her in Kent with the band. I was thinking it would be kind of cool for my friends in Good Company to get all these photos. I'm actually really glad I always carried my camera with me, because a lot of times people would get really pissed off with me and say things like, "You and that damn camera." Well now, all these years later with everyone on Facebook, people are so appreciative that I took all of those photos and I am able to post them. I also had no idea the band had recorded the

Emmylou Harris greets Mary DuShane at the Water Street Saloon on North Water Street on Wednesday, July 9, 1975. Rodney Crowell is at the far right. (Photo by Richard Underwood)

performance that night until much later, and I only heard the recording really recently. It was a great, great night.

Mary DuShane, who played fiddle with the band from 1973 through 1975 and spent just a few years in Kent, can be heard on the recording playing on Hank Williams's "Jambalaya" and in the various photos from the night. She describes the encounter:

Back in July of 1975, Emmylou Harris was not yet a big star. I think most of our audience didn't even know who the heck she was, but all of us musicians, we sure knew who she was because of her work with Gram Parsons. Perry Bocci [Good Company's vocalist and driving force (deceased)] and I used to sing "Grievous Angel," which was a Gram and Emmylou song, so we certainly knew who she was. We liked that particular style of country rock, which was a lot better than what else passed for country rock at the time—these sort of head-bashing southern rock bands that wore cowboy hats. Before we ever even knew Emmylou was going to walk through the front door, we thought she was just a goddess.

When Emmylou showed up that night at the Saloon, she had her steel player Hank DeVito with her, and she also brought Rodney Crowell, and I think he must have been playing bass that evening. I like the photo of her and me next to each other, flanked by members of Good Company—Perry Bocci, Bob Smith, R. T. Mansfield, and Steve Downey. Hippie chicks, we were in those days, with our long dark hair.

At one point we got Emmylou and her band drinks, and they were all really happy. You can tell in that recording, because you can hear her say, "It's good to be in a goddamn bar." So they hung out a little, and then somebody in our band arranged for them to get up and take the stage to play some songs, and they had Steve Downey play guitar. And then Emmylou called me up to play fiddle on "Jambalaya," which was the last song, and I think that was about it. After they played, they hung out, drank a little more, and went away.

Even though it was just for that short time that night, Emmylou and I seemed to make some kind of a connection. And if you look at that photo taken that night you can see that Emmylou is reaching out for my hand. We looked at each other and knew that we were two of a kind. Just like Emmylou, I was the only girl in the band. That's how it always was back then. There weren't very many musicians who were women. There were some great female solo artists, but back then there weren't that many women out traipsing around with an all-male band, so Emmylou and I recognized each other in that sense. She was very friendly and easy to talk to.

Later that night while she was still there and our band got back up, I did sing one of the songs that I'd sort of written for her. I said, "I have this song I can really hear you singing." So I sang this song called "Love's Laughing with Me Now" to her, and she said, "Send it to my agent." I regret that I never did. Who knows if something could have come from that?

We did chat for a while, and there's one thing I clearly remember she said to me. At one point, I asked her, "What's it like doing opening sets for James Taylor? What's it like playing places like Blossom?" And she said, "Thirteen thousand people with perfect hair who wouldn't know a honky-tonk if they were in one!" I've never forgotten that. Those words stuck right in my mind. She'd been playing lots of bars. That's how she started out—playing bluegrass and country music in taverns in the Washington, D.C., area.

In the summer of 1975, Steve Downey, lead guitar player for Good Company, was asked to sit in with Emmylou Harris and her band in absence of her lead guitar player, James Burton, who had stayed at Blossom to play for the James Taylor show. Years later, he remembered that night well:

I had been playing in this garage band in town that never got out of the garage. Dave Robinson [of 15-60-75, the Numbers Band] was our drummer, and Paul Braden of Woodsy's Music was the bass player. In the spring of 1975, Good Company's original guitar player left the band, and they were already doing one of my songs, so they asked me to take his place. Actually, I was in this band for only the last six months they existed. The big North Water Street fire in December 1975 ended everything down there for a while.

Good Company did lots of Grateful Dead–type stuff—that California country-folk-rock sound. We were the house band at the Water Street Saloon and played three, roughly one-hour sets a night, starting at around 10:30. The breaks were somewhere around thirty minutes. 15-60-75, playing downstairs in the Kove, did more or less the same schedule. Summer evenings were hot then as now, so when the bands were on break, the sidewalks outside would fill. Each band had its own fans, but there was also a substantial number of people who liked both.

The Kove was dimly lit, except for the stage. The Water Street Saloon was more lighted, some of that from the double doors open to the street. Kent's current local Mexican food restaurant, Taco Tontos, began here in the rear of the Saloon. There were no laws against smoking in bars, and the clubs were filled with haze.

A huge factor in the bar scene at that time had to be that in the state of Ohio the drinking age was eighteen for 3.2 beer. It's just a guess, but this might have approximately doubled the number of KSU students in the clubs, especially in the summers when the nights were warm, the sidewalks were filled, and the clubs were jammed. On any weekend, you could probably hear seven or eight bands within Kent's city limits. People walked from bar to bar throughout the evening, hearing a little of one band, and then some of another, somewhere else.

The night Emmylou Harris came to the Saloon, none of us knew she was coming. I think we were close to the end of our first set when she and her band walked in. It wasn't hard to recognize her, and we just looked at her walking through the crowd and thought, "Wow—that's Emmylou Harris?!" I think I remember doing two or three more tunes before going on break.

On break, I seem to remember us all hanging around the soundboard and meeting Emmylou and her band and someone in our band, probably Perry, asking her if she and her band would be willing to do a few songs with our instruments. I remember all of us more or less huddled around the soundboard in the rear of the club, and the discussion—Emmylou and her group deciding what songs they could do without their guitar player and bass player, both of whom had stayed behind at Blossom because they were also in the headlining band.

Somehow, it was decided that Mary DuShane, our fiddler, and myself on guitar would be invited to play with them. Of course, this was a big thrill for Mary and me. Emmylou had a rhythm guitarist in her band who would play Bob Smith's bass, and Emmylou would play Perry's beautiful old Gibson electric ES 345. Gerry Simon would remember the name of the pedal steel player [Hank DeVito], who used Gerry's instrument.

Onstage, someone counted it off, and we played the songs. The crowd was on their feet the whole time. Both Mary and I were familiar with the songs and had no difficulties. Emmylou was nice enough to give us both solos. The club was packed, as it was always packed that summer, and everyone was loving Emmylou. I think the crowd was perhaps a little extra pleased with us—seeing Emmylou Harris on our stage probably reinforced our credibility a little. Every little bit helps. And it seemed like she had had a lot of fun. The rest of us did, too.

Steel guitarist and longtime Kent musician Gerry Simon was performing with Good Company when Emmylou Harris and her band walked in. Many years later, Gerry and Bob Smith, Good Company's bassist, remember that night and their times with Good Company:

Gerry: Good Company's very first gigs were at the Deck here in Kent, which was in the basement of the old hotel [now BW3's]. We would play between sets for Ritch Underwood's Monopoly. We chased away his fans. They didn't like us, but eventually we were offered the gig at the Water Street Saloon, although when that happened it was known as Big Daddy's.

Bob: Initially it was just one night, and a couple weeks later we came back for another night and that went okay and it just built on its own success. And then eventually it was four nights a week. On the weekends it was packed, absolutely packed.

Gerry: Before that night Emmylou Harris showed up I was already a huge fan, plus Perry and I loved the album she did with Gram Parsons, and we used to play "Grievous Angel" in the band—we were all in love with her. Perry and I were smitten with her voice, the music, her

look—this beautiful woman. When she walked into the Saloon, Perry had no problem with being friendly towards her but I cowered, and I remember thinking, "That's Emmylou Harris! Oh my god, where can I hide?"—that kind of thing.

She brought her steel player, drummer, and rhythm guitar player. Her steel player, Hank DeVito, used my pedal steel. I had a weird setup, and my steel was weird, too, so he had to quickly relearn his style on it. I was using two amplifiers and the knee levers, and the setup on the steel was not what he was used to. So I just needed to acquaint him with the peculiarities of my particular setup.

Emmylou seemed to have a really good time playing in Kent, although that's not from memory; that's what it seems to me from listening to that recording from the night. She was enjoying herself, because when you play big concerts there is a big distance between the performer and the audience. You totally miss the intimacy.

The Water Street Saloon had a totally different vibe than any other place in Kent. Actually it was pretty different from most other places I've been. We had dogs, kids, just a comfortable place. We had the stage set up with lamps and rugs and tie-dyed stuff. We also had a lot of airbrushed images on our amps and speakers from Dr. Fly. The Water Street Saloon had more of the feel of a living room, which is what we really wanted to have.

Bob: A living room for very strange people.

Gerry: Listening to the recording, you can tell they are using unfamiliar equipment and an unfamiliar sound system, so they sound a little rough compared to how you would usually hear them in a concert situation. Just judging from the steel playing, Hank DeVito is a great steel player, but he was battling it.

Emmylou actually gave us tickets to see her

the following night at Blossom, since she was opening for James Taylor again. So the next day Perry and I saw her play, but we had to miss James Taylor since we had to be back at the Saloon to play our gig.

The first North Water Street fire took place on Wednesday, December 3, 1975. The following day the story about the fire appeared on the front page of the *Daily Kent Stater.* It is my understanding that while the buildings were severely damaged, there was a plan in place to rebuild that strip, until seven months later, on Friday, June 11, 1976, a second fire devoured whatever was left.

Mary DuShane, of the Water Street Saloon's house band Good Company, shared her recollection of that first fire, which marked the end of the ten-year heyday of the North Water Street bar neighborhood. In 1976, that strip was still vibrant, but when a fire took out its entire middle section, an era of downtown Kent nightlife came to an end.

That was an unforgettable afternoon. Good Company had just set up in a whole new configuration. Actually, Perry and I weren't getting along at that point. We used to be set up together in the middle, but we'd had an argument, so we set up with Perry at one side of the stage and me at the other. So, that afternoon we had a rehearsal, and then everybody left the Saloon except for my boyfriend, Bart Johnson, who was the bass player, and myself. Our plan was to go home for dinner and then come back and play that evening with our new stage setup. As we were getting ready to leave, Bart heard a funny noise, like mice in a bag of potato chips. So he ran over and opened the fuse box, which was at the back of the stage on the wall, and he could see flames coming up from downstairs.

Waters Cafe, the Water Street Saloon, and the Kent Kove, March 1974 (Photo by Dennis Rein)

Ubiquitous Kent townie George Condos cleaning in front of the Water Street Saloon, circa November 1975 (Photo by Richard Underwood)

So he and I ran through the connecting door that was the interior door from the Saloon to the stairs that went down to the Kove. We ran down there, and there was an old-fashioned gas space heater about three feet by three feet hanging over the bar down there, and there were all these little orange crinkly flames coming out of it. And the flames had spread across the ceiling. There were these beautifully aged beams down there. Just the kind of wood you'd want for your fireplace. So Bart grabbed the fire extinguisher that was down there and he sprayed it all over place and then he stopped spraying for two seconds and then it went. It started burning again because that space heater down there was gas

The aftermath of the first North Water Street fire, which took place on Wednesday, December 3, 1975 (Courtesy of the *Chestnut Burr*)

and it just kept running. So Bart looked at me and said, "We gotta get out of here."

Well, later we found out the back door of the Kove had been locked, and had we not gotten upstairs when we did, we'd be dead, because we then ran back up the stairs and Bart said, "We gotta get our equipment out of here." I looked at Perry's incredibly beautiful antique Guild arch-top guitar with the F holes, and I said, "Bart, you gotta open the closet so I can get the keys so we can get the guitar"—idiot I am.

R. T. Mansfield [Good Company soundman] asked me later, "Why didn't you grab all the [good] microphones?" I said, "I don't know." I wanted Perry's guitar, and I got it and I put it in the case. Bart ran out on the street and he hollered for Gerry Simon [Good Company pedal steel player], who was by then half a block down the street. Bart yelled for him to get back to the Saloon, and so Gerry came in and he grabbed his pedal steel guitar—he unplugged it and just grabbed it all set up without the case and he rushed out to the sidewalk. Lucky for me, my fiddle was at home.

Bart grabbed his bass and his amp and then maybe one other thing, and then when we went back in for another load it was dark—the fire had eaten through. And then we stood out on the sidewalk. Just moments later the fire trucks came screaming up North Water Street and the guys broke through the front doors with an ax, and the flames shot across the sidewalk from where the wooden steps went down into the Kove. So that's how close that was, and that's how hot that fire was. It makes me shiver just to think about right now.

After the fire, the Numbers Band had a meeting and decided they had to keep going. But Good Company also had a meeting. We looked at each other, and we said, "We're done." Shortly after the fire, we had this big benefit at the KSU Rathskeller to help pay for all the equipment lost in the fire, but after that the band was over, and I was back in Minnesota by Christmas, and I was done. My time in Kent was over, but the friends I made in Kent have become lifelong, and I have visited Kent ever since I left thirty-eight years ago, and I've been visiting every year for the last few years, including this past Labor Day. So even though it's been a very long time since I lived in Kent, the time I spent there was a pretty important time in my life.

The property where the Water Street Saloon once stood on North Water Street, 2013 (Photos by Jason Prufer)

Good Company Gone; Numbers Band at JB's

By Rob Tomsho

Daily Kent Stater

January 7, 1976

Good times for many Kent people were burned out in the blaze that destroyed the Kent Kove and the Water Street Saloon Dec. 3. For the members of Good Company and 15-60-75, however, the loss was greater. Their places of employment and most of their amplification equipment were destroyed.

As a result of an $8,000 bank loan, 15-60-75 has replaced their equipment and are playing JB's Down on Water St.

Robert Kidney, the group's guitarist and lead singer, said he was generally pleased with the sound at JB's, finding it less muffled than the Kove. But he added concern that the layout of the new bar forces the audience to be farther away from the band than he prefers.

"When the Kove got crowded the audience was forced to move closer to the band, here (JB's), the crowding forces the audience farther back and away from the band," said the thin and monastic looking Kidney.

"The band will be moving upstairs to JB's Up as soon as renovations are completed," Kidney said. He described the new floor plan as similar to the Kove, with the stage along one of the side walls.

In addition to the changes in atmosphere and the destruction of equipment, Kidney said the fire has forced the band to postpone work on some original material they had hoped to begin performing soon.

Kidney said the band's first album would, hopefully, be available this month.

The album is a live presentation of mostly original material recorded last year at the Agora in Cleveland.

While 15-60-75 has survived the Water St.

fire, Good Company, their country counterparts from the Water Street Saloon, has disbanded.

The group had been experiencing some internal difficulties, according to bass player Bart Johnson, but the fire that destroyed most of their equipment was the final blow and the members have gone separate ways.

Guitarist Perry Bocci is visiting Mexico, and violinist Mary DuShane has moved to Minneapolis. Steel guitarist Gerry Simon and guitarist Steve Downey are trying to form a new band, while Johnson has joined a jazz band and drummer Rick Shore remains in the area.

Johnson said that the money from the recent benefit concert at the Rathskeller helped ease the losses but the band members had not yet been able to totally replace their equipment.

Roxy Music played at Kent State on Sunday, February 15, 1976.

Roxy Excites Sellout Crowd

By Michael Bloomfield
Daily Kent Stater
February 18, 1976

The Roxy Music concert last Sunday was a perfect display of Roxy's own brand of rock. A late start and the lack of talent on the part of opening act, Angel, marred what could have been a flawless night of music.

Angel led off the show playing music which their lead singer kept insisting was rock 'n' roll. It could have been called very loud noise.

Roxy Music, from the opening strains of "Sentimental Fool" to their energized encore of Dylan's "A Hard Rain's Gonna Fall," put on a highly intense, exciting rock show. The repertoire was taken mostly from their last three albums along with a few of Ferry's solo numbers. Songs included were "Mother of Pearl," "The Thrill of It All," "Love Is the Drug" and "Whirlwind."

Ferry, wearing Mountie pants, boots and a red shirt in lieu of his usual khakis, was always moving, dancing, strutting and marching.

Edwin Jobson's keyboards were the backbone of the group, with Phil Manzanera's guitar and Andy Mackay's wind instruments standing out.

A highlight of the concert was Jobson's violin solo during "Out of the Blue." Roxy peaked on the final number, a long version of "Do the Strand."

Roxy was a joy to watch because they seemed to have as much fun playing their music as the audience had listening to it. Mackay and Manzanera leaning on each other while trading licks and smiles was indicative of the entire mood of the band.

Bryan Ferry of Roxy Music on February 15, 1976, in the Kent State University Memorial Gym (*Daily Kent Stater* photo by Chuck Humel)

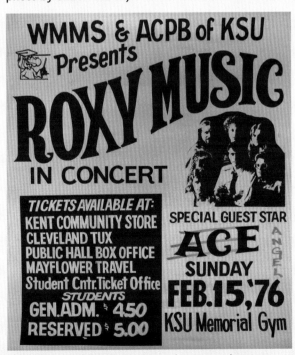

Advertisement for the Roxy Music concert in Kent (From the collection of Mark and Mary Hughes)

It seemed like Roxy Music could have played all night. By the reception they received, it was obvious the sellout crowd wished they had.

J. Geils Band headlined the largest concert ever put on in the city of Kent on the Kent State Commons on Saturday, May 15, 1976.

Play "Punch-and-Kick Style"
By Rob Tomsho
Daily Kent Stater
May 18, 1976

They started setting up tents in a steady drizzle Friday night. By Saturday afternoon there were more than 10,000 people spread out over the Commons waiting for a free day of music.

While rumors in town the day before suggested crowds of up to 30,000 and the possibility of another Altamont (a 1969 rock festival marred by violence) occurring in the Tree City, the crowd of cowboys, bikers, straights, crazies and even some dogs got along well.

Under a friendly barrage of Frisbees, the crowd drank gallons of beer and wine and set up a conglomeration of tents, tarps, banners and blankets that made the Commons look like a refugee camp after a laughing gas attack.

Livingston Taylor opened the show with a fine set of acoustic music. Unfortunately, some of the folks in front expected J. Geils to play first, but Taylor, undaunted, played on.

More than one person in the crowd said, "He sure sounds like James," but there is room in the world for two people who play as well as the Taylors.

Earl Slick followed with a competent, if lack-

J. Geils Band headlined a free outdoor concert on the Kent State Commons on May 15, 1976. (Photos by Richard Underwood)

luster set. The band was tight enough but lacked anything outstanding.

The crowd was ready for some familiar material when the Michael Stanley Band from Cleveland came on. The band is quite popular in this area, and I fear I border on sacrilege in criticizing but I must.

The band has been playing together for quite a while now and while they show great enthusiasm on stage, it doesn't make up for the lack of tightness in many of their vocal harmonies and even an occasional wrong chord in some material from their newest album.

Whatever the opening bands lacked, The Outlaws made up for. Playing material from their first two albums, they brought much of the crowd, even some who were previously unconscious, to their feet and rushing toward the stage, Confederate flags and beer bottles raised.

The raw energy of the Outlaws' performance was not totally unlike an Allman Brothers concert one might have seen five years ago. While their performance was not without its flaws (some of the guitar leads got scrambled when played together), it was, on the whole, excellent.

The Outlaws are a young band and on the way up. They manage to be exciting and energetic without letting overambition rule their performance. Their vocal harmonies were especially bright as was most of their playing, making for an excellent but brief performance.

J. Geils came on with the raw punch-and-kick style that everyone expected. They manage to play funky and wild but remain tight musically. Their energy on stage spreads into the audience like a massive adrenaline injection.

Vocalist Peter Wolf has flash, style and a unique gravel-bottomed voice that flows like butter. J. Geils on guitar and Magic Dick on harp work especially well together, throwing their riffs back and forth and intertwining them like true rock and roll veterans.

Ronnie Van Zandt, lead singer for Lynyrd Skynyrd, belts out a song during the group's set in the Memorial Gym on November 10, 1976. (*Daily Kent Stater* photo by Doug Mead)

Lynyrd Skynyrd and Manfred Mann's Earth Band played in Memorial Gym on Saturday, November 6, 1976.

Skynyrd, Mann Concert Is Brilliantly Boring
By Tony Seel
Daily Kent Stater
November 10, 1976

KSU was given a taste of two rock genres when Lynyrd Skynyrd and Manfred Mann's Earth Band played to a sold-out house in Memorial Gym on Saturday night.

Skynyrd's hard rock was in certain contrast to Manfred Mann's jazz-influenced rock.

The opening act, Manfred Mann, presented a set that was marked with inconsistencies. The English band's show was filled with boring, unimaginative and trivial solos. Their generally listless and lifeless performance was marred, however, with brief flashes of brilliance.

The flashes of brilliance that climaxed Manfred Mann's performance were not music but lighting. During "Blinded by the Light," there was a superb strobe effect with the lights blinking in unison with a drum solo. The song ended

Patti Smith played at Filthy McNasty's in downtown Kent on Thursday, June 15, 1978. (Photos by Frank LaPinta)

with two flashes of bright light that temporarily blinded the audience.

Lynyrd Skynyrd started with "Workin' for MCA," "Gimme Three Steps," "Saturday Night Special" and "Cry for the Bad Man." They also played "Smell of Death," a new song which they added to their repertoire last week.

The band continued the show with "Tuesday's Gone" "One Step Over the Line," "Call Me the Breeze," "T for Texas" and ended the set with "Sweet Home Alabama."

They returned for an encore and gave the sellout crowd their rendition of Robert Johnson's "Crossroads" and their own "Freebird." After a slow start, "Freebird" turned full circle into a bombastic rocker.

The volume of the applause was excluded only by the group's own thundering loudness.

Although the Skynyrd sound is powerful, their stage show is not. Bare-footed Ronnie Van Zandt, when not singing, elects to bandy about the stage, lending nothing to the visual presentation. Fortunately, their playing almost overshadowed this.

Patti Smith played at Filthy McNasty's in downtown Kent on Thursday, June 15, 1978.

Patti Smith Enraptures Fans
By Joe Cali
Daily Kent Stater
June 1978

"I can't believe she's here in Kent!" That phrase was repeated over . . . and over . . . and over . . . in a manner resembling the intense repetition of the star's lyrics " . . . horses . . . horses . . . horses . . . horses."

And like horses they came, packing Filthy McNasty's Thursday evening and filling it with an atmosphere of energy and rowdiness as they awaited the arrival of their goddess, Patti Smith.

Yet "goddess" cannot be used as a description for Smith. Mythology has given us the names of many goddesses, but Smith's name has not been among them. Recordings have brought us the fine vocal qualities of superior songstresses, but Smith's voice has not been grouped with these either.

A better description for Smith would be "sultry." Smith is a goddess and a songstress in her own domain, proven this night by her abilities to enrapture the audience with the mysterious power her material possesses.

Her chanting, singing and stage performance completely locked the audience into the frame of mind Smith was obviously experiencing herself. Her delivery was inflamed with the bitterness of her messages, no matter how puzzling they were.

Smith performed an 80-minute set consisting of material from her *Horses, Radio Ethiopia,* and *Easter* albums to a standing-room-only crowd. Filthy's was as wild as ever. Smith and her group escalated the audience with performances of "Easter," "You've Really Got Me," "Be My Baby" and "Gloria."

The peak of the evening arrived when Smith performed her top-ten number, "Because the Night." Smith knows and loves the fact that she has a hit and she sparkled in the glory of the audience's enthusiasm for the song as she performed it.

Smith's group was also in good shape, providing tight backgrounds, vocals and instrumentals. Unfortunately, the sound system was not in good shape, and the entire performance had an overall muffled sound to it.

The Smith concert is the first in a series of top rock names being brought to Kent by Filthy McNasty's throughout the summer. Other acts scheduled to play the club include Head East and the Climax Blues Band. Also tentatively scheduled to appear are Brand X, Robert Palmer, Rick Derringer and the Sanford-Townsend Band.

Peter Gabriel played at Kent State on Saturday, October 21, 1978.

Peter Gabriel, Jules and The Polar Bears KSU Gym October 21
By Bill Camarata
Scene Magazine
October 26–November 1, 1978

How would you expect any other concert to start? Lights down, applause, a shuffling of lights on the stage, an announcement and music. No way for Peter Gabriel. While the lights were still up, he walked out from the audience onto the stage, sat down at the piano and started to talk. A few people applauded at first; nobody knew what was really going on. Here he was, the star of the show being as casual as can be. He said that there was a very important person to be introduced; it was his "personal psychiatrist." He walked off stage and brought on a large inflated Teddy Bear. He set it on the piano and sang "Me and Teddy Bear Ain't Got No Hair" while accompanying himself on piano.

After this, he put on a day-glo vest and gloves, donned a back-pack flashlight beam and as the black-light stage went up and the house lights went down, he played a game called "Find the Musicians": he flashed his light out into the audience and the band showed up out

Peter Gabriel played at Kent State on Saturday, October 21, 1978. (Courtesy of the *Chestnut Burr*)

KENT STATE UNIVERSITY

·ACPB·

in cooperation with WMMS presents

peter gabriel

opening act to be announced

Sat. Oct. 21
8:00 p.m.

Kent State Memorial Gym

Tickets Available Now at the
Student Center Box Office and all Ticketron Locations

	Reserved Seats	General Admission
K.S.U. Student	5.50	5.00
Non-Student	6.50	6.00

50c more day of show — *No bottles or cans*

Advertisement for Peter Gabriel in Kent (Courtesy of the *Daily Kent Stater*)

of nowhere, all dressed in the same day-glo garb with lights. They set themselves and opened with "On the Air." From then on, it was major musical bliss as a collage of tunes from his two albums were performed, including "D.I.Y." and "Perspective," which had a really long end section, with Timmy Capello's sax and Peter's voice playing on each other.

"Waiting for the Big One" was a highlight, with Peter singing from the balcony using his wireless mic and, upon making it to the stage, jumping on drums for the ending of the song. For an encore, "The Lamb Lies Down on Broadway" from the Genesis album of the same name was done.

The house lights went up, but the crowd would not stop going. Clapping, chanting, stomping, shouting, nothing would stop them—except another encore—"Here Comes the Flood."

It was a great show for Peter and the members of his band, including Larry Fast on synthesizers, Tony Levin on bass (with his clean-shaven head) and Sid McGinnis on guitar.

The opening band, Jules and The Polar Bears, left something to be desired. Jules, the lead singer, seemed overly pretentious and out of tune. He tried to play guitar by only using his thumb to play the neck. Jules's backup band was good, but the overall act requires much polishing.

Stephen Stills headlined at Kent State on March 10, 1979.

Bluesy Bramlett Brightens Show
Stills "Disappointing" in Memorial Gym concert
By Joe Cali
Daily Kent Stater
March 30, 1979

Stephen Stills performed on March 10, 1979, in the Memorial Gym. (*Daily Kent Stater* photo by Gus Chan)

Stephen Stills, renowned member of Buffalo Springfield and Crosby, Stills, Nash & Young, as well as solo performer and song-writer.

Such a name would be thought incapable of giving a bad performance. Unfortunately, Stills' struggle to bring his career to the heights of its past has produced no visible sign of that return. And the performer's Memorial Gym concert three weeks ago was a rather poor display of the virtuoso's talents—and a sadly disappointing show.

Stills has been seeking the key to success since embarking on a solo career. Once a prince of acoustic wizardry, Stills left that musical style for a more rhythmic rock—à la "Love The One You're With" and "Sit Yourself Down."

However, his albums since then have emphasized his growing use of electric guitar. Early in the show, Stills mumbled some inaudible gibberish about an electric guitar being a suitable substitute for an acoustic one. Perhaps he thinks so—many of his fans obviously did not.

Not that Stills can't play the electric guitar. Rather, his use of powerful runs through the performance displayed a rapport he shares with his instrument. During renditions of "Precious Love" and "For What It's Worth," Stills seemed to be conversing with his guitar, much as B. B. King does with his instrument, Lucille.

In fact, the majority of material Stills performed was done well. His vocals were exhilarating—initially. Yet, as the evening wore on, they grew a little bit hoarser, a little bit flatter and a lot less enjoyable. His attempts to cover his quickly fading voice with a capella ballads and softer pieces were not successful.

Members of Stills' touring group apparently recognized their leader's faltering, and, cut by cut, began playing longer solos, extending spotlight vocals and harmonizing to a fuller and greater degree.

Yes, Stills disappointed, If not for the surprisingly powerful vocals of keyboardist Michael Finnegan and fine flute and drum solos of Joe Vitale, the show might have been a disaster.

One of the brighter spots of the evening was the vocals of blues belter Bonnie Bramlett. A lack of recognition by audience members may have left them wondering who this fine female was and where she came from. But Bramlett has been on the scene for quite some time, emitting thunder-like sounds from her voice and taking the throne as the blue-eyed blues queen of the 1970s.

Bramlett provided lead harmonies for Stills during much of the performance, and their blended, blues-oriented duets produced sounds often superior to some performed solely by Stills. Bramlett's lead vocals added the only ray of sunshine to an otherwise gloomy, reggae-tinged arrangement of "Love the One You're With."

▶ 121

Opening for Stills was Irakere, an 11-piece outfit from Cuba. The group performed a number of cuts from its debut Columbia album of the same name. Their excellent up-tempo brass and percussion arrangements displayed a massive amount of versatility, and gave the audience an unusually good opening performance.

Stills, who discovered the band on his recent tour to the Communist country, said (of Irakere) he stole that nation's "finest latin-afro-cuban-rock band." Judging from the group's showmanship that night, he is correct.

Bo Diddley Backed by the Numbers Band (15-60-75)

September 12, 1980

Recently I was leafing through an old *Chestnut Burr* yearbook from the early 1980s when I found this incredible photograph of legendary rock-and-roll architect Bo Diddley jamming with another guitar player somewhere in downtown Kent. The photograph had so many mysteries to it. What is Bo Diddley doing playing in Kent? Who is this other guitar player next to Bo? What is the date of this photo? Where specifically are they playing in town?

So, I scanned the image and threw it up on my Facebook wall: "Bo Diddley and unknown guitar player in Kent."

After only a few responses, someone chimed in: "Guy on the right used to play with the Numbers Band. Ask Terry Hynde [about him]!"

Soon, someone added: "Side guitarist may be Michael Stacey of the Numbers Band."

This photo was a catalyst that lead me to discover the Numbers Band's music. The more I learned about this extraordinary Kent band, the more I learned about how much Bo Diddley meant to these musicians.

The earliest incarnations of the Numbers Band were drenched in the influence of Bo Diddley and those awesome boogie blues. By 1980, the band's sound had completely changed from Bo Diddley–esque blues to a high-intensity level of multilayered jazz fusion, but its members still had his hits committed to memory.

As to be expected, the *Daily Kent Stater* was all over this show. Several preview ads and a small article appeared in those issues leading up to the show, and a full review with photos appeared in the issue immediately following the performance.

Bo Diddley and Michael Stacey (of the Numbers Band) performing at JB's Down on Friday, September 12, 1980 (*Chestnut Burr* photo by John Neitzel)

I spoke with most of the band's prominent members who played with Bo on North Water Street on that September night, and all of them still glowed when recounting the experience.

Vocalist and multi-instrumentalist Jack Kidney recalls the experience:

I must have been six years old when I saw my first Bo Diddley album cover. It belonged to my sixteen-year-old cousin. The red plaid jacket and the rectangular box guitar left an indelible mark on my consciousness. By the time I hit my twenties, I was copying harp parts off the same recording and had listened to just about

everything he'd recorded for the Chess Brothers in Chicago. I thought I knew Diddley.

Here's the scoop. In the early 1980s for $2,000, a round-trip ticket from somewhere in Florida and one night in a hotel, you, too, could have Bo for the night. We were the house band at JB's [bar], and JB's had acquiesced to fork over the cash. The Numbers Band would open, then back up Mr. Diddley. Unbeknownst to Bo, we were ready to kick ass behind him. We'd been covering him for years. "Can't Judge a Book," "Who Do You Love," "Mona," and "You Don't Love Me" were some of our most requested songs. We had singlehandedly kept his name alive in our neck of the woods. Our drummer, David, could have written a doctoral thesis on how to employ the nuance and give life to the world-famous "Bo Diddley Beat."

David and I went down to pick up Bo at the airport.

We're standing there watching these people walk up the stairs after de-boarding when I asked, "How will we recognize him?" David laughed. "He'll be the one that's Bo Diddley." About a

Bo Diddley before his second performance at JB's Down with the Numbers Band on Saturday, May 9, 1981. *Left to right:* Roy King, Michael Stacey, Bo Diddley, Jack Kidney, Robert Kidney, and an unidentified man. (Photo by Richard Underwood)

minute later, there he was. No doubt, David was right. The black fedora was a dead giveaway, not to mention the huge guitar case he was hauling. We drove him back to Kent. We went directly to the club for a rehearsal—after all, he was slated for a two-hour show. That's a lot of songs.

Bo was all business. He'd been through this routine at least a thousand times with every little Podunk band across the country who had singlehandedly kept his name alive in their neck of the woods. He plugged in, tuned up, and started playing the rhythm that had put him on the map more than thirty years ago. It oozed out of the amp. I was captivated. It was the essence of rock and roll. It stood on its own, no accompaniment needed.

He told me exactly what he wanted from my harmonica: "Just the beat, man." I could have played it in my sleep. David started playing the drum part he'd been playing since late adolescence. Bo came to an abrupt stop, turned to David, and said, "I don't play that old s—— no more." That comment hung in the air for an amount of time that's immeasurable. What he wanted out of the drums was Rock Drum Beat 101. Kind of a *boomp, bop, boomp, bop* thing. I was disappointed. David was, well, I don't know what David was, but it wasn't good. Then Bo played a little three-note figure and told us, "When you hear this one, two, three, the song ends." He meant *every* song. Rehearsal was over. It had taken about fifteen minutes. I drove Bo to his hotel.

JB's was packed that night, wall to wall, a fire marshal's nightmare. All the boys and girls had come to see us kids make good while backing up the legend. Included in our opening set was a tip of the hat to Bo, yet another version of "You Don't Love Me." He stood and watched us from behind the bar, with a slight hint of appreciation in his eye. The crowd was beside itself.

My brother Bob got down off the stage, [and] Bo took his spot. It was time. "If that diamond ring don't shine, Bo Diddley take it to a private eye." It was heaven. I was playing music next to a guy who'd been staring at me from album covers since I was six. I lunged into the harp and played exactly what he'd told me, that's all. Beautiful. I was there to soak it in, just like everybody else. We were cranking out his hits, one after the other, one, two, three, same beat, new song.

About three tunes in, Bo caught my eye. He looked at me and rolled his index finger. He was throwing me a solo. I couldn't believe it. I took the verse. The crowd went nuts. Crowds are apt to do that when one of the locals gets called off the bench. He rolled his finger at the end of the verse, so I took another and another. He was having me solo on every song. The crowd was loving it, and I was out there, in that land somewhere, never wanting to return. David, on the other hand, was not having a good time. When he would try to demonstrate that he could play the drums or make a contribution to the proceedings, Bo would turn around and snarl at him and toss off some discouraging words. The show eventually came to an end. I was exhausted and perplexed.

The next day, I took him back to the airport for his flight home. We were alone in the car. We made small talk, and then I said, "So, you heard the band. What advice would you give us?" He said, "Well, if I was you boys I'd learn some country music; it's coming back, and it's gonna be big." I asked for it, couldn't believe it, and if we had taken it, y'all could be line dancing in front of us.

I did have a realization on the way home. While I was playing my ass off the night before, Bo was just killing time. One more thing. He flew up from Florida about a year later. David managed to be out of town. I hope he had a good time.

The Numbers Band saxophonist Terry Hynde recalled the night:

It seemed awfully bright in there. I don't know if they were taping or what, but I could see everybody's faces. Everything was really well lit, and I just remember everybody all packed in together, not really moving around or anything, just sort of stuck solid because it was so packed.

There was an incident with Bo Diddley that I can remember. The first time we played down there, the whole band set up before I came in, and neither Bo nor the band knew what exactly to expect out of each other, so before the performance I went up to Bo and said, "Is it okay if I sit in?" And he said, "Sure."

It was pretty exciting, and when it came time for the actual show, everything was just fantastic! I played the whole night. I took all kinds of solos here and solos there. He was cueing me for solos. It was really fun. The whole night was just so fun.

So then eight months later, which would have been that following spring, we had Bo back again at JB's. So I set up like last time and as the show begins I jump up onstage with my sax and start playing and Bo looks at me and says, "Get the f—— out of here. I don't want any of that s—— up here!" He threw me offstage! He didn't know who this guy was with a saxophone coming up! He wasn't going to play with me! Yet I was the same guy who played with him all night eight months before.

Michael Stacey, the rhythm guitarist in the Numbers Band from 1974 to 1989 and the sole member photographed with Bo on this night, described his experience:

I don't remember how this show came to be, actually, but I do remember that we were always interested in getting blues acts into town. I can't remember if we were directly involved in getting him booked or not, but I do remember being aware that if he was in fact booked into JB's that he would need a backup band.

Bo Diddley and Chuck Berry both used to travel with just a guitar. If you booked them to play your club, you had to supply them with an amp and a backup band. I remember the first time seeing him in the basement at JB's Down, he had this cowboy hat and was wearing this red polyester jumpsuit. We were all excited to play with him, and once we all met up down there he said, "Well come onstage; we're gonna have a rehearsal." So we all get up there, and he just really quickly starts running us through some different beats, and before we could even get a feel for how to play with him, he says, "Okay, sounds good. We'll be fine." So we didn't actually rehearse anything!

We already had a couple of Bo Diddley tunes in our repertoire anyway, so we were familiar with his signature beat. Plus, we also did lots of blues, so if he wanted to play straight blues we could do that, too. The band was pretty well versed in those rhythms and stuff, so it wasn't like we had to have special rehearsals for this show because we were already doing it.

I thought he was a genuinely nice guy, and he was talking about living in Florida. He made lamps. I remember him saying, "Yeah, I make lamps and mosaics and stuff." He really liked one of the guitars that I had, and I almost talked him into trading me one of his square ones, but in the end he said he just couldn't do it, since he was the only one in the world who plays those things, and he just couldn't let one go.

But he was a real nice guy. The thing that struck me is that I've also met Chuck Berry, and Chuck was like the opposite side of the coin. Chuck was very bitter, and both Chuck Berry and Bo Diddley were sort of screwed over by the business. Both of them had their signature rhythms stolen out from under them, and other artists made millions of dollars off of their signature sounds. Bo Diddley, though, just shrugged his shoulders at this and said, "That's the way it goes, you know?" He was still playing as much as he wanted to, and by then he was getting recognized a lot more.

I remember JB's was packed. It was like shoulder to shoulder, and people were really looking forward to him. Plus, it was sort of the height of our popularity, too. So we opened for him and played a set of our stuff, and people were really into it, and then when he came on everything went up a level. It was really high energy in the room, and playing with him was great. I was always more of a basher rhythm player than a soloist. I can play solos, but I was a good rhythm player, and I sort of had the feeling he wasn't used to that—being onstage with someone who could play rhythm strong. I think he was having a good time, too. It was really a nice night. I remember it fondly.

I have that photograph hanging up in my cube at work. It sort of reminds me that I wasn't always a cube geek, you know? Sometimes people look at that picture, and they say, "Who is that?" And I say, "Well, that's Bo Diddley." And they say, "No, the other guy," and I say, "That's me thirty years ago!" [laughs] It was a great, great night.

The Numbers Band front man and leader Bob Kidney recalled that evening:

I think the manager of JB's set up the show. In that period they were trying to bring in some out-of-town people based on the history of the Kove, which had burned down by then.

We do "Mona," which is a Bo Diddley song, and we do "Not Fade Away," which is a song that has that Bo Diddley Beat. We also used to do "Who Do You Love," and [the Numbers Band drummer] David loved that beat, and he studied that beat, and he had that beat down, and he was all excited about Bo Diddley.

A distinct memory I have from that night is being in the back room with him and he was getting his guitar out and stuff, and I just talked to him for a little bit. [Mostly,] I wasn't talking to Bo Diddley, though; I was talking to Ellas McDaniel [the man behind the stage persona]. I said, "Yeah, I do one of your songs. It's one of my favorite songs," and he said, "Oh yeah, which one is that?" I told him, "You Don't Love Me (You Don't Care)," and he looked at me weird, and he didn't even remember that song. And then I reminded him that Little Walter played on it, and he said, "Oh yeah, yeah, yeah. Really, you like that song?" [laughs] That was his reaction and I went, "Yeah, I like it. It's a f—— killer song." I still play that song; it's a great song! And the original version is incredible."

It also must be noted that playing with Bo Diddley wasn't the first flirtation the Numbers Band had with great musical artists and icons— not even close. In their very earliest days, they were the band to play with when you rolled through Kent. For instance, they shared bills with Bruce Springsteen and Tom Waits.

In the early 1970s, when some of the great forgotten old blues artists became notable again, it was the Numbers Band who embraced those guys and presented them on North Water Street, down at the Kent Kove. Bob Kidney hosted Mississippi Fred McDowell and played with him as a duo at the Kent Kove in the band's earliest days, around 1971. In this same period the Numbers Band also served as blues legend Johnny Shines's backup band at the Kove. Some legendary nights with a Numbers Band–Hound Dog Taylor double bill at the Kent Kove still live in musical memory.

The Numbers Band itself had some quite notable musicians. In the early 1970s, Gerald Casale, who would later cofound DEVO, played drums and then moved to bass guitar. Casale actually replaced a guy named Rod Reisman, who would later become DEVO's first drummer. I don't even need to mention Terry Hynde's sister Chrissie, whose band the Pretenders later covered the Numbers Band song "Rosalee."

In the mid-1980s, Sex Pistols' front man Johnny Rotten and Cream vocalist-bassist Jack Bruce both covered "The Animal Speaks," which Bob Kidney wrote and performed with the Numbers Band for years. The tune also appears on the Numbers Band's most notable album, *Jimmie Bell's Still in Town.*

And—just as cool—in 2006 Jack Kidney got to be a session musician for alt-rock pioneer and Pixies front man–founder Frank Black for his roots album *Fast Man Raider Man!*

But really, these are just footnotes (albeit incredible footnotes) to the almost fifty-year legacy of the Numbers Band.

Diddley Thrills JB's Crowd

By M. Daniel Jacoubovitch
Daily Kent Stater
September 16, 1980

Rock 'n' roll patriarch Bo Diddley's heavenly voice, outer-space guitar playing and earthly presence held sway over his frenzied minions at JB's Friday night.

Supported by Kent's Numbers Band, 51-year old Mississippi born rock 'n' roll originator delivered two sets of 50s hits and some new songs to a wildly appreciative standing-room-only crowd.

Dressed in a gold-trimmed, wide-collar shirt, red pants, a black hat adorned with a silver-mounted turquoise triangle, and sporting two diamond-studded gold rings on his right hand, the stocky musician cut an imposing figure as his big, smooth voice sailed over the powerful, infectious chords he drew from his rectangular electric guitar.

The Numbers Band was in especially fine form for their opening set of original songs and stylized, staccato, horn-embellished reworkings of R&B standards. The audience crowding the steamy, low-ceilinged basement was primed for the star's appearance by the time the band closed its set with "You Don't Love Me," a song Bo recorded in 1955.

Diddley accepted as his rightful due the enthusiastic reception he was given by his audience as he came onstage. After exhorting the crowd to say "yeah" several times, he broke into his 1955 hit, "Bo Diddley." People sitting on the dance floor soon had to move to make way for those who wanted to dance. The Numbers Band, minus bandleader Bob Kidney and one of its three horn players, was right behind him; the rhythm section pounding and pushing as the horns squealed fills and responses in and around the hypnotic beat.

Looking out at the audience through heavy-framed tinted glasses, mugging and moving gracefully as he played, Bo had the crowd firmly in hand. The beat that has become his trademark (commonly described as "shave-and-a-haircut, two bits") had the audience swaying under the spell of some tribal incantation.

"You are in my classroom now," he said. "You're gonna clap your hands, stamp your feet, jump up and down and have a good time." The audience followed his orders.

His second song, a show ballad, had couples on the dance floor rubbing together lasciviously. Bo's sweet, soulful singing and haunting, echoey guitar prompted public displays of affection in greater number (and of greater intensity) than common in Kent Taverns.

Four of the seven remaining songs in his nonstop first set were hits he recorded in the 50s: "Hey, Bo Diddley" (1957), "I'm a Man" (1955), "Diddley Daddy" (1955), and "Who Do You Love" (1956).

"I'm a Man" was particularly powerful for its extended introduction, during which Diddley drew purring, grunting sounds, wolf whistles and space noises from his guitar.

Other highlights of the first set included Bo's drumming during part of one song, and a solo during which his voice and guitar worked together to produce otherworldly sounds transcending their individual sources.

Bo opened his second set with a reprise of "Bo Diddley" eliciting thunderous shouts of "Hey, Bo Diddley" from the audience at appropriate points in the song.

High points of the enthusiastically received second set included a rendition of "Mona" (originally recorded in 1957) and a slow ballad during which he sang first the low, then the high part of a 50s doo-wop vocal back-up. The voice-and-guitar solo on that song was played to a young blonde on stage who blushed crimson as Bo's guitar produced sounds that could only be interpreted as indecent proposals.

The evening closed with Bo playing one last trademark-beat song as two women danced wildly on stage.

Bo Diddley returned to JB's on Friday, May 8, 1981.

Bo Diddley Raises Roof
By Vicky Fresh
Daily Kent Stater
May 12, 1981

Alan Freed once introduced Bo Diddley as an "act that's gonna rock and roll you out of your seats." He didn't know how right he was.

Bo Diddley, the first rock performer in history, and still one of the best, played two hot shows with the Numbers Band Friday night at JB's and the only thing not moving was the tables.

Diddley has been in the rock and roll business for 27 years. He celebrated his anniversary May 5, and is proof that age will never be a factor in delivering marvelous music.

Before the show, Diddley said that tonight "we're gonna raise the joyful noise of rock and roll," and with that statement, he hit the true mark of the music—rock and roll at its best is a prayer and a celebration, and nobody, but nobody celebrates it like Diddley does.

He joined the Numbers Band on stage after a tremendous set by the band, and proceeded to raise not only a joyful noise, but the damn roof as well. Diddley and guitarist Mike Stacey fairly exploded from the intensity of the evening. These two men played with each other, off each other, in spite of each other. One would start a line and the other would finish it. All night, these two guitarists teased, coaxed and ripped searing music out of their instruments and their hearts.

Both men were in top form all evening. Terry Hynde's sax playing was everywhere and perfect. Jack Kidney, Bart Johnson, and guest drummer Roy King all performed with inspiring precision and passion, putting things exactly where they needed to be throughout a set characterized by the word "masterful."

It is shows like these that make the job worthwhile.

Diddley, 52 years old with no end in sight, said that he has no intention of quitting. "I have years to go. Quitting would be depriving the world."

The world has not always treated Diddley with the respect he deserves. Back in the fifties, before Freed labelled what was going on "rock and roll," the sound was called "race music," and no white radio stations would touch the stuff.

While innovators like Diddley and Chuck Berry were going unplayed, people like Elvis Presley, who took his style from those performers, garnered all the fame.

Diddley is not bitter, though. "That's the way it was. It didn't have to be that way, but it was. I was a victim but at the same time I helped open the door for other black performers."

In 27 years, thousands of people have run through those doors, each one either surviving or more commonly self-destructing. Diddley has managed to stay around longer than anybody else, and as he approached the audience to say, "I'd like to thank each and every one of you for my survival in the rock and roll crisis. 27 years I've been in rock and roll for you."

I heard various audience members thank *him*, and well they should.

In all these years, we've heard good rock and great rock, but Bo Diddley, by virtue of his simplicity and rhythmic grace, leaps beyond the greatest.

The Waitresses, with opening band Unit 5, played at JB's on Wednesday, May 13, 1981. (*Daily Kent Stater* photo by Dean Nettles)

GUEST CHECK

TABLE NO.	NO. PERSONS	CHECK NO. 89932	SERVER NO.

JB's

244 N. Water Street, Kent, OH 44240

Wednesday May 13

The Waitresses and Unit 5

$4.00

TAX

Advertisement for the Waitresses and Unit 5 playing at JB's (Author's collection)

The Waitresses, with opening band Unit 5, played on Wednesday, May 13, 1981.

Waitresses, Unit 5 Entertain at JB's

By Vicky Fresh

Daily Kent Stater

May 15, 1981

Old friends, big crowds and new sounds can make JB's the best place in town, and thanks to Wednesdays night's performances by the Waitresses and Unit 5, that's exactly what happened.

The Waitresses, comprised of KSU graduate Patty Donahue on lead vocals, ex–Tin Huey man Chris Butler on guitar and vocals, Tracy Wormsworth on bass, Dan Klayman on keyboards, Ex-Television drummer Billy Ficca on— you guessed it—drums, and Mars Williams on horns, including a Tibetan Monk horn, are one of those groups, that for a variety of reasons, are a pleasure to welcome to town.

For Donahue and Butler, it's more of a welcome back. Tin Huey was one of those bands that sparked the whole whoopla over Akron being the "Liverpool of the Seventies/Eighties," Donahue is a graduate not only of KSU, but of the scene as well, so having the both of them back in town, and on the same stage, sparks excitement that can barely be contained.

Such was the atmosphere Wednesday. JB's, which usually doesn't start to fill up until very late in the evening, was quite crowded by nine. People were milling about, saying hello to friends they hadn't seen in years, and the excitement and anticipation kept building until finally, the music started.

Unit 5 hit the stage first, and rocked and rolled their hearts out through a set that showcased their talents in a way that they haven't been for some time. Apparently even JB's sound system was willing to cooperate for the evening.

The audience, which had been singing along to the PA for some time hit the dance floor with the very first note, and they stayed on the floor the whole night. Unit 5 came back for a splendid encore, "Panic in Detroit," and left, leaving behind a heated-up crowd for the Waitresses to further excite.

And so they did, opening with "Quit," and going straight through a set that featured songs off their forthcoming record on Stiff. One reason the Waitresses' set was so good was that it started good and got better. The segue between "No Guilt" and "Wise Up," the second and third song they did, was perfectly executed, as the shift in beats was accomplished without a miss.

From there, the band launched into their single "I Know What Boys Like," which, Donahue said, is currently in the Los Angeles top ten.

The band itself sounds like a combination of styles that managed to avoid any one stylistic pitfall while actually coming up with something original.

The rhythmic interplay between Wormsworth's bass and Ficca's drumming, which set the tone for some heavy dancing, also set the pace for a band that knows exactly what it's doing. Williams' assorted horns, and Klayman's keyboards, fill in the sound, giving it a fatter and welcome edge.

Add to this Butler's guitar and Donahue's happy, crystal clear voice and anybody with half a brain can easily figure out why, as Donahue said before the show, they've been getting bonuses from bars they've played.

"Everywhere we go, we've been breaking crowds. I don't know why, but there've been record-breaking crowds."

Wednesday night finished the Waitresses' tour of All Night Diners, which has lasted five months.

For a band that's been on the road that long, they sure looked to be having a lot of fun. Donahue mentioned earlier that they all got along pretty well, but nowhere was that more apparent than on stage.

The band was enjoying itself, trading grins and comments, and in general having a great time. The crowd brought them back for a delicious second set, and the fun and the dancing just kept on happening.

Finally, though, the Waitresses left the stage, and were quickly surrounded by a massive crowd of congratulations and well-wishers.

Some nights just should not be missed, and I'm ecstatic that I didn't miss this one.

Hall and Oates played at Kent State on Sunday, November 8, 1981.

Hall and Oates
Dramatic Show by Singers Excites Enthusiastic Crowd
By Anne-Marie Stoj
Daily Kent Stater
November 10, 1981

The stage in the Memorial Gym went dark. Two men came out and lit cigarettes. The audience went crazy. It knew who was taking the stage: Daryl Hall and John Oates.

Hall and Oates took the stage Sunday night and started the concert with a single from the *Voices* album, "How Does It Feel to Be Back." This is one of the few songs that features Oates on vocals.

Hall and Oates played at Kent State on Sunday, November 8, 1981. (*Daily Kent Stater* photos by Gary Harwood)

Hall was dressed in a baggy green suit, black T-shirt and white tennis shoes. Oates wore purple pants, and a white athletic T-shirt, with a blue bandana around the neck.

The duo did another cut from the *Voices* album, "Diddy Doo Wop (I Hear the Voices)" and again the audience screamed and clapped. "Mano a Mano (Hand to Hand)," a new single from the *Private Eyes* album followed.

The band played "Rich Girl," an older hit which prompted the evening's first standing ovation. The next song, "She's Gone," was, at times, too loud and overbearing. The approach was too dynamic. The song was not all bad—the saxophone solo was performed exceptionally well.

"Kiss on My List," the number one song from the *Voices* album was next, and the members of the audience swayed back and forth in their seats. The song, however, was not nearly as polished as the recorded version.

Hall and Oates introduced the band members next. On lead guitar was G. E. Smith (married to former *Saturday Night Live* member Gilda Radner). On Bass was Tom Wolk, who played his bass guitar from behind his neck and sang, "I'm So Glad I'm Living in the USA."

Drummer Mickey Curry displayed his talents by playing "Wipeout," and on keyboards and saxophone was Charlie DeChant, who had already won the audience over from his previous solo.

Hall himself was featured in the next song, the duo's first big hit "Sara Smile." Hall gave a nice performance, but he seemed to want to overdo the song. Hall came to the front of the stage and sang and screamed the end of the song a cappella. An enthusiastic fan came up to the stage and gave Hall a carnation which he tossed aside.

It was a dramatic performance, but perhaps too dramatic.

As "Sara Smile" ended, the band started

"Wait for Me." This was one of the best performances of the evening. The vocals blended well together with the instruments.

At last, the duo performed "Private Eyes," its number one song. The tune lacked the quality of the recorded version, but was generally well done, and the audience gave the duo another standing ovation.

"You've Lost That Lovin' Feeling," was next, and the audience finally got up on its chairs in response to the music. After another ovation, Hall announced the end of the concert. Fans threw roses as the band left the stage.

Bics flickered in the gym, as the audience cheered Hall and Oates back. The encore song, "You Make My Dreams Come True," was met with thunderous applause.

"Thank you, Kent, we'll see you next time," Hall said, and again the band left the stage.

Once more, the audience screamed for them, and the group came back on stage. This time, the duo did two selections from the *Voices* album, "Gotta Lotta Nerve" and "United State." Hall and Oates left the stage and the concert was over.

The duo's performance, in general, was good, with a nice variation of songs. The lighting was exceptionally well done.

After the concert, the fans interviewed thought the show was great but it should have lasted longer.

"It was the best thing I have seen on campus," said Linda Spichty.

Another student, Ann Carney, thought the show was excellent. "I would have liked a private interview with Daryl Hall," she said.

Finally, student Tony Dascenzo summed up the performance "That concert was excellent, the light show was beautiful and the music wasn't too loud."

Opening for Hall and Oates was Karla De-

Ad for Hall and Oates (Courtesy of the *Daily Kent Stater*)

Vito, one-time backup singer for Meatloaf, who also sang back up with Linda Ronstadt in the Broadway musical *Pirates of Penzance.*

DeVito gave a very impressive performance. She and her five-man band opened with the title song from her new album, *Is This a Cool World or What?* DeVito, dressed in white shorts and top, carrying a parasol, won the audience over.

DeVito had a stage presence that was overwhelming, as she danced and paraded across the stage. Her voice was strong and dynamic, with a thin and vibrant quality.

DeVito's music selections included "Big Idea" and "Heaven Can Wait," a song with a religious motif. She followed with a remake of "Midnight Confession." DeVito sat on the front of the stage and sang "Just Like You," a song she wrote.

DeVito and her vivacious personality were warmly welcomed by the crowd.

"This is only our third gig," she said, and added that it wasn't easy.

For only the third performance, DeVito is on her way to becoming a polished, professional act.

Koko Taylor brought the blues to JB's on Saturday, April 17, 1982.

Can Having the Blues Be Fun?
Koko Taylor Makes It Seem So
By Joanne Draus
Daily Kent Stater
April 20, 1982

From the moment she belted out the first notes of "Let the Good Times Roll," one could sense that Chicago blues artist Koko Taylor was about to deliver a fun-packed performance at JB's Saturday night. Ironically, Taylor proved that having the blues, or at least expressing the feeling, can be fun.

"If you came here to hear anything other than the blues, you're not gonna hear it," announced rhythm guitarist Carlos Johnson, a member of Taylor's band, the Blues Machine, just before the group performed two eye-opening songs without Taylor. But, when she finally took the stage in her white evening gown, Taylor did provide the audience with something other than the blues—a good time.

Taylor and the Blues Machine, which consisted of Johnson, lead guitarist Johnny B. Moore, bass player Bay Williams, and drummer "Youngblood," performed two sets of energetic blues standards like "Sweet Home Chicago" and "Hoochie Coochie Man," new numbers like "You Can Have My Husband (But Don't Mess with My Man)," and several songs from Taylor's recent Alligator Records release, *From the Heart of a Woman*.

While the musicians performing with Taylor did not appear on the album, the sounds produced were incredibly similar. Johnson's churning rhythms on "Keep Your Hands off Him" and Moore's twanging leads on "Blowtop

Koko Taylor brought the blues to JB's on Saturday, April 17, 1982. (*Daily Kent Stater* photo by Henri Adiodha)

Blues" were particularly reminiscent of the album's sound.

Taylor's gutsy, throaty voice did not seem to correspond with her pleasant, mother-like stage presence. She constantly smiled and talked to the audience between songs, and it seemed as though she was performing strictly for the fun of it. Taylor was a success in that the feeling of fun was transmitted to the people—and it affected them.

Even though JB's was packed to full capacity, fans managed to find enough room to dance to slow numbers like "I'd Rather Go Blind" and to fast songs like "Tryin' to Make a Living." After Taylor ended the performance with her million selling 1965 single "Wang Dang Doodle," the boisterous audience called her back for an encore, and Taylor returned to perform one last song.

The Numbers Band performed one set of the most exciting music heard in the area— whether it be called blues, jazz, rock or fusion.

Songwriter, guitarist and vocalist Bob Kidney drilled sound out of his guitar while piercingly singing the mesmerizing words and melodies that he has written, from the sultry "Summer Fever" to the sizzling "Here in the Life,"

Guitarist Michael Stacey added a touch of raw rock 'n' roll to each song with his searing solos and dramatic stage presence, especially on his own composition, "Telephone Girl," on which Stacey sang lead vocals.

The jazz element of the band's sound was produced by the always energetic saxophone and flute player, Terry Hynde. Harmonica player, keyboardist, saxophone player and percussionist Jack Kidney displayed diverse talents in both blues and jazz performance styles. Bass player Bart Johnson maintained a driving beat on his custom made fretless bass, and drummer Dave Robinson's intense concentration was apparent throughout his impressive performance.

Blues duo Daniel Jacoubovitch and Anderson Hawes began the evening with acoustic traditional songs by blues greats like [Big] Bill Br[oonzy], Willie Dixon, Eddie Taylor and Bo Diddley.

Jacoubovitch's deep, round voice and Hawes' high-pitched, often humorous vocalizations accompanied Jacoubovitch's basic blues guitar riffs and Hawes' early departure left Jacoubovitch to perform alone for most of the duo's set. Jacoubovitch then played both guitar and harmonica.

Sonny Rollins and Pat Metheny played at the University Auditorium on Monday, April 19, 1982.

Jazz Masters Certainly Provide Fine Show
By Mark Morilak
Daily Kent Stater
April 20, 1982

When two music masters get together on the same stage, one thing is always certain—that nothing is certain.

Sonny Rollins alone would undoubtedly have been enough for the crowd of about 150 last night at the University Auditorium. But when the tenor saxophonist was joined by contemporary guitar master Pat Metheny, the end product was enhanced beyond what anyone might have expected.

Rollins, who came up with the likes of Miles Davis and Clifford Brown during the height of the be-bop era, departed from what many might have expected. In his 75-minute set, he presented a repertoire that he was able to retain full control of while continuously varying styles.

When Rollins wanted to play swing, he swung. When he wanted to play bebop, he did that, using the techniques which brought him the status of genius during the 1950s.

But in the end, it was Rollins' mastery of improvisation and his composing talents that brought him his greatest success. Rollins managed to manipulate phrases effortlessly, almost playfully, often taking a particular phrase and repeating it several times using the same notes while varying the rhythm.

Metheny, considered one of the foremost guitar players in modern music, joined Rollins to

Sonny Rollins played at the University Auditorium on Monday, April 19, 1982. (Courtesy of the *Daily Kent Stater*)

show his own improvisational talents as the two held a good-natured trade-off of solos.

"Coconut Bread," one of Rollins' calypso-oriented pieces, featured a variety of short solo passages by all four members of the group (including Bob Cranshaw on electric bass and Ron Barage on drums). "Here You Come Again," the Dolly Parton-popularized song, was performed in classic bebop style, as Rollins built from the basic melody and chord progression of the tune, adding his own embellishments while moving in a swing tempo.

"Penny Saved," a medium-swing tempo piece, provided Metheny with his first opportunity at an extended solo for the evening, and he responded by toying with his instrument in the higher registers, darting in and out of lower registers on occasion and, in general, holding the audience spellbound with his mastery. Rollins responded with an equally ebullient effort, although the electric pick-up on his instrument occasionally muffled the sound, losing some clarity on the lower notes.

For the remainder of the set, Rollins weaved his way in and out of various styles, opening various opportunities for Cranshaw and Barage, the lesser-knowns, to demonstrate their capabilities. But there was always the continuous interplay between the masters.

Concluding the set with another of his Latin-flavored pieces, Rollins left the stage, declining to return for an encore, but leaving having made his point. He may not have been the old Rollins, the bebop master of the 1950s who later emerged as a legend for having practiced at nights on a bridge over New York's East River.

But he certainly hasn't lost anything.

Son Seals played in Kent on Saturday, September 4, 1982.

R & B Swooning by Seals Packs JB's
By Paul Pinkham
Daily Kent Stater
September 10, 1982

If B. B. King is the king of rhythm and blues, then Son Seals must be the prince.

Seals brought his Chicago-based blues band to a packed JB's (upstairs) Saturday night. The number of local blues artists who were in the audience serves as a testimony to Seals' greatness.

The band's two sets consisted of blues standards which they played flawlessly. Much of the crowd spent a good portion of the night on the dance floor.

Bassist Strapper Mitchell brought the band to the stage after a warm-up set by Kent's 15-60-75 (The Numbers Band). The band played several tunes, featuring Mitchell's crisp, clean bass and guitarist Mike Gibb's vocals, before Seals took the stage.

Seals then took complete control, taking the band through several blues standards as well as tunes from the band's new album. He possessed a strong, gutsy singing voice and his constant exhortations to dance and party worked the dancing crowd into a frenzy.

CHICAGO BLUES

JB'S
PRESENTS
THE
BOSS
OF THE
BLUES
SON SEALS
WITH O.T. AND THE SMOKERS

Son Seals played in Kent on September 4, 1982.
(Courtesy of Michael Staufenger)

The main attraction, though, was Seals' guitar. His leads were simple but scintillating, adding to the band's high-energy sound.

Seals spent much of the evening trading leads with fellow guitarist Gibb. Seals' influence on the younger guitarist could be plainly heard, both in Gibb's guitar playing and his singing. At times, Gibb sounded almost like a Seals clone.

Terry Hynde and Jack Kidney, 15-60-75's two saxophone players, sat in for several tunes with the Seals band. Hynde in particular blended well during his solos.

The Seals band was rounded out by keyboardist Pat Hall and drummer David Anderson, Hall played unpretentiously, taking an occasional solo to let listeners know he was still there, while Anderson kept a steady beat, contributing to the band's tight sound.

The Numbers Band performed its warm-up

function well. The band has a very tight sound. Hynde said the band will be releasing an album "probably in a couple of weeks."

On Sunday, October 17, 1982, the Clash played at Kent State.

Casbah Club Comes to Kent
Intense Clash Show Overwhelms Audience
By Cathi Ciha
Daily Kent Stater
October 19, 1982

"Everybody hold on tight!"

Joe Strummer's advice in The Clash's signature song "This Is Radio Clash," was to be heeded Sunday evening when the group plunged into its intense, hour and 40 minute set.

The Cleveland reggae band, Spirit I, opened the show. The group's low-key, 45-minute set included covers of Bob Marley's classic "Jammin'" and 10cc's "Dreadlock Holiday." But it wasn't much preparation for what was to come.

When The Clash manned the "battle stations," it became clear why "Combat Rock" is such a fitting title for this tour. The area on the floor intended for dancing became a battle zone for those in the near-capacity audience who wished to get closer to their heroes. And what was happening onstage was as overwhelming as a blitzkrieg.

Lead singer/guitarist Strummer paused to welcome everyone to the Casbah Club, a nickname for his tour's gigs, before launching into the title cut from *London Calling*. Going at a breakneck pace, the band avoided the more commercially successful songs until the middle of the set. One got the feeling that the group was testing the audience to separate the longtime

Advertisement for the Clash in Kent (Courtesy of the *Daily Kent Stater*)

On Sunday, October 17, 1982, the Clash played at Kent State. (Photos by Earl K. Miller)

fans from the ones newly acquired since its music has finally been accepted by commercial and album-oriented radio stations.

Early in the set, The Clash gave the audience a taste of its own jazzed-up reggae, playing "One More Time," a more obscure cut from *Sandinista!* the group's triple-release from last year.

Then Strummer stepped out of the limelight for a while, playing bass while Paul Simonon sang "Guns of Brixton."

Simonon, who fluidly danced nonstop during the show, thrived on the attention from fans flattened against the stage. With an occasional wink, nod or grin, he acknowledged an outstretched hand or the call of his name. Standing right at stage's edge, he didn't flinch as those close enough reached out to touch his pant leg or boot.

Strummer propped himself in the corner of the stage during "Brixton," making faces at the audience, but remaining very low-key. Getting his guitar back and shedding the black sunglasses he had been wearing, he livened up again for "Somebody Got Murdered," on which lead guitarist Mick Jones did vocals. Although Jones lacks the flash and aggression of many lead guitarists, his earnest expression and high spirited dancing made him even more interesting than the usual heavy metal "slasher" style.

Jones was back at the microphone later in the 24-song set to sing "Train in Vain," and in the encore for "Should I Stay or Should I Go?"

Despite the two very able musician/entertainers on either side of him, Strummer still was the focal point. Emotion enhanced his entire performance, as he worked himself into a screaming frenzy from the beginning. When not singing, he jumped on the platform with drummer Terry Chimes, or hunched over his guitar, his Mohawk shaking furiously as he played.

He was so involved in "Junco Partner," his guitar often hung idle as he gestured emphatically. And he successfully ignored the crudity of people in the audience ignorant enough to spit at the stage.

"Rock the Casbah," The Clash's latest single, still sounded fresh with Simonon's variating the original bass riff. The audience didn't need Strummer's encouragement to sing along.

The only time things slowed down was during "Straight to Hell," the mournful Viet Nam commentary. Even the audience quieted a bit. Maybe the piercing eyes of the Amerasian child in combat clothes depicted in the slide-show backdrop touched a few people as much as Strummer's haunting vocals.

"English Civil War," an updated version of "When Johnny Comes Marching Home," from the second album, *Give 'Em Enough Rope*, caught some of those less familiar with early material by surprise, but was still eagerly received. "Tommy Guns," also from the second album, ended the set, punctuated by Chimes' energetic, precise drumming which appropriately sounded like pistol fire.

But the audience would not let The Clash leave so easily. After a wait which wasn't nearly as long as it felt, the stage lights came up again, The Clash came back, beginning the first encore with "Charlie Don't Surf," which is based on a scene from the movie *Apocalypse Now*. The group also played "I Fought the Law," one of the rousing anthems from the early days of punk in England.

Still unsatisfied, the audience called the four back for more, and they complied by grinding their way through the reggae cover "Police and Thieves," following it up with "London's Burning," both from the first album. Following an enthusiastic rendition of "Clampdown," the band

The Clash in Kent (Photo by Earl K. Miller)

The Clash in Kent (*Daily Kent Stater* photos by Hoda Bakhshandagi)

The Clash in Kent (*Daily Kent Stater* photo by Hoda Bakhshandagi)

finally delivered the song many in the audience had been clamoring for all evening—"White Riot." This time, when the Clash was through, there was no arguing.

Todd Rundgren played at the University Auditorium on Saturday, April 24, 1983.

Rundgren Doesn't Let Down Expectant, Enthusiastic Fans

By Thomas Wills
Daily Kent Stater
April 26, 1983

A large banner proclaimed "Todd Rundgren for President" to the sold-out University Auditorium Sunday night, and the response of 977 fans was enthusiastic.

They knew it would be a good show, and Todd Rundgren did not let them down. Rundgren, dressed in black, displayed his solo talents on guitar and piano and unveiled his "home movies"—experimental videos—to a mellow audience.

Rundgren opened with "Love of the Common Man" and "Cliché," two selections from his 1976 *Faithful* album, which highlighted his versatile vocal range. Moving from 12-string acoustic guitar to acoustic piano, Rundgren then played "It Wouldn't Have Made Any Difference" to the ecstatic crowd.

"Well, 1983 had been a year of change already," he said. "Some people just can't deal with change." An artist who strives to avoid commerciality, Rundgren said his constantly changing musical direction confuses people.

"They said, 'This album sucks—it's nowhere as good as the last one," he said. "Well, I have a song to go with that rap." On piano, long hair over his eyes, Rundgren performed "Too Far Gone," with the message, "It's better to keep moving on."

The artist then roused the audience with his 1978 single, "Can We Still Be Friends."

Rundgren then brought out his toys. "This guy is really into the video game," he said. "Of course, this is not a new thing with me—I've been into it for six or seven years. I brought some home movies with me."

Colorful experimental films, set to oriental keyboardist Tomita's interpretation of two Claude Debussy compositions, were generally well received by the audience. "As you can see, this would be an *excellent* time to take your drugs!" Rundgren joked.

Rundgren then performed "The Viking

Song," from 1972's *Something/Anything* and "Compassion," from 1978's *Healing*, to a somber audience. "Lysistrata" followed, from 1982's *Swing to The Right*.

Lysistrata was married to an Athenian army general in ancient Greece, Rundgren explained. She refused to have sex with her husband until he stopped pillaging Sparta.

Rundgren said that tactic would not work today. "Today's new army got sucked in by a new, contemporary rock 'n' roll type ad campaign," he said, crooning "Be All You Can Be." "You can be a doorstop in Nicaragua," he said.

Switching to electric guitar, Rundgren performed "Tiny Demons," from *Healing.* After joking through a technical difficulty that darkened the auditorium, Rundgren then performed a wild, theatrical version of "Lord Chancellor's Nightmare song," from *Todd* (1974).

The video screens came to life again as Rundgren performed "Bag Lady." The film showed disturbing scenes of New York City street people.

Next was a piano instrumental, "Drunken Blue Rooster." "This highlights my peculiar piano-playing style, to which I use every finger except *this one!*" He held up the middle finger and asked, "Can everybody see that?" This piece featured a prerecorded piano arpeggio, because Rundgren said he cannot play one. "Saves me endless hours of practicing!" he said.

The audience was invited to participate in "Bang the Drum All Day," from his latest, *The Ever Popular Tortured Artist Effect.* Rundgren played tom-tom and cymbal as five audience members assisted on percussion.

"Hello It's Me," Rundgren's most successful single, was notably absent from the roster. "Having a hit does have its disadvantages," Rundgren said. "People are always saying, 'Hey Runt—Hello It's Me, Hello It's Me.'"

Todd Rundgren began his show in the University Auditorium with two numbers on a 12-string acoustic guitar, "Love of the Common Man" and "Cliché." Rundgren's solo performance showcased both old and new material. (*Daily Kent Stater* photo by Mickey Jones)

Musician and video artist Todd Rundgren sings and plays percussion to a backing tape of "Bang the Drum All Day," from his album *The Ever Popular Tortured Artist Effect*, in the University Auditorium. (*Daily Kent Stater* photo by Mickey Jones)

Obviously having a good time, Rundgren asked the crowd, "How many people here have MTV?" Several hands raised. "Then you all know how truly exciting the new music and video experience can be—Zzzzzz!

"However, I've got to live up to my responsibilities," he said, showing a new video of "Hideaway" from *Tortured Artist.*

Rundgren then removed his jacket and performed a medley from his 1973 *A Wizard, A True Star* album, backed with taped music and vocals. "I Saw the Light," his second 1972 single, followed, also augmented by tape.

The 90-minute set closed with "One World" on acoustic guitar as the audience clapped along. The sound in the auditorium grew deafening as the crowd screamed for an encore. Perhaps fearing the ceiling would collapse, Rundgren returned twice and performed "The Wheel" from *Another Live,* and "The Dream Goes on Forever," from *Todd.*

The Stray Cats played a Halloween show on Sunday, October 30, 1983.

Stray Cats Full of Treats, but not Tricks at Ball

By Lorraine Welsch
Daily Kent Stater
November 1, 1983

The only things missing were the crepe paper streamers and the spiked punch.

At their concert Sunday night, the Stray Cats turned Memorial Gym into a séance filled with all the fun and frenzy of a '50s prom. Indeed, their show was as slick as their pompadour hairdos.

Perhaps the show was a little too slick. The Cats played a quality set that lasted about an hour, but one got the feeling the band had been down this road many nights before coming to KSU.

The New York trio opened the show with "Baby Blue Eyes," from their first American LP, *Built for Speed.* The crowd of about 3,300 responded enthusiastically; however, the Cats

seemed determined to control the show's pace to suit their own liking.

The band kept the energy level high, but never lost command of the show. Lead singer Brian Setzer was the focal point, strumming and crooning in a tiger-striped blazer, black pegged pants and bolo tie.

Bassist Lee Rocker and drummer Slim Jim Phantom had a ball in the background. Rocker slapped his bass and road it like a horse, while Phantom stood to play his minimal drum set. Both came on stage puffing cigarettes.

The Cats continued with two songs from *Built for Speed*, "Double Talkin' Baby" and "Rumble in Brighton." Setzer changed the line from " . . . there's a rumble in Brighton tonight" to " . . . there's a rumble in Kent State tonight." The crowd loved it, even though Setzer had a hard time getting the words "Kent State" to fit in properly with the rest of the chorus.

The Cats' first two selections from their new LP, *Rant n' Rave with the Stray Cats,* were met with a lukewarm reception. "Something's Wrong with My Radio" and "Look at That Cadillac" were well done, but many simply did not recognize the new material. *Rant n' Rave* is number 20 on the Rolling Stone album chart.

There seemed to be only a small number of hardcore Stray Cats fans in the audience. The majority was composed of people familiar with *Built for Speed* and those just out to have fun.

One thing was certain, however. The crowd was determined to have a good time. Most were in costume: Space monsters, cigarette packages and numerous Boy Georges danced and swayed throughout the show.

The Cats had no elaborate stage or light show, save a mirrored star ball that twirled from the ceiling during the schmaltzy "Lonely Summer Nights." Drummer Phantom, in a black cowboy suit with white stitching and red gloves, almost resembled John Travolta in *Grease*.

After winding the crowd down, the Cats cranked the key once again and launched into "Stray Cat Strut." "You cats ready to do a little strut?" Setzer asked as the band began to hum the melody. Setzer grabbed a bottle of beer, toasted KSU, and the crowd was on its feet singing.

The band's final number of the set was their new single, "(She's) Sexy and 17." Setzer wailed. The zoot-suit Rocker spun his bass. Phantom threw his drumstick to the crowd. The band left the stage with the crowd screaming for more. Considering that most had paid $9 or $10 admission, it seemed almost proper to scream for more than the 10 songs the Cats had performed at this point.

The Cats returned for two encores of three songs each. Opening act 14 Karat Soul, a five-man a cappella group who did backing vocals on the Stray Cats' new album, joined the band on stage for "I Won't Stand in Your Way."

The first encore also included a cover of the Buddy Holly classic "Oh, Boy," and "Rock This Town." "Rock This Town" seemed to be the band's favorite song to perform, with Setzer hunkering over his guitar and Phantom atop his drum stand.

The Cats' second encore included "Rebels Rule" from *Rant n' Rave*, and "Jeanie, Jeanie, Jeanie" from *Built for Speed*.

The band closed with a cover of Elvis Presley's "Jailhouse Rock." It seemed fitting that the Cats should close with a song from the man who helped invent the music that has vaulted them to fame.

Opening for the Stray Cats was the Times, a Cleveland-based trio. The band played an energetic half-hour of techno-pop with a nice human touch.

The Stray Cats played a Halloween show on Sunday, October 30, 1983. (Photos courtesy of the *Chestnut Burr*)

Lead singer Dennis Richie did a fine job reaching the crowd, especially during "Vikings" and "Dance Music."

The members of this band played off each other well and seemed to know what each was doing during their time onstage.

Richie seemed as if he couldn't decide whether he wanted to be Simon LeBon or David Bowie on this particular night. Perhaps he should try being himself, especially since he has a rather arresting stage presence and is backed competently by drummer Randy Blaire and keyboardist Scott Thomas.

Following the Times' performance, 14 Karat Soul sang a short set. Their a capella numbers included "Boogie Woogie Bugle Boy" and "Why Do Fools Fall in Love." The crowd loved this brief but stellar performance.

The Stray Cats helped turn Halloween into a rowdy, sing-a-long good time for their audience. Those who didn't attend the show could have gotten the same effect from a Halloween night at home with some albums, a few friends and (no pun intended) a few choice spirits. One cannot help wondering, however, if the rockabilly wave the Stray Cats are riding this Halloween will ebb by next October.

Waiting Is Thing to Do after a Show
By Brian Mooar
Daily Kent Stater
November 1, 1983

It seemed silly. And in retrospect, it seems sillier.

"Gate-crashing" at concerts would seem to be an activity limited to high-schoolers and teeny-boppers, but after the Stray Cats concert Sunday evening, it seemed to be the thing to do. About 100 die-hard fans waited outside the se-curity barricades, hoping to get a glimpse of the members of the three-man band.

After a while, I decided it was time to leave, even though my curiosity had not yet been satisfied. While walking out the door, a row of cars parked against the building caught my eye. A few people followed me until we came to a window which had been covered by a large black canvas. It had obviously been placed there to stifle the progress of wandering eyes.

Undaunted by the obstruction, Craig, a KSU sophomore, climbed on the back of a nearby automobile and made his way onto the window ledge.

"Oh my God!" Craig announced, "They're in there."

As a small crowd began to gather, I made my way onto the ledge and confirmed Craig's findings.

About that time, Beth, a friend from high school, happened to be walking with a few friends, assuring each other that the Stray Cats had left long ago. As I clutched onto the ledge, I motioned Beth over to the window.

"They're in there," U said, totally caught up in the moment.

"THE STRAY CATS ARE IN THERE!" she screamed frantically, drawing a crowd of about 25 people, who immediately began to scale the walls in hope of getting even the smallest glimpse of their idols.

Suddenly, the members of the band became aware of our presence. At first, they seemed faintly amused and crawled up on tables and chairs to tease us.

Beth, who by this time was on my shoulders, began to beg them to let us in as she pounded on the window. Apparently Slim, the band's drummer, pulled the canvas away from the door momentarily.

Slim smiled and waved cordially as he pointed and exposed his posterior to the screaming crowd. We had been mooned.

Seconds later the police and concert security chased the bulk of the crowd away. About five people, including myself, remained.

About 35 minutes later, eight shivering people remained when the security people told us that we were going to have to go home.

But Beth, Karen and Mary had other ideas. They refused to leave the cement walkway they knew the Stray Cats would pass on the way to their van. When they were politely threatened with prosecution, they decided not to press the issue.

As we were walking away, I asked Beth, "Are you going to give up that easily?"

Before she could answer, someone spotted the Stray Cats walking toward the van. "Oh my God," one of the girls shrieked as she ran into the waiting arms of the security man.

But while he was occupied with the shrieking girl, three more slipped past him. He allowed the rest of us to pass through unmolested. "You're all crazy, do you know that?" he cried out at us.

Setzer was the only one who had not yet reached the van and was immediately mobbed by the girls who began kissing him. He seemed to be enjoying himself. They paused for a few minutes and then tried to drive on with eight excited women clinging to the van, begging for one last kiss. The vehicle stopped, and Setzer popped out to kiss a few of the girls, one of which happened to be wearing a sweatshirt with "I Love You Brian" painted on it.

Once again, the van started away. The girls chased it for about 150 yards, then gave up and walked back, comparing which member of the band they had touched, kissed or managed to

The Stray Cats in Kent (Courtesy of the *Chestnut Burr*)

get an autograph from. All of them agreed that the long, cold wait was worth it.

Black Flag played in Kent on Saturday, October 13, 1984.

Black Flag Raids JB's with Its Music

By Lorraine Welsch
Daily Kent Stater
October 16, 1984

I just knew my date with veteran hardcore band Black Flag Saturday at JB's Down was bound to be some enchanted evening when singer Henry Rollins made a special stop to show me his incredible collection of tattoos.

"They move, too," he said, pinching his flesh to animate the tarantula emblazoned on his shoulder between the words "Creepy Crawl."

"Here's a scary one," he continued, buckling his forearm to make a skeleton wiggle.

"And how about this?" he cried, lifting his mop of curly black hair to reveal the words "Search & Destroy" stenciled in inch-high letters from shoulder blade to shoulder blade.

Rollins has tattoos in other places, too—plenty of other places. But the artwork was second to the music as Black Flag pounded its way through a fast 90-minute set of "classic" and new material.

From the openers "Obliteration" and "Re-venge" to the title cut from the band's new LP, "Slip It In," Black Flag provided plenty of mood music for the stage-diving, slam-dancing faithful.

You couldn't have shoehorned another person in the place. Bodies flew in the air. Ceiling panels came crashing down. Benches were ripped from their moorings. And the music was good, too.

"Can't Decide" and "Keep Me Alive" kept the frivolity at a height, Rollins leading the screaming while the rest of the three-man, one-woman outfit kept pace.

Black Flag, from Los Angeles, has been around since the late 1970's—a long time considering the life span of many hardcore bands. They've gone through some staff changes over that time, but always seem to mount a relentless attack.

While Black Flag omitted older songs like "White Minority" and "No Values" from its set, the band's new material is consistently fresh and strong, qualities hard to maintain in the high-level burnout hardcore arena.

Indeed, Black Flag's staying power is admirable. The band was a contemporary of early hardcore outfits like The Avengers, The Germs and other bands long since dissolved by disillusionment or death.

As its performance Saturday showed, Black Flag has the ability to continue in a forward direction, leaving musical, physical and social debris in its wake.

The Red Hot Chili Peppers' 1984 Punk Funk Explosion at JB's Down in Kent

November 17, 1984

As a teenager in the early 1990s, when the Red Hot Chili Peppers were making their world domination known with albums like *Mother's Milk* and *Blood Sugar Sex Magik,* I had begun to hear whispers that these guys had made an appearance at Kent's JB's Down very early in their careers.

What especially hits me about this story is that something like this could be happening on any night in Kent, even today. On any given night you can see live music in more than ten different venues, and you never know what the future holds for some of this talent—a college town can be a breeding ground for great art and music.

And that takes us to this late-autumn night in 1984 down on North Water Street. November 17, 1984, was only three months after the release of the Red Hot Chili Peppers' self-titled first album, and the lineup that came to JB's featured Anthony Kiedis, Flea, Jack Sherman, and Cliff Martinez—the same as on that first album. Legendary Red Hot Chili Peppers guitarist Hillel Slovak had quit the band before the recording of its first album and wouldn't rejoin as a full-time member until the following year.

More than twenty-five years later, John Teagle, the show's promoter, recalled the night the Red Hot Chili Peppers came to Kent:

I got involved with promoting at JB's in the early/mid-1980s [by] being involved in the whole late 1970s Akron scene.

So then when I started actually playing in bands, we were playing these same places. At the end of 1983, I was asked to manage the bar at JB's Down, and I thought that it might be an interesting thing to do. So my fiancée at the time, Becky Armstrong, and I ran the place, and the two of us lived across the street for a while.

Basically, I was the one who funded bringing the bigger bands to JB's by selling off my old guitars one at a time to kind of keep some money coming in. We didn't manage it real efficiently. We gave away way too much as a kind of communal hangout, but I would guarantee the bands coming in from out of town $300 to play for us. That was my standard top guarantee. By being willing to put up $300 out of my pocket I got some great national touring acts into Kent. And this was always against the door. I always gave the traveling bands 100 percent of anything after their guarantee, the opener, and PA outlay were recouped. And for that same guarantee, I got the Red Hot Chili Peppers.

Back then, there were a whole bunch of bands touring, living out of vans. If you put them up, they didn't have big contracts or riders or anything like that; it was more of a communal thing. A lot of these guys were just happy they had a place to play when they came through. A lot of times, the people that came to JB's Down to see all that punk music didn't even know who most of the touring bands were.

Somewhere around the time that I booked the Chili Peppers I got this other band called What Is This, which was the other half of the original Chili Peppers. What Is This had Hillel Slovak and Flea from the Red Hot Chili Peppers, and Jack Irons played drums (he later played in Pearl Jam).

I can't remember quite how it worked out, but I either got What Is This through the Red Hot Chili Peppers or I got the Chili Peppers through What Is This. I knew the Chili Peppers

soundman through a band out of Cincinnati, called the Erector Set, that I used to book. And I think he called me, or I may have gone through booking agent Frank Riley.

At the time, the Chili Peppers were just breaking, and they had one album out. There certainly wasn't any kind of fanfare, like, "OH MY GOD THE RED HOT CHILI PEPPERS ARE COMING TO KENT! WE GOTTA GET READY!" Nothing like that at all. They were just another band coming through. I don't think the crowd knew who they were. I think they just trusted it as something like, "Okay, it's JB's Down on a Saturday night; we'll see 'em 'cause there's nothing else going on."

When they showed up they were very pleasant. I mean they were California guys and we had a good working relationship with them at least for that one night. I remember talking to Anthony Kiedis, and I wouldn't say we had a conversation, but we certainly chatted a bit and had a beer together, nothing intellectual or anything like that. We probably talked about some of the other California bands that I'd had or that maybe I should be getting. I talked to all the members in the band at some point, but, you gotta remember, they were just another band on another night at JB's, so it wasn't like I was meeting my heroes on that night or anything.

The show itself was almost a riot, it got pretty wild. They did what they did right from the start. They were funky, punk obnoxious with the expected stage banter and all. There were probably a hundred people there. The JB's Down stage at the time was in the middle of the room on the north wall, so people spread out around the stage. You had the two wings, so people crammed right into the middle.

I remember Flea being fun to watch. He's a character, and he was pretty out there. There was a lot of bantering back and forth between people in the crowd and the band. At one point when they were playing, some of the punk rock girls were yelling stuff at them and then Anthony would just dish right back pretty firmly and quickly until people got offended. During the show, the guitar player, Jack Sherman, walked off in the middle of the performance! Maybe it was something somebody yelled out. There was a lot of fighting within the crowd. Then Cliff Martinez [their drummer] came and was trying to console him and get him back on-stage. This whole time I'm just thinking to myself, "Oh yeah, this is another punk rock ploy," and their soundman was like, "No, no, no, they have never done this. This is serious."

In the other cities, the punk rock crowds would dance and get wild and get right up to the stage, but in Kent there weren't as many people going to these shows, so nobody had to push forward in order to see. People just kind of migrated to the back and hung out. We didn't really give these people the hero worship that a lot of these bands were accustomed to.

I'm thinking when Black Flag played for us at JB's there were enough people where they would crunch forward. So it wasn't like MTV where you have all these people piling up against the stage to see the Red Hot Chili Peppers. It was more like local art student kids who were just like, "All right, prove yourself. Let's see what you got." And that was very common in Kent. It could be an almost brutal crowd if a band came in with a rock star attitude.

The last that I saw those guys in the Chili Peppers was after the show, when F Models drummer Steven McKee took Anthony and Flea to a party up towards campus. There was some kind of story with that. I didn't go to the party. I had to stay and clean up the bar. It was a fun night.

Was it a fun night? Perhaps it depends who you ask. Some of the people who had been in the audience the night the Red Hot Chili Peppers came to Kent remembered bits of the evening years later. One of those "yelling girls" recalled some of what happened after the show.

I think we lived on the fourth floor of College Towers, but, hell, I'm not sure. I remember how the fight started, and it was —— and me out front of JB's, and Flea came up to us and said, "Are you actually going to go in or are you going to be really punk and hang outside all night?" To which —— replied, "Happy Easter, Asshole," which was [Flea's] line in the movie *Suburbia*. This enraged Flea, who proceeded to call us all kinds of names and stomp inside. The band continued to berate everyone in the audience, and we all started throwing stuff at them. Then they came to our apartment, and we did mess with them A LOT, disconnecting the calls, et cetera, and they ended up leaving.

Her roommate had a similar, if fuzzier, memory of the night:

I don't remember very much. We all drank a lot that night. I do remember that they didn't like to be heckled and started berating us over the mic. We had the bartender invite them to our apartment afterwards just so we could mess with them. Flea used our phone to make a call, and someone pulled it out of the wall and disconnected his call. Stupid stuff, but honestly, that's all I remember.

Well-known Kent local David Jerome Bragg definitely was there:

I got along with Flea very well. We joked around a lot and had a good time laughin' at stuff, but Anthony kinda rubbed me the wrong way, too much ego I think. They definitely thought Kent was strange, and it was in those days. What a great place to be in the 1980s.

These fragments of memory give context for Steven McKee's recollections of the night the Red Hot Chili Peppers played JB's. McKee, as Teagle said, did bring Flea and Anthony Kiedis to that College Towers party.

I was in a band called the F Models, and we were pretty much the house band at JB's for a couple years. We played there two, sometimes three times a week. Johnny Teagle did the booking, so we were privy to anybody who came to town. We didn't open up for the Chili Peppers, but we did play the night before, opening up for the Gun Club.

The night that the Chili Peppers played there were two other bands on the bill, the Subterraneans and In Fear of Roses. The Chili Peppers had a video "True Men Don't Kill Coyotes," which was on MTV at the time. I believe that was probably their first video off of their very first album. So when it was announced they were coming to JB's, there was already a lot of buzz about them, plus nobody sounded like them at the time.

The show itself was crazy. Their performance was just super intense, they were just awesome. Nobody had ever seen anything like them. They were just super high energy. Seeing the Chili Peppers in a 150-seat club, even at that stage of the game, was pretty awesome.

I just remember this confrontation with these girls in the front area who were heckling, and the band stopped in the middle of their song and released this tirade of obscenities! I wish somebody would have recorded that, because it was absolutely incredible.

A present-day view of College Towers on Rhodes Road, where Anthony Kiedis and Flea of the Red Hot Chili Peppers attended a party on Saturday, November 17, 1984 (Photo by Jason Prufer)

After the show, I ended up hooking up with Flea and Anthony. I don't really know why that happened, but we just sort of gravitated towards each other, and I just thought they were cool and they needed a ride and that was it. I had a van. I actually loaded up some of their equipment and stuff. Their guitarist, Jack Sherman, disappear[ed], and I [took] Flea and Anthony to this party on one of the upper floors of College Towers.

So we get to this place, and we knocked on the door, and who opens the door but one of the girls who was in the middle of the confrontation! It was her party, which I didn't know! We weren't well received over there. There were a lot of people I knew that were like, "I can't believe you brought them here!" I remember thinking, "What the hell, I didn't know." It apparently was a bigger deal than I thought it was. I didn't know those girls were gonna be there. It was such a ridiculous situation. We stayed there for a little bit, and we were pretty much run out of there by all these girls, but it was actually kind of funny.

After that I ended up taking them back to their hotel, the Red Roof Inn over on I-76 and State Route 43 in Brimfield, where I had a couple beers with them. I was there for maybe an hour, an hour and a half or something. It was late by that time—maybe two or three in the morning—and they had somewhere to go the next day. We finished our beers, gave each other a hug, and parted ways.

I actually spent a total of about five or six hours with them that night, and I remember some of the conversations I had with Flea and Anthony. I remember them asking what was up with Kent. At the time in Kent, it was cool to act like you didn't like the bands. I don't know why people were like that, but it was cool to not clap and to boo and stuff, and they were just amazed by that. And I remember Anthony saying that this was the weirdest place they had played in their life. I'm sure they played weirder places afterwards. I actually remember reading an article a year or so later where they brought up Kent, Ohio, and what a bizarre, strange place it was. I also knew they had changed drummers, and we talked about how they ended up with Chris Martinez.

They were cool surfer dudes who were as personable and friendly as you can imagine, and you could tell they were excited to be on the road traveling and touring and playing. You could tell that was what they wanted to do and that's what they'd always do. We talked about playing in bands and who they'd played with before. They were definitely on the prowl, but they didn't get a very good reception at that party so we all went home alone. It's a cool memory to have.

Joe Walsh spoke at a press conference in the Kent State Student Center on Friday, October 3, 1986.

A Banner Weekend at KSU

Walsh May Play for Memorial

By John Gerome

Daily Kent Stater

October 7, 1986

Rock singer-guitarist Joe Walsh said Friday he plans to organize a potentially major benefit concert sometime this year to help fund the $500,000 May 4 Memorial.

"I feel it's right. It's time and this needs to be done," Walsh said at a press conference in the Student Center. "It is time for May 4 to be recognized as a tragedy so we can get on with the subject of education."

The concert is still in the planning stages, he said.

"I'm aware of members of my peer group being concerned with what happened on May 4. I would contact them and I think they would respond," he said.

"It should be in Ohio, and anybody's liable to show up. I am convinced it could turn into a major event," he added.

Walsh, on campus for last weekend's Homecoming festivities, was a student at KSU in 1970 when four students were killed when Ohio National Guardsmen fired into a crowd of Vietnam War demonstrators.

"I will work hard at it (the benefit concert) because I was here and I am proud of my college," he said.

"We should build the Memorial in the hopes that nothing that tragic will ever happen again," Walsh continued. "I hope we can put it in the history books and get on with education."

Walsh spoke with KSU President Michael Schwartz before making the announcement. Schwartz was in Columbus Monday and was unavailable for comment.

Walsh, 38, is one of the most well-known guitarists in rock. He began his musical career in the bars of downtown Kent in the late 1960s–early '70s with his band the James Gang. The group disbanded after producing two hits, "Walk Away" and "Funk 49."

After moving to Colorado, Walsh and his band, Barnstorm, recorded three albums, one of which contained the classic "Rocky Mountain Way."

He joined the Eagles in 1977, making his debut as the group's lead guitarist on the album *Hotel California,* which went platinum.

During this period of his career, Walsh also released a solo album titled *But Seriously Folks,* which included "Life's Been Good," a song about stardom that has become his trademark tune.

Since the Eagles disbanded in 1980, Walsh has recorded three solo albums.

He said in an interview Friday he is about two-thirds finished with his fourth, which he described as sounding like "nothing you have ever heard before."

It has been 11 years since Walsh last performed at KSU, and he indicated Friday that he was happy to return.

"In the past, it wasn't time to come back," he said when asked about his long absence. "This year I felt it was time."

"It hurts a little to come back," Walsh said, noting the May 4 tragedy. "There are a lot of mental things involved."

Walsh, who served as grand marshal of Saturday's Homecoming parade, said he was "honored at the invitation."

"I hope they know what they've done. I'm capable of random chaos at any time," he said with a chuckle. "I'm liable to play 'Louie Louie' or 'Funk 49' instead of the National Anthem."

Although he didn't go that far, Walsh did pull a few off-stage antics that have contributed to his popularity over the years.

During a live broadcast on WMMS FM 100.7 Friday morning from the Student Center, Walsh attempted to call Ravenna Mayor Donald Kainrad to express his displeasure about Kainrad's verbal attack on rock 'n' roll. But Walsh was told Kainrad was out of town.

Kainrad appeared on a Cleveland television station last week and suggested the future Rock Hall of Fame be renamed the "Hall of Shame," because he said it promotes illicit sex and drug use.

Friday, Walsh said, "Rock 'n' roll has always been dissected and torn apart."

Walsh said he often misses his days in Kent because, "In those days I wasn't Joe Walsh, the famous rock star. I was just another musician playing in a very, very artistic community."

Joe Walsh played at Kent State's 1986 Homecoming on Saturday, October 4. (Courtesy of Kent State University Libraries. Special Collections and Archives.)

Joe Walsh played at Kent State's 1986 Homecoming on Saturday, October 4.

Life in the Fast Lane
Walsh Classics Keep Sell-Out Crowd Cheering
By Karen Bells
Daily Kent Stater
October 7, 1986

Joe Walsh fans were treated to nearly two hours of classic rock 'n' roll tunes and trademark Walsh guitar virtuosity at Saturday night's concert in the Memorial Gym.

Walsh, a renowned rock musician and former Kent State student, kept the receptive crowd of nearly 6,000 fans cheering throughout the sold-out show.

Dressed in a Kent State hat and football jersey, he took the stage at 9:20 P.M. following a well-received 45-minute set by the opening act 15-60-75, The Numbers Band.

The show began with a segment Walsh called "A Few Minutes with Old Buddy Joe," during which Walsh did a few solos, talked with the audience and told jokes.

A psychedelic backdrop and lights recaptured the mood of the era when Walsh attended Kent. Members of the audience carried "Joe Walsh for President" signs, referring to his semiserious and highly publicized candidacy for president of the United States in 1979.

Describing himself as a "sixth-year junior in good standing," Walsh said he majored in English while at Kent "because I wanted to learn how to talk good."

Walsh, who was obviously enjoying himself onstage, joked about getting a kiss from the Homecoming Queen. He had the audience join him in a standing ovation for the Golden Flashes, in honor of the team's victory Saturday afternoon over Central Michigan.

He kept the crowd laughing throughout the night with his off-beat humor.

Joe Walsh as grand marshal for Kent State's Homecoming in front of the Robin Hood on the northeast corner of Lincoln and East Main Streets on Saturday, October 4, 1986 (Photo by Alex Gildzen)

"Please," he requested, "don't anyone drive home drunk; crawl home drunk—I plan to."

The crowd cheered when Walsh, who was a student here at the time of the May 4, 1970, shootings, announced that he will make "a very serious donation to the May 4th Memorial project."

The 12-song set began with a heartfelt solo performance of "Indian Summer," After a solo introduction of his most recent hit, "The Confessor," Walsh was joined onstage by his longtime cohorts, drummer Joe Vitale and bassist Rick Rosas.

The band joined Walsh in a powerful performance of "The Confessor." He brought the crowd to its feet with energetic performances of his James Gang hits "Walk Away" and "Funk 49."

Walsh kept the atmosphere casual as he lay down on the stage while Vitale performed his "Funk 49" drum solo.

"Do I really have a Maserati?" he asked. "I don't know—it seems logical. I know I've got a limo." The crowd cheered during Walsh's intro-

duction to "Life's Been Good," one of his most popular hits.

He went on to rock the enthusiastic fans through "Rocky Mountain Way" and "Life in the Fast Lane," a popular song from his days with The Eagles. Walsh finished the concert with two encores, ending the performance with "All Night Long."

He topped off the show by throwing his Kent State hat into the audience and tearing down the drum set in a celebrated, destructive Walsh style.

The opening band 15-60-75, The Numbers Band, opened the show promptly at 8:00 P.M., rocking through an impressive 45-minute set.

Overall, Saturday's concert was good, despite the noticeable absence of such Walsh classics as "Space Age Whiz Kids" and "I Can Play That Rock 'n' Roll."

Walsh ended his show by telling the audience, "Be proud that you go to Kent State. I am."

The Ramones played in the University Auditorium on Saturday, November 15, 1986.

Crowd, Not Music Was Best Entertainment at Ramones

by Karen Bells
Daily Kent Stater
November 18, 1986

The scene at the University Auditorium on Saturday night looked more like a riot than a rock concert as punk rock fans rushed the stage and slam danced into each other.

The crowd of about 1,000 people gathered to experience the 80-minute set of brash punk rock music delivered by The Ramones.

From the minute the leather-clad, New York City–based band took the stage, it commanded the full attention of the audience, keeping the people on their feet, moving to the rapid-fire attack of rough, loud music.

The set opened with "Teenage Lobotomy," as hundreds of fans rushed toward the stage to dance, gyrate and slam into each other.

The music was a series of fast but simple songs, most less than three minutes long. It combined a strong background of guitars with deadpan lyrics, often indecipherable as singer Joey Ramone half slurred, half snarled them into the microphone.

Although their music didn't seem to reflect any great amount of talent, The Ramones' bizarre and enjoyable show revealed the reason their concerts consistently play to full houses.

Fans stood on their seats and yelled, jumped about erratically and sang along as the band whipped through such Ramones classics as "Rock 'n' Roll High School," "Loudmouth" and "Sheena Is a Punk Rocker."

the **RAMONES**
UNIVERSITY AUDITORIUM Nov. 15 8:00 pm
$11 general public Advance tickets: $6 students

On sale at KSU ticket office
$11 night of show
ACPB

The Ramones played in the University Auditorium on Saturday, November 15, 1986. (Courtesy of the *Daily Kent Stater*)

Bass guitarist Dee Dee Ramone belts out a punk rock tune at the wild-n-crazy concert in Kent on November 15, 1986. (*Daily Kent Stater* photo by Karen Schiely)

157

Some spike-haired fan made several acrobatic leaps from the arm of his chair into the sea of dancing bodies as other people were picked up and passed overhead by fellow enthusiasts.

The band, clad entirely in black and looking every bit the part of a New York City street gang, raced from one song to the next, barely allowing enough time for guitarist Dee Dee Ramone to bark his trademark "1-2-3-4" command before each song.

It didn't matter that one song was, for the most part, barely recognizable from the next, or that the words were sometimes a bit garbled.

What mattered was that the music was fast, hard-hitting and danceable. Everyone seemed to enjoy themselves, with the possible exception of the security guards lining the front of the room, who spent the evening plastered against the stage with fans screaming lyrics into their faces.

The Ramones, who announced they were celebrating the 10th anniversary of punk rock, demonstrated how they helped shape the sound of this musical institution in the last decade as they ripped through "I Wanna Be Sedated" and "Rock 'n' Roll Radio," two of the show's highlights.

After about an hour the band left the stage, only to be lured back twice for encores by the chanting, cheering crowd. The audience then was treated to another 20 minutes of music, including "Do You Wanna Dance?"

In addition to Joey and Dee Dee, the band is rounded out by Johnny Ramone, sharing guitar with Dee Dee, and drummer Richie Ramone, the most recent addition to the lineup.

The concert, sponsored by the All-Campus Programming Board, opened with a 40-minute set by the Bangorillas, a rock band from Youngstown, who entertained the crowd with songs like "Say Goodnight."

Gregg Allman and Dickey Betts played Filthy McNasty's in downtown Kent on Wednesday, January 28, 1987.

Allman Rocks McNasty's—Southern Style
Blues Influence Evident in Old, New Material
By Lisa Bales
Daily Kent Stater
January 30, 1987

"We got some good stuff for you tonight," announced Dickey Betts to a crowd of a few hundred at McNasty's on Wednesday night.

And he was right.

The two original members of the Allman Brothers Band, Gregg Allman and Dickey Betts, were back to play some of the finest southern blues.

Ten years ago, the Allman Brothers Band had five platinum and three gold albums to its credit, and was one of the highest paid rock acts in the United States. Success turned to tragedy, however, when two band members were killed—Duane Allman (the founder) and Berry Oakley.

With the reformation of the band, the blues musicians erase any negative doubts about their ability to make a comeback. The concert is direct proof that these men are once again serious musicians.

Betts, with his Gibson guitar, kicked off the eight-song set with "Hideaway," a great instrumental piece featuring talented guitar licks. When comparing the old material to his new songs, there is very little difference—it all has that strong bluesy influence.

Allman opened his set with "Ain't My Cross To Carry" followed by "Old Time Feeling," which demonstrated obvious musical skill. "Running Water" allowed the crowd to reminisce.

Allman's band included Chaz Trippy, en-

Gregg Allman sits down at the keyboard during a concert at McNasty's. (Photo by Richard Underwood)

Former Allman Brothers Band member Dickey Betts joined Gregg Allman onstage for a set of old Allman Brothers songs to close the show. (*Daily Kent Stater* photo by Lucy Royer)

ergetically hitting the bongos, Danny Toler on lead guitar, Frankie Toler on percussion, Bruce Waibel on bass and Tim Heding on keyboards.

New material such as "Faces without Names" is featured on his new album, which is expected to be out Feb. 1. It is obvious that Allman is a product of his own influences. He has a soulful voice in the style of Otis Redding and Little Richard, and the audience responded positively to it.

It was time for both men to share the stage as sort of an Allman Band reunion. On the first few notes, fans were able to recognize the familiar tune "Whipping Post."

The Replacements played in Kent on Friday, November 13, 1987.

Replacements Know How to Rock 'n' Roll
By Michael Gallucci
Daily Kent Stater
November 17, 1987

The Replacements are the greatest rock 'n' roll band in the world.

Forget that their latest LP, *Pleased to Meet Me*, is one of the greatest albums of '87. Forget that '84's *Let It Be* and '85's *Tim* are two of the best albums of the '80s. It's just that the Mats (the Replacements' nickname) are a helluva band, doin' it like it really matters.

And last Friday's show at the University Auditorium proved this. I've seen the Mats a couple times before, but this was the first time they really seemed to care. Yeah, they were drunk. Yeah they lost drummer Chris Mars before the show. But, yeah, that's what makes 'em great.

Kickin' off with "I.O.U.," the Mats let go 27 songs, a third of them being covers. With the exception of their version of "Hitchin' a Ride,"

The Replacements' lead singer and rhythm guitarist Paul Westerberg takes a break from "boinkin' around the stage" by mellowing out to the song "Unsatisfied" at the concert in the University Auditorium. The concert was sponsored by the KSU All Campus Programming Board. (*Daily Kent Stater* photo by Lucy Royer)

Plus, they did the typical boinkin' around that the Mats are loved for (well, at least why I love 'em) In the middle of "I Will Dare" Paul broke into "If I Had a Hammer"; he told the crowd to shut up so they might learn something; he had the crowd lift him over their heads during "Nightclub jitters"; he changed words (typical Mats); he told the crowd they were tired of doin' their own songs (another typical Mats); finished the evening with an unfinished "I Don't Know," and (the greatest action I've ever seen *any* band do on stage), Paul kissed Tommy on the lips.

And for those who missed the point, the love and the whole damn rock 'n' roll spirit of that gesture, didn't deserve to be there. And for those who did miss any of that, they just don't understand rock 'n' roll. But the Mats do.

Great White, Tesla, and Badlands played at Kent State on Friday, October 14, 1989.

Gym Concert a Headbangers' Heaven
By Mike Raymond
Daily Kent Stater
October 17, 1989

which they did in '85, this was the finest set of covers I've seen the Mats do.

They did Prince's "I Could Never Take the Place of Your Man"; "Hear You Been To College" (for the predominately KSU audience); "Honky Tonk Woman"; "I Wanna Be Your Dog" (head Mat Paul Westerberg changed one of the verses to "Saw Iggy in Paris, he . . . sucked"); "The One I Love" (great jab at the now acceptable R.E.M.), and (after bassist Tommy Stinson's attempts at starting the song several times throughout the evening), a blistering version of "Anarchy in the U.K."

They also dipped into a grab bag of songs from their first three releases, doin' hot pieces of "Takin' a Ride," "Color Me Impressed," "Within Your Reach," "I'm Trouble" and "Go."

It was a night of headbangers' heaven—or is that hell?

A jammed near-capacity crowd of almost 5,000 filed into the Memorial Gym Saturday night ready to rock. Black and more black was the proper attire for this show.

It was a concert where no matter what the bands Badlands, Great White or Tesla played or did, the crowd would have begged for more.

Tesla, billed as headliner, proved itself worthy of such a title. The obvious influences were there, especially in lead singer Jeff Keith, who struts, shakes, looks and, to stretch the truth a little, sings or screams, like Aerosmith's Steven Tyler.

Probably what made Tesla a more formidable headliner than Great White is that they seemed more sincere in what they were doing. They were trying to be creative on stage, such as in the acoustical guitar dual between Frank Hannon and Tommy Skeoch before "Heaven's Trail."

Tesla has been called the last "T-shirt and blue jeans" band. Only one member, bassist Brian Wheat, actually wore them, but these guys got down into some nitty-gritty old-fashioned rock 'n' roll.

Great White played nearly 75 minutes, much of which was dominated by the foul-mouthed talking of lead singer Jack Russell.

If there's a stereotype that still exists about lead singers who try to create a cheerleading effect by saying "You sing it . . ." or "Everybody clap their hands . . . ," Russel fits it perfectly.

The shirtless Russell, his right arm in a sling, pranced back and forth in a sleazy David Lee Roth manner, and yelled obscenities at the crowd. But the audience didn't mind—they just kept bobbing their heads while cheering the singer's antics along.

And when Great White played, it was obvious the crowd came to hear the big hits, "Rock Me" and "Once Bitten, Twice Shy." Even the 10-minute milking of the latter, including the stereotyped sing-along, didn't bore the most avid headbangers in the back.

Probably the best attraction of Great White's show was the monstrous drum kit of Tony Montana.

Badlands began the set and was received rather well, judged by the number of head bobs. This is a band sure to headline its own show, if it withstands the test of time.

Iggy Pop played at Kent State on Saturday, October 20, 1990.

Iggy Pop Still "Bad Boy" of Rock
By Jon Epstein
Daily Kent Stater
October 24, 1990

The Iggy Pop concert held in the University Auditorium Saturday night created a certain sense of uneasiness in my otherwise unshakeable self-image. You see, I have taught in the auditorium and will be doing so again in the near future. Iggy Pop pointed out to me the arbitrariness of what we sociologists like to call "norms." When he yelled, "Rock it, motherfuckers," he was rewarded with screams of approval from the 700 or so people who attended the show. If I yelled "rock it motherfuckers," to the intro-sociology class I'm the graduate assistant for, I would be in deep trouble. Maybe it's a question of presentation. Either that or a self-esteem issue. Needless to say, my relationship with the University Auditorium will never be the same.

Iggy Pop has been the ultimate bad boy of rock 'n' roll for longer than most people reading this article have been alive.

While it is possible that the twinkle in your parent's eye, which became you, was inspired by Iggy, I hope it wasn't. This type of inspiration would indicate a certain degree of what psychologists refer to as "dysfunction."

Two decades ago, when you were gestating, Iggy Stooge (now Pop) was keeping himself busy by rolling around on broken beer bottles, inventing stage diving, smearing himself with peanut butter, getting his butt kicked by irate music fans who felt he had violated norms of peace, love and other groovy things which that generation was supposed to stand for (think about that for a minute), and shooting heroin.

Almost as an afterthought, he was also creating wonderfully obnoxious music, which would go on to inspire the entire punk rock movement.

The Sex Pistols' bassist Sid Vicious couldn't hold a candle to Iggy Stooge. In comparison, Sid was a rank amateur and a whole lot more pathetic. No matter how out of control Iggy has become, he has always managed to stay alive and create a certain kind of twisted art in the process, two things Sid Vicious never got the hang of.

The crowd at Saturday's concert was as diverse as I've seen, possibly mirroring Iggy's longevity.

The youngest person attending was my five-year-old daughter, who, incidentally, offered up the best and most concise concert review I have heard in quite some time. "Daddy, that funny man sure is loud."

So loud, in fact, that I could hear it outside of the Business Administration building as I walked to my car during the last encore. I could compare the volume, using Hunter Thompson's words, to "an F-14 at takeoff."

Rock 'n' roll is a fine thing, by God. Judging by the way the auditorium rafters were shaking, and by the amount of paint and screws falling from the walls and chairs, I would predict that the university administration is going to have to put some long overdue money into renovating the auditorium.

Maybe rock music does serve a higher social purpose.

The oldest person there, as far as I could tell, was the geriatric daughter of someone who has long since shuffled off to Buffalo.

No kidding, she was eighty if she was a day.

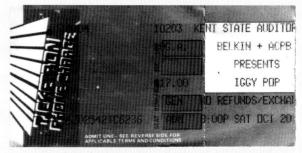

Iggy Pop played at Kent State on Saturday, October 20, 1990. (Author's collection)

No one can tell me that rock isn't music for the masses. I found myself wondering which Iggy Pop rock 'n' roll gem was her favorite. "I Wanna Be Your Dog?" "Raw Power?" "Metallic K.O.?" "Butt Town?" The mind boggles. I finally settled for "Lust for Life." It seemed appropriate.

If the person in question is reading this article, please call me. I would really like to meet you.

Opening for Iggy was a band called Manu Negra. What they did is kind of hard to explain.

Picture a band made up of representatives from a number of European countries playing a combination of calypso, rap, hard rock and techno-pop and you should get a pretty good idea of what they were about.

I predict they will be a big hit on the "dare to be weird with no regard for musical talent" variety of college radio stations. The 14-year-old sitting next to me with the razor slashes on her forearm seemed to enjoy them a lot.

In an age where rock music is defined mostly by trends, instead of talent, Iggy Pop stands out as a true legend.

Saturday's concert was rock music as it should be: Loud, obnoxious and totally inappropriate. Which, come to think of it, is why I fell in love with rock 'n' roll to begin with.

Legendary Vermont Jam Band Phish Descended upon the MAC Center

November 12, 1994

This is one of Kent State's most storied and well-documented shows, and because it took place on Saturday, November 12, 1994, a good amount of archival materials and memories are still intact. This was the first major concert to be held in this venue since its 1992 renovation and rededication. (The Memorial Athletic and Convocation Center had previously been the Memorial Gym.)

The show was a complete sellout, and the party atmosphere before the concert was in typical legendary Phish preshow fashion. The Student Center parking lot and the C parking lot adjacent to the Michael Schwartz Center were filled with hippies, gypsies, and Volkswagen buses ripped out of some festive Grateful Dead show. This was commonplace for a Phish concert but highly unusual for Kent, Ohio.

Phish, on tour for its *Hoist* album, was completely in its musical prime. This was Phish's only ever appearance in Kent, and by the following summer the group's growing popularity meant it was playing only the largest sports arenas, stadiums, and summer sheds.

In 2005, Phish released a small chunk of this concert (tacked onto the end of another show) as part of its LivePhish.com series. Also of note is that the entire fall 1994 Phish tour was professionally recorded for its official release, *A Live One.*

I was sitting in the third row on the floor, and I distinctly remember that just before the performance, balloons were batted around in that floor section. First, there was one, then three, and then what seemed like hundreds of balloons of all sizes. The lights went down, and Phish came on to a roaring applause. The stage was littered with those balloons. I think the stage security

On November 12, 1994, Phish played at Kent State. Before their performance, balloons were batted around at the front floor section. (*Daily Kent Stater* photo by Jeff Camarati)

had all the balloons popped and out of the way by the end of the first song.

Kent State graduate Dan Soulsby, the All Campus Programming Board Concert Committee chair for the 1994–95 school year, was the chief promoter for this concert. The show was 100 percent his idea, and he and his staff made this entire thing happen. Dan, who was only twenty-two years old when Phish came to town, shared his memories of the concert with me almost two decades later in early 2011.

None of this would have been possible without the help of a great staff of ACPB board members. It was a team effort.

We were talking about doing a show at the MAC Center because it had just been renovated so the Undergraduate Student Senate wanted to do a big show and fill the place up. At that time there weren't too many bands that could put 6,000 people comfortably into a venue like that, and I narrowed it down to like five different bands. I actually had the *Kent Stater* post in the paper a questionnaire about "Who would you want to see play in the new MAC Center?" The whole time, though, I was trying to convince the powers that be that if we brought Phish to the MAC Center we could sell the place out.

A lot of the college kids knew who Phish was, but the problem was the people who had to write off on this thing and hand out the money, i.e., the fraternity kids on the Student Senate, had never heard of them. I mean, you can ask ten different people on campus what's in and what's hot right now and you'll get ten different answers. So, they were worried about giving me the money, but just before the school year started, they gave me like the largest budget ever given to a KSU concert committee ever, with the goal for me to bring a headlining band to Kent State.

I went after Phish not too long after that survey went out, and on September 16, 1994, we made them a formal offer of $37,500 plus 85 percent of net profits to play in the MAC Center on Saturday, November 12, 1994. Phish was cool with it, and by October 6, we had a signed contract between Phish and Kent State University. We also got 20 percent of the money from all of the merchandise sold at the show, which is big, so it had the potential to generate more money for the university than anything I'd ever seen.

At that time, they would have much rather played some place like Kent State than somewhere up in Cleveland. Their album *Hoist* had come out in March of 1994, and this concert was like eight months later. I think *Hoist* had become their most commercially successful album up until that time. By the fall of 1994, Phish was just starting to gain a lot of popularity and more commercial success, and it was *Hoist* that really had propelled them into the mainstream.

I actually got into an argument with Phish's management, because I insisted that we have a special student ticket sale before they went on sale to the general public. I didn't want them going onto Ticketmaster or anything until our students got the first opportunity to buy the tickets. I knew that they had a lot of Phishheads traveling with the band who pick up tickets, and I didn't want some scalpers buying up a whole bunch of great seats to try and sell back to our students in the weeks leading up to the show. I said I wanted our students to have first crack

at 'em, and they did. They showed in numbers to the special sale, and most of them bought the maximum they could buy.

I want to say that the concert sold out like within just a few days, and it shut up all the naysayers pretty quick when they saw how fast tickets sold. The people at the *Kent Stater* and the student government had no idea who Phish was [until] after we sold out the MAC Center, and then they were believers! Of course, now that we had a sold-out Phish concert on our hands, this led to all kinds of other problems.

[Leading up to the event,] I remember several meetings with the police force, and they were extremely worried about all this illegal activity that they perceived would be going around in the parking lot, like they thought this was going to be some kind of San Francisco Hell's Angels rally or something, and I was telling them, "No, it isn't going to be like that."

They were really worried there were going to be all these hard drugs. It almost got to the point where they were going to cancel the whole event, so I told them, "I already signed the contracts, and we're gonna have to pay them the money anyways." They made me hire so many police. I thought it was funny, because I told them so many times that you don't need this many cops. But they said, "If you're gonna have it, you're gonna need to hire all of our police force." The chief was worried. They were telling me all this misinformation about the kind of angry crowd they were going to attract, that I knew was just plain wrong. I kept telling them, "Ummm no . . . It's not like that." In the end, they made me hire twenty-two police officers, thirty-eight hall security officers, and eighteen campus security persons for one show.

In the semesters before we did Phish, I booked De La Soul with A Tribe Called Quest, the Lemonheads, and Koko Taylor, and they didn't make me hire thirty-some police officers. For this one it was like overkill. Think about how many exits there are for the MAC Center. It's like, what are they doing? What were we paying these people for?

I think [Phish] showed up the night before. I don't believe we put them up. I think they stayed on the buses, because I remember those big tour buses pulling up behind the MAC on the Friday and then there being a bunch of students standing outside and trying to meet them. I had to have the campus security guys put some gates around the buses so the students wouldn't try to get autographs or bug the band.

I remember the sound check. I remember going to the MAC Center and there were like a dozen security people getting into place and then just our staff and my sound guy working with the Phish sound guy. And Trey was on stage alone, just soloing, testing out his pedals, which I thought was so cool. The sounds he was making, it was like an orgasm for your ears. I remember thinking it was kind of cool that a band that was as big as Phish were still doing a sound check. I was just in awe watching Trey play guitar, and then the whole band came onstage and finished out sound check.

Since I was the head promoter, I got to eat dinner with Phish, so after the sound check I walked with the band over to the Schwebel Room. On the way they were asking me about the Kent State shootings; luckily I had taken a class called Peace and Conflict Studies and learned all about it and I was able to answer all [their] questions. I didn't take them to the memorial or anything, but I pointed out the area since it all happened behind the MAC Center. During our dinner I didn't want to start gushing or acting like a fan, so we just did like small talk.

I remember saying things like that I had never been to Vermont, stuff like that.

[Then, before the concert,] I remember the anticipation leading to the opening of the doors and the police and security thinking that the gym was going to fill up in like five seconds, but I knew they were going to file in slowly. It wasn't general admission or anything, but the security was acting as if it was [a huge arena show].

I didn't have time to [see what was going on in the parking lot outside the show]. I really wanted to. We were so busy inside the MAC just making sure everything was set up right. We had a bunch of volunteer ushers to show people where their seats were who got to see the show for free, and I [had] to throw one of them out, because I'm like, "Dude, you're not showing anybody where their seats are. All you gotta do is just show 'em where their seats are with your little flashlight and then you can watch the show." And then I came back twenty minutes later, and this guy was just still dancing, so I had to call security and told them to kick [him] out.

I was running around so much backstage and in front of the stage that I can't even remember the whole set, but I know it's online and I'm looking forward to downloading it. I remember my parents came down to the show, and I asked my dad about what he thought. He was impressed that they were actually really good musicians.

During the set break, we were having problems with the folding chairs that we had set on the gym floor. They were zip-tied together, and people were pulling the zip ties off and pushing them away, and the fire chief and those people were worried about that because of the fire codes. I remember trying to handle that by bringing down more volunteers, whose job it was to just keep the aisles clear so the crowd could still dance.

I remember getting a check for Phish [right after the show] and sitting down to go over the numbers for the night. We had to write them a check, and we had to get our checks from them for 20 percent of the merchandise sold. I'd never seen numbers in the hundreds of thousands before. It was over $100,000 we were talking about! Ya know, when you're in college you're lucky to have $3 in your pocket and 99 cents left on your [meal] card, so [this] was just mind-blowing. I remember breathing a sigh of relief that there were no EMS incidents.

Phish Concert Owes Success to Much Planning

By Ann Milanowski
Daily Kent Stater
Tuesday, November 15, 1994

Although a concert may begin for fans when the lights go down, the evening of the event is simply the culmination of months of hard work and planning for the members of the All Campus Programming Board. Saturday's Phish show was one of ACPB's semester-long goals.

Preparation for the sold-out show began last summer. Planning a concert for ACPB is the responsibility of several chairs: the concert, concert publicity, house and stage productions chairs.

These board members work together to unify the multistep process, from booking an act to hiring security. "Before anything can be done, we must determine the budget through allocations from the Undergraduate Student Senate," Dan Soulsby, ACPB concert chair said. "Then we must reserve the facility and begin to pursue talent."

Soulsby, a junior communications major, spent most of the fall semester trying to recruit a band

to play a concert in the MAC Center. The recruiting process was initiated in September with a band survey conducted at the Black Squirrel Festival. And although Phish only received 10 percent of the student votes, they were chosen to play since they were the only act available.

The Phish concert was the first to be held in the Memorial Athletic and Convocation Center, and Soulsby said he wants to make better use of the facility in the future. "The Great White and Tesla show in 1989 was the last concert held in the old gym," Soulsby said. "Everyone wants to put Kent State back on the concert scene, especially after the renovations and addition of Ticketmaster."

The main source of pursuing talent is through POLLSTAR magazine, which publishes touring dates and box office summaries. "You have to find someone who can sell 4,000 to 5,000 seats and then check out the information on when they are playing," Soulsby said. "It's tough to get a show in because we are in the Cleveland/ Akron market." ACPB had to compete with Belkin Productions to bring Phish in concert. However, the organization won the offer since it had more money at its disposal.

After an offer is made and accepted by the band, their agent sends back a rider that contains the agreement specifications. This is 30 to 40 pages, including information ranging from lighting and dressing room requirements to the band's special requests. "For instance, Van Halen requests two bowls of all brown M&Ms," Soulsby said. "We have to go through the rider and cross out everything that we can't provide, such as alcohol, and then send it to be signed off by the Office of Campus Life and we can finally send it out."

The agent sends the contract, which is then edited by a group of administrators and the board members. When it is returned, the contract is usually accepted or declined within several working days. At this point, the other chairs begin work on ticket sales, advertising and security measures.

However, the Phish show has proved a unique experience since they are operating on a larger scale than usual. "With the smaller shows, it's mainly the campus that we target," said Amy Franjesevic, ACPB concert publicity chair. "But with a show this big, we couldn't just sell on campus. "For Phish, we did some radio spots and advertised in *Scene Magazine*," Franjesevic said. "But the majority of our budget went to advertising in the Daily Kent Stater."

Franjesevic, a senior visual communications major, said dealing with agents about advertising can hinder creativity. "It sometimes seems like you are working against them, not with them," she said. "They've got a specific way of doing things, and so do you. They want only a specific ad with a particular typeface used for their ad, or they say that we can't give out many complimentary tickets."

In addition to advertising, the house productions chair arranges the security, ushers, campus security, police and oversees hospitality. The newest member of the ACPB board, Bryant Compton, took over the position when its old chair resigned last month. "I came in from scratch and had to get my feet wet up to my head and watch out for the alligators," Compton said.

While Compton takes care of security needs and numbering seats, one of his major tasks is catering to the band's needs. "With the dressing rooms, breakfast, lunch and dinner, I have a small crew helping me," Compton said. "But as far as hospitality goes, if they need something,

I am their man." Compton said he must comply with all special requests in the contract. For Saturday night's performance, this included a dinner of poached salmon with lemon.

Finally, it is the responsibility of the stage productions chair to arrange light and sound specifications and set up equipment on the day of the show. "Our production has been intense for the past week, and this is the first time we have put in a big rig, or a flying sound and light system," said Brent Walla, ACPB stage productions chair. "For such a large scale show, our crew was impressive, and it's been a steady operation of a major production."

After all the months of hard work, the concert was a big success. The band drew a 5,800 maximum-capacity crowd. Many fans drove long distances or took buses to come to Kent State for the show. "Phish is probably the most amazing live act around today," said Michele Angis, a sophomore philosophy major at Syracuse.

"It isn't an odd thing for me to come to see them here in my home state, it's worth the drive." Jeff Kemp, a University of Guelph student, came from Canada to see the show. "They aren't playing in Canada on this tour, and though it was a six-hour drive, this was the closest show," said Kemp, a doctoral student in environmental engineering. "I'm into the Internet news groups and that's how we heard about the show."

Members of ACPB were pleased with the show and said they may decide to plan another concert in the MAC Center for next semester. "I feel like it's a big achievement to sell out a venue that hasn't been used in 5 years, and we haven't had a sold out show since Hall and Oates in 1981," Soulsby said.

Kent band Dink signed with Capitol Records in June 1994.

DINK

Next Stop, the World
By Angela Gent
Daily Kent Stater
May 2, 1995

The menacing force of Dink: Sean Carlin, Jan Eddy Van der Kuil, Rob Lightbody, Jeff Finn, and Jer Herring (Courtesy of the *Daily Kent Stater*)

Kent homeboys and rock audio-visual dynamos Dink may have penned a two-record deal with Capitol Records last June, but that certainly doesn't mean they're lounging around soaking in the sun.

"We're working constantly. We're not sittin' back smoking cigars," says Rob Lightbody, the group's singer/guitarist.

He's not kidding, either. Since signing the deal, the band has been caught up in a whirlwind of activity. The band kicks off a month-long tour with industrial madmen and Dink comrades KMFDM tomorrow in California. They will be making a stop at the Nautica stage in Cleveland for WENZ 107.9 FM's birthday bash May 25.

But the tour isn't the only thing on Dink's platter these days.

The quintet is also awaiting MTV approval for their latest video, for the single "Get on It." The video was shot at the Daily Double in Akron in early April and was directed by Californian Nancy Bennett.

Guitarist/vocalist Jer Herring says he was leery about having Bennett shoot the video at first.

"It was really bizarre because we really liked Nancy's treatment for 'Get On It,'" he says. "But when we got her video resume, so to speak, she'd done stuff for En Vogue and Tori Amos, this VH-1 stuff."

"Personally, I was nervous, but it looks nothing like an En Vogue video," he said laughing. "She did a terrific job."

Herring says the context of the video, including the familiar local setting, was important to the band.

"We wanted to do something with some local flavor . . . more local than the last time," he said. "We also wanted something that set moods and threw images."

Herring says the new video includes two separate settings and a lot of little colored light bulbs. He said band members were shot in still photographs wearing clothes covered in the band's practice space in downtown Akron, while the rest of the video was shot at the Daily Double.

Dink's last video was the major national promotion that got the band rolling. It began on a chaotic morning in October.

The event of the day was the filming of the band's first video "Green Mind," a whirling dervish of trash and body parts. It wasn't long before the video ended up in the hands of MTV and soon began rotation, appearing six to eight times a week, Herring says.

For the five members that are Dink, "the whole video-making process is a trip," Lightbody says.

He says some of the fun came from looking at the directors' treatments, which are one- to two-page descriptions of what the director would do for the video.

"Oh man, some of that stuff is so hilarious to read." he says.

Apparently the band was impressed by Ben Stokes' treatment, because he was chosen to direct "Green Mind." Of course it didn't hurt he had directed videos for Nine Inch Nails, Ministry, Public Enemy and Revolting Cocks.

A month after filming "Green Mind," the band embarked on a month-long tour with Pop Will Eat Itself and Compulsion, after which the band took a much-deserved break for the holidays.

But then January swept in not only a new year but another tour for the five. This time, Dink found itself on the bill with Belgian techno devils the Lords of Acid, who were venturing out on their first-ever American tour. Along the way, the band stopped at The Roxy in Los Angeles, First Avenue in Minneapolis and The Limelight in New York City. It was a trip that left the band in a somewhat harried state of affairs, Lightbody says.

"There's times when you'll be doing eight, nine days in a row of shows, getting in the van and driving to another, and you'll be physically exhausted." he says "Sometimes you don't physically feel good, but nobody cares about that. You just want to get out there and do it. When you're successful, you can totally lose your mind, and you don't feel bad anymore."

And for the frantic Lightbody, the stage often becomes a platform on which to exorcise his personal demons.

"It's definitely an altered state when it's going good and you're really rocking." he says. "Sometimes you'll come off the stage and go,

'wow what just happened?' and you don't even know, you're totally somewhere else. You don't get that feeling flipping burgers."

Herring, too, says the new found rigors of touring can become a little much at times, and given Lightbody's comment about touring in a van with eight people for two months straight, "I can sum it up in one sentence: the van smells funny," it's no wonder.

"It's a little overwhelming when you think about being out for two months." Herring says. "It's hard to get used to. You miss your friends and it'd be nice to crawl into your own bed."

Amidst all the fun of touring, Dink was invited to MTV's *120 Minutes,* a two-hour program of alternative videos. Lightbody says the experience proved to be literally an eye-opening one.

"We hadn't slept at all the night before," he says. "We did a show in Boston and got in the car and drove to New York to that at like 8:30 in the morning.

"So, when everyone looks dazed and stoned on *120 Minutes,* it's because they do it at some ungodly hour in the morning. It isn't 'rock time,'" he says.

The segments on *120* aired March 12, and the band also appeared on the FX channel's *Sound FX* music show later that week.

But despite the band's growing success and contrary to some local beliefs that Dink members have gotten too big for their britches, the members of Dink have not succumbed to self-centered, arrogant fancies. In fact, they are quite humble when asked about their success.

"I don't know how it happened," says Lightbody. "I guess it was the right bunch of people at the right time.

"We never started out expecting anything out of this. It seems it happened naturally somehow, go figure."

Herring echoes Lightbody's sentiments exactly, adding, "Part of it was that we worked hard and put ourselves in a position to get attention." But then he adds "I don't know how the hell it happened. I'm just glad it did."

Herring says the whole trip is still like a dream.

"It's definitely work, but I still have to pinch myself and say 'Yep, I'm making a living playing music. This is really happening.'"

Lightbody says they don't deny their hometown roots either, saying the band has broken the habit of people in the business who refer to Dink as from Cleveland rather than Kent.

And although Lightbody says he'd like to stick around home base in Kent, there's certainly no moss growing under the feet of Dink. Herring says the band will probably release another single and tour again before heading into the studio, probably in early '96, to record their next album.

And where from there?

"The world," Lightbody says. "I hope we'll be going to Europe soon—Japan, Australia and all that good stuff. If nothing else I want to see the world with this.

Peter, Paul and Mary performed before a crowd of about 3,800 in the MAC Center on May 4, 1995. *Left to right:* Paul Stookey, Mary Travers, and Peter Yarrow. (*Daily Kent Stater* photo by Jeff Camarati)

Peter, Paul and Mary performed in the Kent State MAC Center on May 4, 1995.

Peter, Paul and Mary Sing Tribute to May 4

By Tina Grady
Daily Kent Stater
May 5, 1995

Have you ever heard of punk rock–folk music? That's exactly what would describe the female duo from New York City that opened for Peter, Paul and Mary.

The Murmurs' psychedelic acoustics kept the audience's attention although the older generation present didn't seem to appreciate them as much as the students.

Leisha [Hailey], with rainbow-colored hair, and Heather [Grody], with pink hair, admitted to being a bit nervous about the performance but that didn't stop their sweet voices from carrying a melody.

During the song "Bumble Bees," their playing was interrupted when both of them broke guitar strings. The audience was a bit disappointed, but they came around during the group's popular song, "You Suck."

Although the songs contained some obscenities—and the group did apologize for them beforehand—they decided to perform it anyway.

"There are some things you can compromise and some things you can't," Heather said. "This song means a lot to us."

After performing a few other songs, including "Make Love Not War" and "Sleepless Commotion," a song about domestic violence, the Murmurs ended their 30-minute set with a pleased audience.

After a short intermission, the long-awaited arrival of Peter, Paul and Mary had finally come.

As the trio made their entrance, the cross-generational audience of at least 2,000 people exploded with applause. Then silence prevailed as the crowed stared at the stage, waiting for the famous group to begin.

"Being with you today is an extremely moving experience," said Peter Yarrow, referring to May 4. "It's been an honor to be with you friends."

They considered it such an honor that all the proceeds from the concert will be used to set up a May 4 scholarship fund.

Opening up the set with "No Easy Walk," the power of folk music captivated the audience. Somewhat calm after this, the group then went on to perform their famous children's song.

"It's a song of hope," Peter said as the crowd cheered, realizing what song would be next. "When you're a child, you believe in magic dragons."

The audience sang along with Peter, Paul and Mary for the first part of "Puff, the Magic Dragon," then the group just played while the crowd performed the vocals.

Although a bit aged from the Vietnam War–protest era, the threesome's voices and guitar-playing skills have not diminished.

Mary's voice in particular was very strong when the group performed Pete Seeger's "Where Have All The Flowers Gone."

Midway through the set, Peter, Paul and Mary, accompanied by special guest bass player Noel, played and sang some of their solo songs. Some of the crowd didn't seem to pay as much attention during these, but as soon as the group came on with "If I Had A Hammer," the audience erupted with applause while beginning to dance.

Giving them a brief moment to settle down afterward, the group then closed with Bob Dylan's "Blowin' in the Wind." Except for the crowd singing along with Peter, Paul and Mary, the entire place was silent. Many people held hands while swaying back and forth, and others shed subtle tears.

At the song's conclusion, Mary said we need to promote, "peace, justice, equality and an end to racism—and all of us working together."

The audience couldn't get enough. Peter, Paul and Mary, along with The Murmurs, performed "This Land Is Your Land" as an encore.

Everyone danced, clapped and sang, leaving the show on a happy and peaceful note.

John Densmore visited Kent State on Thursday, November 2, 1995.

Writer on the Storm

John Densmore from The Doors Performs for KSU

By Kim Miles
Daily Kent Stater
November 3, 1995

Clutching their Doors albums, books and posters, about 200 students and members of the '60s generation filed into the University Auditorium Thursday night to see John Densmore, drummer from The Doors.

John Densmore, original drummer for the band the Doors, spoke November 2, 1995, in the University Auditorium. (*Daily Kent Stater* photo by Chad Mossholder)

A pony-tailed Densmore stepped onto the stage at about 8:30 P.M. and was greeted with a roar of applause and a standing ovation.

"But I haven't done anything yet." he said. The crowd laughed and then he got down to business.

"You are probably tired of hearing about Kent known for the killings. . . . Well, I would just like to say, tonight's performance is dedicated to Allison Krause and company . . . done," he said. Densmore lit an incense and told the audience that's how the Doors always started their shows.

"Something we copped from (East) Indian musicians," he said. "It puts us in a collective mood to play . . . us being you and the band. For this brief time together we are leaving the outside world behind."

And that's just what we did. We left the world behind and for an hour went back in time to the '60s and relived the music, the drugs, the life. Densmore took us on the trip the band made from college dropouts to fame and fortune as entertainers.

The auditorium was dark except for a light clipped onto a music stand from which Densmore read parts of his book, *Riders on the Storm.* On stage sat Densmore's original snare drum and cymbals he played as a member of The Doors.

He played his familiar beats and sang some of Jim Morrison's lyrics. To further explain what life was like in a rock 'n' roll band, Densmore brought along some film of a rehearsal and a recording session.

Densmore told the audience little-known facts and quirks about the band. Morrison never wore shoes and always had a book in tow. Densmore had an addiction to Pepperidge Farm Bordeaux cookies.

Linda Benjamin, from Louisville, saw The Doors in Cleveland in 1968 and said Thursday night's performance helped her relive those moments.

"I was in love with Jim Morrison," she said. "I had his picture in my locker. I still have his poster up at work. I was crying at the beginning. I didn't know what to expect, but I loved all of it. People talk a lot about how Jim (Morrison) self-destructed but we were all doing it. We were just kids. We were innocent. We were kids loving each other and having fun."

Crosby, Stills and Nash participated in the 27th annual May 4 commemoration.

Pausing to Remember "Four Dead in Ohio"

By Marti Bledsoe
Daily Kent Stater
May 6, 1997

Left to right: May 4 survivor Alan Canfora, Graham Nash, Stephen Stills, May 4 survivor Tom Grace, and David Crosby (Photo by Michael Pacifico)

Approximately 3,000 voices sang the chorus of "Ohio" along with rock trio Crosby, Stills and Nash Sunday on the Kent State Commons, concluding the 27th annual May 4 commemoration.

"We want to encourage them [today's students] to stand up, to be counted the way those kids did," David Crosby said before he went on stage. "We don't want their deaths to let these kids be intimidated. We don't want the bad guys to win here.

"The bad guys intimidated those kids by killing them and tried to say 'You can't have a voice. You don't have the constitutional right of assembly, you don't have the right to protest. We'll kill you if you do it.'"

Crosby, Stills and Nash, who played at Kent State for a $1 charge, also performed a sold-out show at the Agora Sunday, where they finished with the song "Ohio" as their encore selection. The trio is scheduled to be inducted into the Rock and Roll Hall of Fame in Cleveland tonight.

Graham Nash said, in an interview following the Agora show, that "Ohio," written by Neil Young when he was with the group, sounded different at the Kent State performance than at the Agora concert.

"It's very hard to get angry in blazing sunlight and when you can see beautiful kids out there smiling at you," Nash said. "When you bring the show into a place like the Agora ballroom and the lights go down and you can only

see the first two or three rows, you can project your anger about what happened 27 years ago much more directly when you can't see them.

"When we played Kent State earlier today, when we came back, we began to really think about why we were at Kent State, and that made us extremely angry, which came out in 'Ohio' tonight."

Stephen Stills said the best part for him about being on the campus was a chance to make a point that society needs to keep conversing in order to avoid a tragedy like the one in 1970.

Ronald Kuby was the keynote speaker at Sunday's ceremony. Kuby, a civil rights attorney and former law partner of William Kunstler, focused on the fact that the people responsible for the Kent State shootings, from politicians to National Guardsmen, were never brought to justice. Kuby said by remembering the tragedy, people can bring them to justice.

"There was never any justice for the four students who died in Kent. The men who pulled the triggers, the men who gave the orders to shoot, the men who called in the National Guard were never brought to justice," Kuby said. "Not a single guardsmen was ever convicted for a crime. There's nothing we can do about that but one thing—we can remember it.

"Any people that allows its government to murder its own children, and then forgets the victims, is a government and a people that fundamentally has no claim to morality."

Other speakers at the ceremony included: Al Long and Tom Papp, Vietnam veterans; Kendra Lee Hicks, an 11-year May 4 Task Force member who spoke in honor of Allison Krause; Carol Meyer, a Task Force member who spoke in honor of Jeffrey Miller; Wendy Semon, co-chair of the Task Force who spoke in honor of Sandra Scheuer; Mac Lojowsky, a Task Force member who spoke in honor of William Schroeder; Mwatabu Okantah, Pan-African Studies instructor; Chic Canfora, eyewitness to the events of May 4, 1970; and Jena Brown, the high school essay contest winner from Minerva High School.

"If we lose sight of basic human principles on our college campuses, there is no hope for a better society," Chic Canfora said. "If we are ever to rediscover the potential of students to mobilize and affect change again, then it must begin here."

Margaret Mlocki, a sophomore psychology major, is an Alpha Xi Delta sorority member. Sandra Scheuer was a member of the sorority when she died in 1970.

"I was there for the speech (about Sandra)," Mlocki said. "I felt like I knew Sandy even though I wasn't born. The whole time I felt like I shared our ritual.

"The wind blowing was like her being here. It was awesome that 27 years later I could still feel someone who died when I wasn't even born yet."

The Europe Gyro scene in the late 1990s launched the careers of local bands in Kent.

Bands Begin European Tour

By Matt Stansberry
Daily Kent Stater
October 17, 1996

You can feel the pulse on the sidewalk as you stroll by. The muffled sound of the Marshall cabinets draws people in.

On this night, the music is not coming from J.B.'s or the Loft. It's coming from Europe Gyro.

Europe Gyro has been a musical catalyst in Kent for more than two years. Local bands often get their first breaks here, said Bert Solis of the local band KLC, who also books the shows.

The shows always are free, which helps attract more of a crowd. The bands don't get paid. That is why there is no cover, but the bands do get something in return.

"Free food, free beer, jam some jams—it doesn't get any better than this," said Soma bassist Dave Tenney.

Shows are on Sunday and Tuesday nights from 10 P.M. to 1 A.M. More experienced bands play Tuesdays, Solis said, while bands with less experience jam the Sunday slot.

"All I need is a tape, but a band bio would be classy," Solis said. "The trend is real heavy, but I'd like to get some jazz in here."

Ryan Balis, bassist/drummer of Fake, explained why many bands get their start here: "It's just the easiest place to play."

Europe Gyro has launched the careers of many local bands, Solis said.

Hate Theory and The Butterfly Effect, Northeast Ohio rock bands, got their start at Europe Gyro. The Butterfly Effect has moved on to play

Europe Gyro (Photo by Travis Estell)

the larger Cleveland scene, and Hate Theory will be playing with Pro Pain later this month.

August 9 was the two-year anniversary of shows at Europe Gyro, bands from other areas also show themselves there. The Akron-based band Soma made their debut at Europe Gyro on Sept. 17.

"Kent has a lot of support for local music," said drummer Jeff Novak. "It's a new market to expand our boundaries."

Bands from the Cleveland area that play at Europe Gyro include Cows in the Graveyard and Reason Seven.

Dark, smoky and loud, Europe Gyro is a great place for aspiring musicians to connect with an audience.

"It's small, it's loud, but it's personal," said Soma guitarist Zigmond Novak.

When heavy bands like NDE and Hate Theory play, things can get pretty rough, Solis said.

"We let people mosh, but when things get broke, the music stops," he said.

For Kent bands that do not have time to play other places, Europe Gyro gives them an opportunity close to home.

"The Gyro's a great place to play music and hang out with all of our friends," said Jason Prufer, rhythm guitarist of the Kent-based band Amazing Larry. "Most of us are students at KSU, and this is where we're able to have a creative outlet."

Black Keys Member Patrick Carney and His Early Days in Kent's Music Scene

July 22, 1997, and August 31, 1997

When an acquaintance of mine, Gabe Schray, posted some vintage Kent photos to his Facebook page, I was blown away to see future Black Keys member Patrick Carney playing at Europe Gyro in the summer of 1997. Back in those days, the Gyro had a really cool scene that involved everyone I knew who was making music. The gigs were easy to book, and they had live music on Sunday and Tuesday nights. Sometimes I would be down there with all of my friends seeing bands made up of people we all knew, and on other nights I would find some whole other scene.

Kent's music scene in the mid-to-late 1990s was certainly vibrant, but it wasn't so centralized, and the music definitely varied. There were lots of little pockets and crews of young musicians and artists around who did their own things and had their own followings. In the late 1990s, there were a lot of different venues in town: Brady's Cafe, the Mantis, the Robin Hood, the Avenue, the Garage, Europe Gyro, and a healthy house show scene. Now, to put this into perspective, 1997 was long after the North Water Street heydays of the Kent Kove, JB's, and the Water Street Saloon. It was a completely different period for live music.

So, the photos of future Black Keys member Patrick Carney as a seventeen-year-old playing with his high school band at Europe Gyro really validated my impression of Kent as a long-running magnet and breeding ground for some really great art and artists.

But the pictures mean something much more personal to the musicians who actually took part in these two shows. They tell stories of these Akron kids playing in bands and coming to Kent,

Gabe Schray, Jermaine Blair, and Patrick Carney performing at Kent's Europe Gyro (Photo by Philip Swift)

Steve Caynon and Gabe Schray at Kent's Europe Gyro (Photo by Philip Swift)

but, more broadly, they dip into the story of one local youth music subculture.

Filmmaker Philip Swift took the pictures. Swift's award-winning 2010 *Sincerely P.V. Reese* is a documentary about a lot of the kids who were in attendance on these nights at the Gyro. That summer, Swift was just about to enter his senior year at Akron's Firestone High School. Fifteen years later, he remembers the shows well:

These photos were snapshots taken in the moment probably with some disposable camera or an actual SLR camera. These are definitely from two different nights. The one that I am looking at right now is Gabe on the left, Jermaine [Blair] in the middle, and Pat on the right. Gabe is wearing a nondescript orange shirt in this one, and in the next one he's got on a Jawbox T-shirt. Also in this one photo Steve [Caynon] has on a Spiritualized T-shirt, and in the other one he is wearing a Nick Cave and the Bad Seeds shirt with what possibly looks like a polo underneath. The two black and whites would be from one night and the three color photos from a different night.

I remember many nights at Europe Gyro, at the Mantis, and at all these other different little venues from that period. I can't even think of them all right now. I couldn't even tell you the exact dates on these shows.

I come from a very close-knit, [large] group of friends. Throughout high school there were these little times where we all had got fed up individually with each other, and so we wouldn't be around as much. Since Pat Carney is in these photos, I would have to say this is 1997. By senior year of high school, he had kind of given up on all of us and moved on. I think he was doing postsecondary stuff from Firestone to Akron University.

Everybody in those photos, we all went to the same elementary school, the same middle school, the same high school, and we were like a big group of friends forever. And Gabe, obviously, I still have a big connection with, and Pat, as busy as he is, he still took the time to text me on Christmas.

So we were all friends, and a bunch of [the guys] were musicians and they all practiced music on some level. Steve had older siblings that were into music, Gabe's dad was really into music production, and Pat's uncle is, obviously, Ralph Carney, who had played on all of those Tom Waits albums and has done work with countless others of that caliber. So all of these people had music connections to begin with.

I never ever had any musical bone in my body. I could never carry any rhythm or play any instruments or anything, and so I was the guy that was there with the camera who would photograph stuff. I also made weird music videos with these guys.

At the time of these Gyro shows, we all worked at the Mustard Seed Market, and because of this we knew people that were a little bit older and who were involved in the Kent scene, so that may have been how these shows got booked. I was just happy to show up and hear some great music and take photos.

I remember on one of the nights I drove to the show with some people, and I definitely remember knowing about a show coming up at Europe Gyro. Every night was kind of the same. Basically, you would show up and you'd be really excited because your nerdy rock-and-roll friends were playing a show at the Europe Gyro and you'd get to be part of the entourage, posse. We, as friends of the band, would always show up way too early and make a lot of fuss outside the venue, [fooling] around and getting in trouble, and then when the show started we were down front just flipping out and loving every note those guys played. Whether it was really good or not, we were always there ready to have a great time.

I was always more about capturing the moment as it happened rather than thinking about framing and composition and such. [In] the other black-and-white photo, you can see Gabe and Steve [are] looking right at the camera, and they are kind of like smiling. It's a weird photo, because everyone seems very happy, but you can't tell if it's because they wrapped up a good show or because they are about to play a good one.

Patrick Carney, Steve Caynon, and Gabe Schray at Kent's Europe Gyro, with Ted Gerbick and Colleen Ganon in the background (Photo by Philip Swift)

Steve Caynon (Photo by Philip Swift)

It's interesting to think about what these photos meant back then and what they mean now. Back then I was proud and happy to be with my friends and see them play this live music. It was always a big event for us, whether it was in the tiniest little basement in someone's house in Akron or the Europe Gyro or the Mantis. And I certainly lived vicariously through all of them getting onstage and performing. So I was always excited to be there to take pictures or shoot some video of my friends playing.

I just wanted to have photos to show these guys so that right after I could say, "Hey guys,

Patrick Carney, Gabe Schray, Steve Caynon, and Jermaine Blair performing at the Europe Gyro. Pat's brother Michael Carney is in the audience (*lower right*). (Photo by Philip Swift)

this is what you looked like while you were playing," or, "Look at you guys smiling at the camera; you guys look like a bunch of goofs."

Gabe Schray is an amazing man and is the most prolific musician I know. He is constantly putting out music, and he is a ridiculous individual and a ridiculous human being. He is always up for bizarre, weird, fun adventures. He is a total goofball, but I love him, and he's great. And Pat Carney obviously now is a multimillion-dollar rock icon almost.

It's interesting to look at Gabe and Pat as these two opposite ends of the spectrum of the Northeast Ohio–Akron music scene. Pat as a huge rock star who goes on *Saturday Night Live* and plays with the Rolling Stones and [is] making a lot of money, and Gabe producing an album every year of whatever he wants to put out. One will be an electronic reggae album and the next album can just be ambient tones.

The third person in these photos is Steve Caynon, who was literally my best friend. We were in kindergarten together; he's definitely the closest thing to a brother I ever had until I married

Katie. And Steve died in 2004, and all we have are these photos and these films we made.

When I teach, I talk a lot about how photography is about capturing less than a second. We can look at these photos of these nights from Europe Gyro and we can ask, "What happened before these photos? And what happened after?" I think before is a little blurry but the after is pretty obvious. And the present is just these guys enjoying the art form that they always enjoyed, which is just rockin' out for their friends.

Musician and artist Gabe Schray, the drummer in the pictures, was a huge part of that old Akron crew, and he continues to play live shows and produce music. He produced and composed the soundtracks to both of Phillip Swift's films, *The Bubble* and *Sincerely P.V. Reese* (in which he also appears). On these Europe Gyro nights in Kent, Gabe was just seventeen. Fifteen years later, this was his take on the photos:

Christopher Whispers started because we were all in high school, and I think just before we put the group together we were all playing louder punk rock than straight rock. But by this time, we had gotten really into bands like Galaxie 500, which was just a lighter, spacier kind of thing that had some actual songwriting. We must have been sixteen or seventeen years old, and that would have been 1997.

At the time this was our exclusive band, and we were all about it, although we would switch around a lot of the same musicians within the different bands. As I recall, right at the beginning of our senior year of high school we decided to take this band real seriously. I think there was a possibility of us opening up for Luna at the Grog Shop, and that was big-time—though that show never materialized.

We actually did some four-track recordings, and I still have the cassette tapes along with hundreds of other cassette tapes in a giant briefcase. I think there were two recording sessions, and those were held in Pat's basement. He had the nicer four-track, and he had the drum set. Those recordings would have been done in the fall of 1997.

Christopher Whispers probably only played three actual shows, and two of them were at Europe Gyro in Kent. The only other one was for a house show in Akron in Jermaine's basement. That might have been it, and those photos that Philip took would reflect both of those public shows.

I do remember a few things. I know that for one of those nights, there was a big bar fight where somebody threw a bar stool while we were playing. And while that didn't have anything to do with us, it was very exciting for us teenagers to be in the midst of a barroom brawl. That was the first and only band I played drums in, and I kind of remember screwing off a couple times during one of those shows and being self-conscious about it. Jermaine's guitar was real noisy, and I'm not sure he ever played the same thing twice. We were probably pretty noisy. We were all seventeen years old and feeling like adults for the first time—playing a real show in a real public place in front of strangers in another town.

There wouldn't have been anyone else on the bill for those nights but us. We didn't know how something like that worked. We didn't really understand that usually for these kinds of shows multiple bands should be booked.

Pat must have booked those two Gyro shows. Even back then he was good at talking, networking. Pat was always precocious and ambitious. He was the first one of us to have a job on his own, which was at the Mustard Seed Market when he was like fifteen, and even before that he was mowing yards when he was ten and eleven, and he had his own lawn-mowing company. And then he had a paper route, too. He was the one saving up to buy the equipment that I still can't afford, and he was always the real go-getter and wanting to do things on his own. So then later he was the one going out and getting the shows.

At the time of these Gyro shows I was not really aware of the Kent scene at all. It was only a few months later that I kind of realized that there was this whole other group of people in Kent who were our peers and doing the same kinds of things with music and bands, though they were a little older, maybe a few years older. The Kent kids were like the cool older kids. The real breakthrough for us into that scene was that we went to high school with a guy, Jeff France, and he was in that Kent band Pankration. Because of that I totally started becoming aware of the Kent scene. But at the time of those Gyro shows with Christopher Whispers we were in our own little weird world.

The breakup of the band was in early 1998. First Jermaine disappeared, and we couldn't get ahold of him anymore. Then we got into this sort of high school argument with Pat, and he wasn't really talking with us. I remember Steve and I being really worried that we wouldn't have the master tapes of the Christopher Whispers recordings. And I think I talked Pat's dad into letting us go down into the basement to get something, and when we went down there, we stole the master tapes. Pat was really upset about that. I don't think they would still exist had I not done that.

That isn't the only time that we had to sneak into his basement studio. Probably around the time of the Black Keys' second album, our band

Intelligent Knives was recording in his basement. We recorded like six songs, and then he went out on tour with the Black Keys for a while, and we really wanted these mixes. And once again, we talked the people he was living with into letting us go down into the basement to mix the record. There is sort of a long tradition of breaking and entering into Pat's basement.

I'm not sure why Kent has this creative magnetism to it. I draw a lot of parallels between my crew in Akron with that Kent crew. People like Jamie Stillman, Joe Dennis, Ryan Brannon, and Jon Finley. Those guys were in Party of Helicopters, and they had this whole big group of friends that sort of stretched out from that band. We all have similar senses of humor and the way we interact with each other is pretty funny. Like once you start to actually get to know them, they were just the same breed of weirdo.

Party of Helicopters was one of like the top five most important bands to me. It was because of them that I had this realization that there's this entire crew of people who we don't know who are making cool stuff. And they were further ahead of me and my crew. Party of Helicopters were putting out records and 7-inch [records], plus Jamie Stillman had his record label, so they just really inspired me.

I remember being really passionate about [Party of Helicopters], and seeing them at the Mantis was like probably in my top favorite shows of all time. I remember being totally swept away by them live, but it just doesn't seem like something an outsider would ever get. In Akron they seem to still have a ton of young fans now. When they did those few reunion shows in recent years, there was a huge crew of these twenty-one-year-old kids that were just freaking out and loving it.

Not everybody in my Akron crew got caught up with the Kent crew, but Steve and I did for sure. While we were at Kent State, we were just obsessed with that scene. Pat got into that Kent crew, too, and that's actually how we kind of started talking again after Christopher Whispers broke up. When Steve and I went off to college in the fall of 1998, there was still this sort of animosity with Pat, but [it] was kind of slowly being stripped away as he kind of became more friends with a lot of those guys. I think Pat was as obsessed with Party of Helicopters as Steve and I were, and then later Jamie Stillman, who was the driving force behind Party of Helicopters, became the Black Keys' tour manager.

In the late 1990s there was a pretty healthy house show thing going on. It was more in the basements of people's houses and in these other odd spaces in Kent and Akron. I mean that scene in the late 1990s meant a lot more to, or as much as, that scene that the Numbers Band or Tin Huey meant to those people in the '70s and early '80s. It gets weird because there are people from my parents' generation that were in the same kind of bands, the local, do-it-yourself kind of bands, and I almost feel like they were shoving that. I guess what I am trying to say is not one is more important than the other.

I guess I should say it would be hard to dismiss Tin Huey and the like. People liked to talk Tin Huey up, but to me it was just like, "Huh? I don't really get this." I like it now, and I can appreciate it now, but back in the mid-to-late 1990s, it was just kind of this baby boomer thing, like them telling us what's important. It just didn't mean anything to me. Later on, Tin Huey kind of embraced my band Houseguest and they were all super cool with us. Some things you kind of have to get away from so that later you can look at it with some perspective. I shouldn't say that that generation didn't influence us kids, because we were all DEVO fanatics.

I did end up playing with Pat again. I was in that Churchbuilder band briefly that he was a part of just before and right at the beginnings of the formation of the Black Keys. Churchbuilder was Pat and his now ex-wife and a couple other people. They were like a pop band, and they were signed to Shelflife Records, an indie pop label. I was just an auxiliary live member. I wasn't on any of the recordings, but I played trumpet and guitar live, so I kind of never refer to it as my band. But they were signed to a legitimate record label, and they recorded a full-length album and an EP, which I think [is] out of print now. That would have been around 2000–2002. I probably played four or five shows with them at the Lime Spider, the Grog Shop, and at the Beachland [Ballroom], which is where they opened for Jonathan Richman.

Thinking about what has happened with Pat now with the success of the Black Keys—at this point it's kind of surreal. I've seen them since the beginning, and every time they would make some kind of move I would think that this was as far as this band could possibly go. One memory that really sticks out is that I traveled to Australia with them for New Year's 2004, '05. They were playing at this giant festival, and I remember sitting backstage and looking out into this sea of people and just thinking, number one, "This is completely insane." But, number two, "This can't possibly get any bigger. There is no way. Where can it go from here?" And I remember sitting back there thinking this was probably it for them. And then every year since then they somehow exponentially get more and more popular. It's pretty fascinating. But yeah, I distinctly remem-

ber that De La Soul came on after them, and I was thinking this is completely insane.

I guess at this point they are as popular as you can get, but we'll see as they continue. I actually got a text or something from Pat recently, saying, "Yeah, I am going to be playing with the Rolling Stones." And I didn't really know how to respond except to say, "Oh, that's really strange." It doesn't make any sense, but that's okay.

Philip must have given [the photos] to me a few years ago. He always had a camera with him; those were the days before digital photography, so it always seemed like he had a 35 mm or one of those little crappy disposable cameras. I like these pictures for just the personal history aspect. I originally posted them to Facebook because they had Steve in them, and we all miss Steve so much.

Looking again at these old photos from the Gyro, I just think of how exciting it was to be doing that sort of creative thing on our own at that age. I think people kind of thought we were weird because we had taken it upon ourselves to seek out these other endeavors. We were trying to carve out our own circuit with our own rules. It was definitely the first sense that we can do these sort of things ourselves—on our own and on our own terms. These nights at the Gyro were definitely the start of something that has been a big part of my life.

As I began writing about those nights at the Gyro, I never thought I would actually be able to speak to Patrick Carney, but after making a few inquiries, I was put on the phone with him almost immediately. He was driving from his home in Nashville to a studio where the Black Keys were recording a new album.

I think we started the band Christopher Whispers in maybe late May of 1997. Steve and I were both listening to a lot of the same music and also hanging out with Jermaine quite a bit. I think it was the three of us that started the band, or at least the three of us started talking about putting a band together first, and then I think Gabe volunteered to play drums or something like that. We used to rehearse in Jermaine's basement, and he was like twenty-two and we were all seventeen. It was cool being in a band with an older dude, because you could make noise at his house.

The name Christopher Whispers was actually a joke. It was like a character that I came up with. We used to sit around and draw comics at school, and we just thought it was kind of a pathetic-sounding name. I think that's why we wanted to use it.

There were definitely two different nights we played at the Gyro, and I know that the first of the two shows was the one where you can see I'm wearing the bolo tie in the photo. But yeah, there were two separate shows. But they both would have been in the same month or six weeks of each other. I think that first show would have probably been in late July, and the second show would have been towards the end of August. And this was the summer before all our senior years in high school.

Back then, Steve and I had another band at one point, called Example Figure Three, and Gabe, Steve, and I had another band as well. And then Gabe and Steve and a few other friends had bands. Yeah, in high school there were about five or six bands existing within a group of like eight people. We all worked at the same place, so basically we would start bands based on what jobs we had at the restaurant; if you had the same job you couldn't be in the

same band together, because more than likely you'd have to both work alternating days.

I'd saved my money up from that job to buy a four-track, and we used to sit around and make demos and stuff, so all the shows that we ever played in high school were booked from sending a cassette tape to somebody. It could be that Jermaine helped book those Gyro shows; that was the first show any of us had ever played at a real bar.

Though we would have known about the Gyro just from coming to Kent. I think the very first show I ever played in a band ever was in Kent, and that was with Steve [and Gabe Schray] and our friend [Greg Adonia] at the Mantis, which is over on North Water Street. And that was probably in 1995, because I couldn't drive. One thing I remember about that show is that right when we showed up, I was the first one at the door and one of the guys who was putting on the show was standing there smoking a pipe or like a bong or something, and my dad, who had driven us to the show, was right behind me coming up to the door. I was lucky my dad didn't see it, because my dad can't smell. So we were aware of all that for sure, like all the different places to play in Kent. I wasn't friends with Jamie Stillman yet, but I knew who Jamie was, and I knew about Donut Friends, and I knew about Harriet the Spy and Sockeye and all of the stuff going on in Kent.

Back at that time there was nothing like Kent in Akron at all. Because Kent is a smaller town more geared towards students, it's always been a place I think that's kind of inherently cooler than Akron. That's how we viewed it. It was a place where you could go see a show downtown on a Friday night at the Europe Gyro or the Mantis or check out some albums at Spin-More Records. And at the same time, my uncle Ralph was a musician and he was in a band called Tin Huey, and they got signed to Warner Brothers playing at a show at JB's in like 1977. Back then, there was like really cool [stuff] coming through Kent into the mid-1980s.

The coolest thing about Kent in the mid-to-late 1990s, though, was really the Mantis, and we knew that you could get decent shows at other places, too. I remember Dave Neeson was booking shows at Susan's Coffee and Tea, though JB's had turned into a frat bar by the time we were old enough to go play shows. There was the Avenue, too, but that was more of a sketchy place. And then there was the Robin Hood, and, I mean, there was always kind of cool [stuff] going on in Kent.

As far as distinct memories I have from those nights, I remember we had a lot of friends from high school who came out. Not that many people were actually there. Maybe there were forty people. I just remember being happy to be playing a show. I felt like Steve and Jermaine and Gabe and I had put an awful lot of time into practicing and getting something cool together.

The photos are fascinating, but to be honest I don't remember much about Philip taking them or really too much about those shows in general. I remember being there, and without ever seeing Philip there I know Philip would be there because he was really good friends with Steve, Gabe, and me. It wasn't until maybe a year ago that someone sent me the one shot with all of us from far away. That was really the first time I saw a picture of that band.

Honestly, the summer of 1997, the first half of that summer, was probably the most fun time I ever had in high school and one of the most fun times I've ever had in my life, and it was mainly because of that band Christopher Whispers, because Steve and I were always listening to new

music and getting into that kind of stuff. When we had time off, we would go to the guitar store or record store. We were just all about music. We were listening to Yo La Tengo and Galaxie 500, the Feelies, stuff like that, and that was influencing the music we were making. I think that was the first time any of us were in a band that was a little more mellow. I don't even think Steve had a single fuzz pedal or anything.

Later, I actually hung out in Kent a lot. Steve and Gabe went to Kent State the next fall, and I ended up kind of [messing] around going to some art school and then going to Akron University, and at Akron U I started hanging out with this band called the Phelps Hex. Phelps Hex were two bass guitars and drums, and they were friends with Jamie Stillman, so we would go visit Kent all the time because the Phelps Hex would play shows with Party of Helicopters at the Avenue, and that's how I got to know Jamie.

Jamie and I were always super friendly, and then at one point the last label that Party of Helicopters was on, Velocette Records, I think Jamie arranged for them to come meet with us and maybe try to sign us [the Black Keys], while we signed to Fat Possum. And through that whole deal I ended up hanging out with Jamie a lot more. A year later, Dan and I had a really strange tour scheduling thing where we had to start our tour in Seattle. So we asked Jamie if he would drive our van out for us and we would meet him there. That was the beginning of Jamie becoming the Black Keys' tour manager, which didn't actually click in fully for another year, year and a half. And then he was the Black Keys' tour manager for the next five years. He was an awesome person to be spending tours with.

It's hard to even think about Kent without bringing up Jamie Stillman, because that was like one of the most alluring things about Kent. All this [stuff] was coming out of Kent and you can all kind of trace it back in some way to Jamie.

I first heard about Jamie Stillman when I was thirteen, and this is like pre-Internet and you know, Kent is twenty miles away. So, for like a fifteen-year-old or sixteen-year-old for your name to just travel to west Akron is the equivalent to being a punk rock superstar in Akron. We had some friends who were a little bit older than us who'd go to Kent [and] would be like, "Jamie's got an 8-track recorder and a cassette and he's got a label and he's got like two bands."

I think at that time the band he was in was called Velocipede, and then Harriet the Spy and all that. It was all very inspiring. They were all coming from a place musically that I wasn't really, but the thing that I always liked about them was that I loved the music that they made. Those guys all listened to such cool [music], and they were always super supportive of every band no matter what the genre or whatever you know. Dave Neeson and Tom Raichel and all those guys and Joe Dennis especially. And basically how Dan [Auerbach] and I figured out how to get the Black Keys going was just seeing Party of Helicopters get in a van and tour like every single summer for six or seven weeks. We just realized that that's what you kind of have to do. And any time the Black Keys would have a bad show or something, I'd always think about Jamie's stories about being on tour and like playing in some kid's basement and his parents came home and [stuff] like that.

That was the thing, just watching Jamie and all those kids in Kent. They would be like, "Oh, you need to make a T-shirt? Here is how you make a T-shirt." Or they'd be like, "Oh, you want to put out an album? You just call United Press, and you do this, and you send them this,

and it costs this much money." They just knew how to make this stuff happen.

Reflecting on these photos and thinking about where my career has gone since these nights in 1997, I can tell you that I know that my seventeen-year-old self would think that my thirty-two-year-old self was cool. I don't think I could have ever imagined most of the things that have happened to me in the last couple of years. From the age of seventeen until I was probably about twenty-three—and this includes a couple years of touring and playing in the Black Keys—the only successful band that I ever saw live was Dinosaur Jr., and they played to like 1,500 people at the Cleveland Agora Theater. So, for me, real success and being in a big band meant to be able to sell out or pack pretty tight a venue like the Grog Shop. I think all that other stuff—I mean I never watched the Grammys or saw a concert at Blossom or the Gund Arena or any of that. So all of that stuff was not even something I was paying attention to.

These shows at Europe Gyro weren't my first shows or anything, but it was the first time I ever played at what was more of an actual venue versus a DIY kind of spot. It was the middle of summer right before our senior year of high school. Those photos and those nights at the Gyro literally mark the end of an era. Everybody's [situations] just changed within months of that.

As I was putting this story together, I went down to the Europe Gyro, or Eurogyro, as it's now officially known, several times, to take photographs and order food, just see the place again. It was the same crowd and vibe that I remember—just different faces. Some nights, the place was packed front to back with kids who

came from who knows where to see a triple bill of bands. On other nights, it was hip-hop DJs. Most of the time, though, I saw that same young rough Gyro crowd trying to eat, drink, and converse over an extremely loud jukebox.

The Gyro remains the exact same gritty establishment that it was back in the mid-to-late 1990s, the very last vestige of an old neighborhood, while everything around it has moved slickly into the twenty-first century. Perhaps visitors stay at the new hotel next door only to be bewildered by all the ratty-looking kids hanging outside of the pizza place.

The Wallflowers played at Kent State on Thursday, December 11, 1997.

Wallflowers Play to Crowd of 4,147
By Dawn Piros
Daily Kent Stater
December 12, 1997

The Wallflowers performed before a standing crowd of 4,147 last night in the Memorial Athletic Convocation Center.

Complete with psychedelic flowers on the wall, chandeliers and velvet curtains, the band portrayed an intimacy that kept the audience captivated.

"Kent is very cool, very, very snowy and very big," Wallflowers keyboardist Rami Jaffee said before hitting the stage.

"The only problem we've had is that there is no way to get anywhere. We were stuck in our hotel all day, there are no taxis in this town," he said.

Jakob Dylan replied, "They're all lies," and jumped onto the stage.

The crowd jumped to its feet as the band opened their set with a remake of Rod Stewart's "Tonight's the Night," which immediately set the mood.

"One Headlight," the band's third song had the audience screaming and clapping along.

"I enjoyed the show very much, and loved the light show too." said Beth Carpenter, 33. "I think Jakob Dylan is the next Bruce Springsteen."

Anticipation was everywhere prior to the performance.

Even third graders showed their enthusiasm.

"I like The Wallflowers because they have a good tune," said Valerie Trizzino, who attended with her parents.

The Wallflowers performing in Kent (*Daily Kent Stater* photo by Dave Rubins)

She pointed to the picture of Jakob Dylan on her large T-shirt and said he was her favorite.

All Campus Programming Board President Shane Crowl said the ACPB will lose a few dollars on the show. "It's a catch-22 situation. We try to offer students the cheapest prices we can because they pay through allocations," he said. "However, we make more money selling tickets to non-students."

Fugazi participated in the May 4, 1970, commemoration.

Fugazi Show Closes off May 4, 1998
By Jennifer Fiala
Daily Kent Stater
May 5, 1998

Fugazi packed the Kent State Student Center Ballroom full of 1,400 screaming fans for a free show as part of the May 4, 1970, commemoration.

"I wanted to come for the commemoration, and I like the idea of student activism as opposed to the events of 1970," Fugazi vocalist Ian

MacKaye said. "The atmosphere surrounding a lot of universities right now is that there really isn't room for activism."

MacKaye said he was invited to Kent State by Steve Skovensky, Kent State alumnus and supporter of the May 4 Task Force.

"Over the years, I've spoken with Steve about coming here, and he's invited us a few times," MacKaye said. "Our schedules just never worked. I just knew that this year we'd be here on May 4."

Skovensky describes Fugazi as a Washington D.C. band that has risen out of the post-punk period to become a national act with a large underground following.

"Fugazi has turned down headlining spots for shows like Lollapalooza," Skovensky said. "They don't do videos or sell T-shirts—it's just about the music."

Fugazi bassist Joe Lally said the band often does shows to support charities and to raise money for causes they support.

"In D.C. all of the shows we play are to raise money for local causes," Lally said. "We would like to be able to improve something in our hometown. I wish we could do it more. One of the great things about being in a band is being able to do something besides play for people."

Because the ballroom only seats 1,400, task force members and security guards had to turn people away at the door.

"It's a fire code, and I feel bad that we can't let more people in," Skovensky said.

"I'm not surprised of the turnout. It seems like every year, the anticipation is upped, and people realize the importance of activism, the legacy of May 4 and social commitment. Fugazi is one of the strongest and most important bands of our time."

The task force set up an information table that displayed the famous 1970 *Life* magazine issue with the body of Kent State student Jeffrey Miller on the cover.

They also had T-shirts for sale, pamphlets and photos of student activism from the era.

Mark Kaminski, a freshman graphic design major said he liked the show but wished it had been held outside.

"I think this is a great show especially because Ian MacKaye is a leader of the straight-edge movement from the '80s," Kaminski said. "It's too bad that the show isn't outside, because a lot of people couldn't get in. I just wish more people were dancing."

The event was sponsored in a joint effort by May 4 Task Force and All Campus Programming Board and co-sponsored by Amnesty International, Lesbian Gay Bisexual Union–Kent, Anti-Racist Action and Coalition for Animal Rights and the Environment.

Arlo Guthrie headlined the Kent State Folk Festival on Saturday, September 12, 1998.

Folk Fest Springs Roots in Kent
By Kevin Necessary
Daily Kent Stater
September 15, 1998

It was Saturday night when Arlo Guthrie finally sang "Alice's Restaurant."

The elusive classic, which Guthrie updated and highly improvised, was perhaps the highlight of the 32nd Annual Kent State Folk Festival, presented by the All Campus Programming Board.

The tune, laden with political commentary

Arlo Guthrie performed songs including "Alice's Restaurant" during Kent's Folk Fest. (*Daily Kent Stater* photo by Lindsay Semple)

Crowds await the start of the 32nd Annual Kent State Folk Festival. (*Daily Kent Stater* photo by Joe McIntyre)

about Presidents Richard Nixon and Bill Clinton, 37 8-by-10 color glossy photos and its usual "instruments of destruction" capped off two nights of local, national and international folk music performances on the University Commons.

The concert began Friday night at 7:00 P.M. with the Celtic sounds of Cathie Ryan, followed by acoustic guitarist and Dave Matthews Band member Tim Reynolds.

As the sun sank further behind the twin stacks of the Heating Plant, the audience was treated to performances by Iris DeMent, Czech "New Grass" artists Druha Trava and the light-hearted songs of Livingston Taylor.

Saturday's lineup began with Music from the Hearth, composer Ken Bonfield with bass guitarist Michael Manring, Kent almnus Joe Crookston and headliners Donna the Buffalo and Guthrie, who received two standing ovations.

But it was not just the live performances that drew audiences to the concert, which on Saturday broke all previous Folk Festival records, ACPB President Brian Hanner said.

It was the chance for the audience to experience a genuine folk festival.

"This is my reason for living," joked Frances Kovacs, a transfer student to Kent State who has attended two previous Folk Festivals.

"I came here to see Donna the Buffalo," Kovacs, a musical theatre major, said. "And the music, because I play folk guitar in my spare time."

Liz Pechersky, a freshman elementary education major, has never been to a folk festival but decided to come on Saturday.

"I don't normally listen to [folk music] but it's pretty good," she said. But it was not the music that made the Folk Festival special for Pechersky.

"It's the food," she said.

But the experience of the festival was not limited to those who had to pay to get in.

To Ken Bonfield, the festival was a chance to have some fun.

"Festivals are my favorite." said Bonfield, one of the artists who performed Saturday night. "Playing outdoors has its own issues.

"It's harder to hear, it's harder to get all the electricity right, but it's absolutely the most fun, at least for me."

Bonfield, who plays in five to ten folk festivals a year around the country, said that festivals give the audience and the musicians a chance to become closer to both each other and to the music.

"When you get to play for people," said Bonfield, "and when you can really get 200 to 2,000 people and bring them together as one, that's a magical thing. The audience is the most important thing to live music. Obviously, it wouldn't be live music without the audience.

"When they laugh at your jokes, and when they understand the music that you're playing, that's magic."

The Folk Festival concerts also affected those who made the show possible.

To Jacelyn Fitzwater, festival arts coordinator for ACPB, the festival was a learning experience. She had never been to a Kent State Folk Festival and was now expected to run the entire weekend.

The Smashing Pumpkins played at Kent State on Easter Sunday, April 23, 2000.

Smashing Pumpkins, Bunny Rock

By Rachel Wenger
Daily Kent Stater
April 25, 2000

When Peter Cottontail's trail crossed the MAC Center on Sunday evening, the poor rabbit didn't know what had hit him.

The Smashing Pumpkins brought their Sacred and Profane tour to Kent State Sunday evening, fully equipped with music from their latest CD, *MACHINA/The Machines of God* and a five-foot inflatable Easter Bunny.

Billy Corgan, the band's lead vocalist, greeted the audience of 4,678, with the air-filled hare and a few words about the holiday.

"I guess this does confirm we're pagans. We came all the way from hell to play this concert," he laughed.

Brad Powell, concerts chair for ACPB and an employee of Belkin Music, said Belkin chose the campus specifically for the Smashing Pumpkins show.

"This size venue really worked for them," Powell said. "This is bigger than the Agora and smaller than the CSU Convocation Center."

With an almost sold-out show, there is no denying the Pumpkins are continuing as a smashing success.

Drummer Jimmy Chamberlin returns on *MACHINA/The Machines of God,* after being kicked out of the band following the release of the 1995 *Mellon Collie and the Infinite Sadness.* Also, former Hole bass guitarist Melissa Auf der Maur has replaced Pumpkins bassist D'Arcy Wretsky, who had been with the group since the beginning.

Fans from Pennsylvania, New York and Ohio traveled to check out the band's new member and lyrics.

Robert Good, an Ohio University student, came from Youngstown for the show. He said he enjoys the Pumpkins' new material just as well as the old.

Billy Corgan of the Smashing Pumpkins performs alongside an inflatable Easter Bunny. The imitation rabbit eventually was sacrificed to the crowd. (*Daily Kent Stater* photo by Alex Capaldi)

Kent State University employees assist in distributing wrist bands for Smashing Pumpkins concertgoers. (*Daily Kent Stater* photo by Alex Capaldi)

"I've liked the Pumpkins since 1991," Good said. "If you're a true fan, you enjoy everything they do. They know how to mix soft and hard rock together perfectly."

Fast-paced, colored stage lights and sweaty fans didn't miss a beat keeping up with tunes such as "Tonight" and "Everlasting Gaze."

Some audience members donned feather boas and leather pants while others slipped in ear plugs.

When Corgan belted out the words to "Heavy Metal Machine," proving the band knows how to have some heavy metal fun, standing floor fans tossed each other around and swayed together in the tightly packed audience.

Kent State student Bethany Mallett, came to see one particular pumpkin.

"Billy Corgan's lyrics are untouchable," she said. "He is in a dying breed of rock 'n' rollers."

Fans were greeted by metal detectors before entering the MAC Center, which is usual concert procedure, said Jim Singleton, head of Hall Entertainment security.

Singleton said even though the music may sound destructive, the fans usually aren't.

"I've probably worked 20 Smashing Pumpkins concerts and we've never had any problems," he said. "The audience just kind of monitors itself. The fans are just here to have fun and to have a good time."

A Smashing Life
Guitarist James Iha Discusses Life in the Band
By Lisa Aichlmayr
Daily Kent Stater
April 25, 2000

James Iha, guitarist for the Smashing Pumpkins, had been looking forward to the concert at Kent

State, but it was also another step in his career with the band.

"The only thing I know about Kent is the Crosby, Stills and Nash song," Iha said. "But I think it will be pretty cool. I think Kent has an interesting history."

Iha's own history with the band started when he joined 11 years ago. He said the biggest highlight of his tenure was staying together and the freedom.

"We get to make music and put out records," Iha said. "I'm not at work from 9 to 5, doing something I'm not interested in. It's a hard schedule, but in the time we have off I don't have to answer to anything. I'm kind of used to it; it's what I do."

Iha said even though he did not write on the most recent album, he has written on others. He said his inspiration can be almost anything that starts him playing. He starts with chord progressions then adds lyrics later.

He said the current album, *MACHINA/The Machines of God,* wasn't meant to be a different style, as some reviewers had commented.

"It was just the songs we wrote and the best collection," Iha said. "It wasn't a decision to make a different album, it was just the way it came out."

Iha said the current album took eight months to record. He said he enjoys playing the songs, but the touring can make them somewhat repetitive.

"There's a repetition to playing five nights a week. It's not that we get sick of it, but we add songs and take some out to keep it fresh," he said. "A lot depends on the audience."

Iha also remembers his first live concert with the Pumpkins.

"I was scared and nervous," he said. "It was one of those 'putting yourself on the line' things. There's no way to see it, there's lights, sounds, and you're either good, bad or whatever."

Finally, Iha shed little light on the origin of the band's name.

"It's one of those names you just come up with," he said.

The MTV Invasion Tour visited Kent on October 14, 2000.

MTV Invades Kent Homecoming Weekend
By Jennifer Johnston
Daily Kent Stater
October 17, 2000

The MTV Interactive Village had students living out their musical fantasies Saturday afternoon. Then Black Eyed Peas, De La Soul and Wyclef Jean performed for their pleasure that night. Both events were part of MTV's Campus Invasion that hit Kent State during the music channel's October tour of universities across the nation. Kent State was one of two universities (along with University of Virginia) where MTV taped segments to air on the network. MTV's visit coincided with Kent State's Homecoming festivities, creating an atmosphere of excitement for those who stayed the weekend.

Seven MTV attractions lined the area between Dix Stadium and Summit Street in the Interactive Village. A giant inflatable MTV logo stood near the street so passing cars could see this was MTV territory. [Attractions] included Techtronica, Rocks Off, Hip-Hop History, MTV's 100 Greatest, M2 requests and Choose or Lose. Many students walking into this invasion walked in with wide eyes and excited smiles, but had mixed reviews once they played around the area.

Camella Johnson, a junior computer information major, said she came there to experience as much of the event as possible.

"This is my first campus invasion," she said. "I am here for the fun and the games and to receive free stuff."

She said she went into the Techtronica IMAX theater, played a little guitar and drums at the Rocks Off area and played around the whole event.

"There was so much interaction," she said. "It was one of the best events that I've been to. It introduced the new technologies that 2000 is bringing."

Cliff Klatik, a Spanish and French translation major, said he came to the event excited at first that MTV was at Kent, but later became disappointed with the Interactive Village. Still, he had high hopes for the concert in the evening.

"That's why we're here—to get free stuff." he said. "It's not that great, but tonight will be better."

A mini IMAX theater called "Altered States" highlighted the Techtronica area. As the music of Orbital, Moby, Orgy and other techno artists pulsed through the air, the screen displayed psychedelic images of tunneling colors and shapes of all sizes. Students could also remix some of their own techno in this area.

The Rocks Off area gave out a 1-800-COL-LECT Campus Invasion erasable note board and CD opener. A leopard-skin couch set up in front of a big screen TV created a homey setting for watching videos from P.O.D., Korn and Deftones. An electric guitar, drums and keyboards set up in the area made it easy for students to live out their rock 'n' roll fantasies. Free airbrush tattoos were available for those not quite ready for something permanent.

The Hip-Hop History area took students through the family tree of music via computer technology and showed them the beauty of street art. The computer family tree had information about present and past artists in the Hip-Hop genre with audio clips and song samples. While one artist painted a mural of his own street art (sometimes called graffiti art,) students could add their own message from the heart to another mural set up in the area.

Female students could clean up, so to speak, by getting free stuff from the 100 Greatest tent. Students could register to win a free gift basket from Neutrogena and try out a variety of facial products and cosmetics. But that's not all . . . they could be virtual guests on MTV as they were interviewed by VJs Brian and Amanda. And what would a trip, virtual or not, be without getting a picture taken in the TRL photo booth? Students could vote for their favorite video in the top 100. A big screen TV playing some of the top 100, including Wyclef Jean's "Gone Till November," was set up, but there was not a comfortable couch to hang out and watch the videos.

Those dreaming of VJ stardom could request a video at the M2 area for a possibility of air on the channel. Each person had to fill out a form promising not to sue the network if he or she looked idiotic when the footage aired. Lateesha Maris, a freshman biology pre-med major, said she was extremely excited after her big break.

"It was fun," she said, "I hope they use it on TV. They should have more things like that."

The Choose or Lose area was an informational attraction. Here you could get a Choose or Lose button and pen for filling out a survey about your school's racial environment as part of MTV's anti-hate campaign. Stacy McPherson, coordinator of educational programs for a World of Difference Institute Anti-Defamation League handed out information pamphlets and encouraged people to fill out surveys at the booth.

"The response has been wonderful," she said. People have been willing to take the time to fill out the forms. Tolerance for differences is what it's all about. It's about respecting people."

The music at the concert had a jumpin'—literally—from opening act Black Eyed Peas through the end of Wyclef Jean's set.

Black Eyed Peas opened the show with hip-hop numbers from their new album *Bridging the Gap*. One of the members of De La Soul, the next group to perform, ran a little late due to a misunderstanding about which hotel he was staying at. That caused a brief interruption, but the other members of the band just freestyled a bit until he got there. It did not hurt their performance. It only encouraged them to talk to the crowd.

Senior accounting major Adrian Clarke said he thought the concert was the biggest show to ever come to KSU.

"I came here to see Wyclef," he said. "It was the best I've ever been to. He really got the audience into it."

Sophomore technology major Bruce Fletcher said he was looking forward to seeing Wyclef.

"I came here to give love to Wyclef," he said. "That's my dude. I've liked him ever since him and the Fugees got together."

Wyclef Jean held a little wrestling match on stage during the performance. He offered $1,000 to any wrestler willing to come up on stage and take down one of his guys. No, The Rock did not show up and rip into some poor unsuspecting college guy, but The Rock's voice, along with other artists were pre-recorded so Wyclef could perform songs the audience wanted to hear. Juan Gaines, an Akron resident, won the money after pinning his opponent in seconds, and Wyclef handed him the money right there on stage.

"Do we got strippers in the house?" Wyclef then called to the audience. A few guys and several girls jumped right up on stage with no inhibitions. One of the male dancers tried to go up to the highest point of the stage to attract attention, but he was chased down by security. "This is the part MTV is going to censor out."

Warren resident Stacy Green recited a poem to the audience about her life after getting the go-ahead from Wyclef. She and Michelle Jones, a freshman nursing major, came to the show determined to meet Wyclef before the night was over.

"I went there with the notion of getting on stage somehow, someway," Jones said. "As soon as he gave the word we were up there. When he called for strippers, we didn't care what it was for."

"I believe I am supposed to be seen and heard," Green said. "I'm not a stripper, (but) you only live once."

They ended up hanging out with De La Soul after the show.

"It was very exciting," Green said. They were well-mannered gentlemen. I felt like a celebrity. It's something I have never experienced before."

Carmella Johnson ended up hanging out with Wyclef and others after the concert when he performed a more laid-back set at the May 4 Memorial.

"The show was awesome," she said. "It was one of the best shows I've ever been to. He interacted with the crowd. After the show, he sat around the memorial and played guitar. It was more like he was a student than an artist. He was really down to earth."

Chuck D spoke at Kent State on Tuesday, February 27, 2001.

Chuck D Sheds Light on Music Industry

by Ryan December
Daily Kent Stater
February 28, 2001

Chuck D set eloquence aside and instead used the language that perks the ear of today's college students in his address last night in the Student Center Ballroom.

"Unfortunately, my jail lecture is the same as my college lecture," he said in his closing words to the crowd of 200.

Speaking in casual and often profane language, he began his "vibe session" by explaining that by studying black music, one inevitably studies black history. Post-slavery integration is lucidly illustrated through the geography of jazz, he said.

He then drifted into Hip Hop history, describing how Jamaican turntablists combined various American instrumental music and toasting, or rapping, in the mid-1970s. He continued defining Hip Hop as a term for black creativity over the last 30 years, as well as a means of cultural exchange.

"The number one rapper is white, and the number one golfer is black," he said. "That's cultural exchange."

This lead him to the focus of his talk. He stressed the confusion of jail, gun and stupidity cultures with Hip Hop culture. The popularity of saggy, baggy pants is absurd, since the trend was born from protective custody in which belts are not issued to prisoners so that they will not hang themselves, he said.

"We have seen rebel mentality turned into thug mentality and be endorsed," he said. "A

Advertisement for Chuck D in Kent (Courtesy of the *Daily Kent Stater*)

Chuck D of the '90s rap group Public Enemy addresses an intimate crowd in the Student Center Ballroom. (*Daily Kent Stater* photo by Alex Capaldi)

rebel has focus and knows exactly who the enemy is. A thug has no focus and no direction."

He offered the life of Tupac Shakur as a perfect example of this.

"You can sell a dead man forever—just ask Hendrix," he said. "You don't have to negotiate with a dead man."

In light of his recent advocacy of free music online, Chuck D described the corporate dictation that powers the music industry. Artists, he said, traditionally make 10 percent profit from each album they sell. By providing their music directly to consumers via the Internet, artists stand to lose little and also gain control of its production and distribution, he said.

"The big fight is about the technology being in the hands of the public before big businesses got it," he said of the recent Napster trial.

Applauding the recent headlines of all-time low consumer confidence, he described the Internet as the harbinger of equity in music.

He also described Radio Attack Terrorists, a group he recently founded to combat corporate control of broadcasting and subsequent one-sided imaging of African Americans.

The group has a Web site on which visitors can deliver e-mail grenades and electronic bombardments showing the sender's dismay of negative and lopsided programming to the stations of their choice. Further measures Chuck D will take include the publication of broadcast executives' phone numbers, social security numbers and addresses. This notion was met with audience approval.

"It's a really good idea to bomb the radio stations by e-mail. They only play who pays them to," said Jason Collins, a senior ceramics major. "It'll mess their system up."

"It was shocking, but I think that profane and sexist music should stop being played," said Rochelle McCrayer, a freshman exploratory major. "I would like to hear more positive stuff, like Jill Scott, on the radio."

Concluding his talk, the influential Hip Hop pioneer recommended that students get the most of their education and experience life outside of their comfort zones. He bragged that his greatest accomplishment was going through three passports.

The Spitfire Tour show was on Tuesday, October 30, 2001.

Spitfire Tour Drops by to Rally Kent State Students

by Jennifer Kovacs
Daily Kent Stater
October 31, 2001

Musicians, including Nirvana bassist Krist Novoselic and Dead Kennedys founder Jello Biafra, encouraged Kent State students to become involved in political activism last night in the Student Center Ballroom.

The May 4 Task Force hosted the Spitfire Tour, which includes musicians, actors and activists speaking on global affairs.

"We always have a fall program, and this year I wanted something big," said Kelley Garbett, co-chair of the task force. "It's an incredibly good show for the amount of money it costs, and it's incredibly unique. They all have an important thing to say."

Adam Werbach, host of the new magazine *The Thin Green Line,* mediated the event. The musicians, who spoke on various political topics, were Novoselic, Biafra, singer/songwriter Jill Sobule, founder of the Joint Artists and Music Promotions Political Action Committee.

Novoselic opened the show by urging students to participate in electoral reform.

"The electoral process is like a rundown greasy spoon," Novoselic said. "You go in and there's one table but only two chairs, and they're reserved for Republicans and Democrats."

Novoselic promoted an inclusive democratic process that would make it possible for third-party candidates to run in elections.

"I really liked what Krist had to say," senior English major Sue Savickas said. "The more informed people are, the easier it is to get younger people to make a difference."

Sobule performed an acoustic set of songs of social commentary, including one on the difference between drug laws for George W. Bush and a kid across the tracks.

Biafra argued against the war in Afghanistan.

"I'm frightened of Bush saying, 'You're with us or with the terrorists," Biafra said.

"We need to stand up and say, 'No, we're not with Bush or the terrorists. Is what we're doing now really the best way to solve the problem?' What happened to rethinking what made these people so mad in the first place?"

Joe Walsh received his honorary degree on Saturday, December 15, 2001.

Graduation Day at KSU—Call Him Dr. Walsh
Rocker Gets Honorary Degree, Campbell Speaks
By Deborah Guziak
Kent Record-Courier
December 16, 2001

Kent State University bestowed an honorary degree on a Rock and Roll Hall of Famer and heard from Cleveland's incoming mayor as 1,650 graduates received their degrees during commencement ceremonies Saturday.

Guitarist Joe Walsh of the Eagles received an honorary doctorate degree during the morning commencement exercises and Cleveland Mayor-elect Jane Campbell addressed the afternoon exercises at the Memorial Athletic and Convocation Center.

Walsh, who received his degree as Joseph Fidler Walsh, was presented with the pink hood

Kent State University President Carol Cartwright congratulates guitarist Joe Walsh on his honorary doctorate degree at commencement exercises at KSU. (*Record-Courier* photo by Richard Sweet)

representing the music doctorate. He attended classes at KSU from 1965 to 1967 but did not graduate. "I've been a junior for 27 years, in good standing, I might add," he joked.

Although he did not speak during the commencement, Walsh said after the exercises that receiving the honorary doctorate was a humbling experience.

"It kind of puts closure on my school days," Walsh said. "It always bothered me that I didn't finish school. This makes me feel very humble to be recognized, and it reconnects me to a time when I was just 'Joe.'"

Walsh left KSU in 1967 to perform in a band called the Measles, which was a popular group in the Kent music scene at that time. He later joined the James Gang. He recorded a solo project in 1973 and joined the Eagles in 1976.

He lived in Columbus as a child and said he came to Kent in 1965 because he felt it was a safe community. He lived in Manchester Hall and was a political science major before converting to an English major.

"I loved Kent," he said. "It was a time that allowed me to be very creative. I played downtown, and received a tremendous amount of encouragement. I still have friends here."

Index

Page references in italics refer to photos and advertisements.